Being and Creation in the
Theology of John Scottus Eriugena

Being and Creation in the Theology of John Scottus Eriugena

An Approach to a New Way of Thinking

Sergei N. Sushkov

FOREWORD BY
David Jasper

☞PICKWICK *Publications* · Eugene, Oregon

BEING AND CREATION IN THE THEOLOGY OF
JOHN SCOTTUS ERIUGENA
An Approach to a New Way of Thinking

Pickwick Publications
An Imprint of Wipf and Stock Publishers
199 W. 8th Ave., Suite 3
Eugene, OR 97401

www.wipfandstock.com

PAPERBACK ISBN: 978-1-4982-9824-7
HARDCOVER ISBN: 978-1-4982-4851-8
EBOOK ISBN: 978-1-4982-9825-4

Cataloguing-in-Publication data:

Names: Sushkov, Sergei N. | Jasper, David, foreword.

Title: Being and creation in the theology of john scottus eriugena : an approach to a new way of thinking / Sergei N. Sushkov ; foreword by David Jasper.

Description: Eugene, OR : Pickwick Publications, 2017 | Includes bibliographical references.

Identifiers: ISBN 978-1-4982-9824-7 (paperback) | ISBN 978-1-4982-4851-8 (hardcover) | ISBN 978-1-4982-9825-4 (ebook)

Subjects: LCSH: Erigena, Johannes Scotus, approximately 810–approximately 877 | Erigena, Johannes Scotus, approximately 810–approximately 877 —Contributions in philosophy of nature. | Philosophy of nature.

Classification: B765.J33 S87 2017 (print) | B765.J33 S87 (ebook)

Manufactured in the U.S.A.   07/28/17

"But woe to you, scribes and pharisees, hypocrites! For you lock people out of the kingdom of heaven. For you do not go in yourselves, and when others are going in, you stop them."

—MATTHEW 23:13

Contents

Foreword

JOHN SCOTTUS ERIUGENA (C. 810–C. 877) was, it may properly be claimed, the most important philosophical thinker in the Western Church between St. Augustine in the fifth century and Anselm in the eleventh century. Under the patronage of Charles the Bald, as far as we know he held no ecclesiastical office, yet his writings are extensive and of supreme importance for Christian theology. A prime channel for the translation of Greek thought into Latin, Eriugena translated the writings of the Pseudo-Dionysius, St. Maximus the Confessor and St. Gregory of Nyssa, as well as writing extensively on the Fourth Gospel. But his greatest work is the *Periphyseon*, or *De Divisione Naturae*.

It is to this great text that Sergei Sushkov gives the closest attention, thereby revealing, in a book of profound learning and careful thought, Eriugena as one of the most original and important minds in Christian theology. Sushkov's writing should never be taken lightly. His meticulous argument demands a great deal of his reader, but he offers the richest of rewards to the serious theological mind, presenting a radical re-reading of Eriugena that addresses the very fundamentals of a new logic and a new way of thinking that lies at the deepest heart of the Christian theology of salvation. Like Eriugena himself, Sushkov is nothing if not a daring thinker. He radically revises earlier scholarship that tends to emphasize the influence of Neoplatonism, Eriugena as a mystical thinker, and the division of God's nature in his theology. Rather Sushkov emphasizes Eriugena's close links with certain forms of Islamic thought, arguing for a correspondence with the philosophical school of the Mu'tazilites in their emphasis on reason rather than authority in the search for truth. Behind this lies the thought of Parmenides and the Pre-Socratic philosophers and an attention to the question of an ontology as what Sushkov calls the "cradle of dialectic."

Here we approach the very heart of this book. For if St. Augustine of Hippo is often regarded as the father of Western theology, then the rediscovery and recovery of Eriugena suggests some necessary revision of that picture enfolded within the startling identification of him as the "Hegel of the ninth century." For in Eriugena, Augustine's metaphysical vision and his hierarchical model of the universe is replaced by a dialectical thinking that is rooted in a treatment of contraries that profoundly respects their integrity and wholeness. In a way of thinking that resolutely sustains the fundamental theological contradiction whereby God simultaneously both *does* and *does not* create, unity overcomes dualism and the oneness of all things in God is sustained.

Eriugena's radical yet rational retraining of the way in which the mind thinks, an epistemology that operates by a dialectical process, is far from consigning Christian theology to the realms of the remotely intellectual or abstract, however. On the contrary, it is absolutely central to the theology of our salvation, for it is only thereby, in Sushkov's words, that the truth is found that it is "in the reality of creation where the creature and Creator are perfectly and inseparably one in the living and indivisible Spirit that the Holy Scripture is explicit about."

The explication of this vision is of the utmost importance for contemporary theological thinking. It is essential to remember that Sushkov's own thinking and scholarly training reflects the mingling of his Russian upbringing and his doctoral studies in Scotland, caught between East and West. It is through this fine filter that he establishes the proper intellectual thread that connects the ninth century Eriugena with the nineteenth century Hegel, providing the careful reader with a theological platform to go yet further in reflections upon immanence and transcendence and to steer "a safe course between the extremes of Radical Theology and Radical Orthodoxy, and thus to address a wide range of calamities that institutionalized religion is currently undergoing in its deep crisis." Furthermore, we may perceive that beyond Hegel, Eriugena's dialectical thinking should now take its place alongside major elements of revisionary thinking in the twentieth century up to our own time, being placed alongside the thought of Martin Heidegger and even into postmodernism itself.

Sergei Sushkov's book, for which we should be deeply grateful, is the result of meticulous scholarship and makes clearly to the reader the thought of a major, and often unjustly neglected, figure in Christian theology, a careful thinker towards unity within broad reaches of culture that provides a model for reason in our present world fragmented as it is by religious differences and intellectual incoherences.

David Jasper

May, 2016

Acknowledgments

THIS WORK HAS BECOME the result of many years of hard labor and research, and I am grateful to all whose guidance, advice, and criticism helped this project to come true. First of all, I wish to thank my supervisor, Prof. David Jasper, whose constructive critique and encouragement, concentration on the key points of the argument and practical advice were absolutely vital at the concluding stage of the project. I am also grateful to Prof. Joe Houston, under whose supervision this research was begun and whose strategy of line-by-line analysis of Eriugena's dense text eventually allowed me to unlock its secrets. I wish also to thank Prof. George Pattison for his deep interest in the ideas articulated in the work, and Prof. Ian Hazlett for providing an opportunity to speak at the annual Perth conferences about the early developments of the work. I would like to thank as well my fellow-scholars whom I met at the Maynooth SPES conference, and above all professors John O'Meara, James McEvoy, Werner Beierwaltes, Willemien Otten, and Jack Marler, for the fruitful and encouraging discussions. I am grateful to Rev. Stella Durand for helping my access to the material unavailable in Russia, and to all staff of the University of Glasgow for being always friendly and helpful. I would like to thank a lot Rev. John Wright, Rev. Aida Younger, Rev. John and Molly Harveys, Billy Gribben, Tim Taylor, and all our friends from the Church of Scotland, without whose hospitality and kindness it would be impossible to stay in Glasgow and accomplish the project. Finally, I am immensely grateful to my wife Nina for her invaluable assistance and support, and to my Mother, and brother Gena, to whom I am fully indebted for my commitment to studies and the first steps towards the horizon broadened.

Introduction

The Central Point

THE RESEARCH UNDERTAKEN WITHIN the framework of this thesis aims to demonstrate that at the heart of Eriugena's approach to Christian theology there lies a profoundly philosophical interest in the necessity of a cardinal shift in the paradigms of thinking—namely, from the metaphysical to the dialectical one—which wins him a reputation of the "Hegel of the ninth century," as scholars in post-Hegelian Germany called him. In particular, L. Noack, while admitting an extraordinary affinity of Eriugena's ideas with those of German idealism, says that the majestic system offered by Eriugena betrays in him a "Hegel of the ninth century, who in a variety of marvelous ways comes into contact with Hegel of the nineteenth century and his predecessors in philosophy."[1] Furthermore, as F. A. Staudenmaier put it in his renowned work (highly appreciated by his colleagues and critics) *J. S. Eriugena und die Wissenschaft seiner Zeit*, the emergence of Eriugena, called by him "a wonder of history," is unsusceptible to explanation "by the conditions of his time and the environment he was put in. He created the future, and therefore remained a solitary figure among his contemporaries."[2] And in unison with this, Th. Christlieb even more vigorously added that "by his anticipation of the main idea of the latest philosophy" Eriugena "went ahead of his time by a thousand years."[3]

Despite these vehement testimonies to what seems to be most intriguing in quite a mysterious phenomenon of the intellectual history of Christendom called "Eriugena", there is surprisingly not much interest among

---

1. Brilliantov, *Влияние восточного богословия*, 43. All translations from Russian into English are carried out in the present work by myself.

2. Ibid., 43–44.

3. Ibid., 45.

the present-day Eriugenian scholars in what makes Eriugena's thought akin to the German idealism agenda or, as said, its "main idea." Werner Beierwaltes's "Revaluation of John Scottus Eriugena in German Idealism"[4] remains almost the exceptional work of the kind in the vast literature on Eriugena published since the *Society for the Promotion of Eriugenian Studies* (SPES) was founded in 1970. Perhaps, A. I. Brilliantov is right when, referring to Schlüter's words, he admits that those who have grasped the depth and vigor of Eriugena's speculation are the exceptional few, which the same C. B. Schlüter explained by the difficulty of access to Eriugena's system for the reason of its close affinity with Hegel's *dialectical monism*.[5] As for Beierwaltes's work, quite unique in its attention to German idealists' enthusiasm for Eriugena's contribution to Christian philosophy and theology, it does not go however so far as to examine the close affinity of his thought with Hegel's *dialectic*. Instead, Beierwaltes seeks to distinguish Eriugena's approach from that of German idealism in order to argue for his deep indebtedness to Neo-Platonist *metaphysics*, resulting in what the German scholar calls "Eriugena's objectifying Platonism" that "stands against a posited objective idealism."[6] And this makes the implications of Beierwaltes's work quite archetypal for Eriugenian studies[7] but, in my view, unfair to Eriugena himself. Any attempts to neglect the role of dialectic in Eriugena's system and subdue it to the schematism of Neoplatonic metaphysics are misleading and counterproductive. Even an appeal to the Neoplatonic understanding of dialectic, if such were made to secure a deeper insight into Eriugena's discourse, would prove to be of little help.

Indeed, as follows from the *Enneads* (a collection of Plotinus's separate treatises set in a certain order under this generic name by his disciple

4. See Beierwaltes, "Revaluation," 190–98.

5. See Brilliantov, *Влияние восточного богословия*, 18.

6. Beierwaltes, "Revaluation," 194.

7. According to A. I. Brilliantov, since A. Stöckl's *History of the Middle Ages* (*Geschichte der Philosophie des Mittelaltern*. 1. Mainz, 1864, S. 30–128) there has established a tendency in the West to reckon Eriugena among Neoplatonists. Finding him nonorthodox from the Catholic point of view, Stöckl considers Eriugena a non-Christian thinker permeated with Neoplatonic ideas through and through. "Eriugena's allegorical mode of interpretation of the Holy Scripture and his rationalistic attitude to Church authorities," A. I. Brilliantov writes, "fully restore, according to Stöckl, the standpoint and method of ancient Gnostics . . . Enslaved by the Neoplatonic ideas, he is always led by them to the conclusions that contradict the Church doctrine" (Brilliantov, *Влияние восточного богословия*, 27). And further Stöckl asserts about Eriugena: "He entirely upholds to the Neoplatonic pantheism, taking up the ides of emanation and cosmological process of Theogony . . . All the Neoplatonic elements scattered throughout the Patristic Age were assembled in his doctrine, and being thus brought together gave rise to an integral idealistic and pantheistic theory" (ibid., 28).

Porphyry), the father of Neoplatonism understood dialectic as a method or discipline of reasoning that aims to give proper definitions to all things. While approaching them, dialectic defines, according to him, "what each is, how it differs from others, what common quality all have, to what Kind each belongs and in what rank each stands in its Kind" to be real.[8] In a sense, therefore, dialectic appears to Plotinus to be a mode of *distinction* of a particular thing from other ones, resulting in ascertaining the distinctive qualities common to them all, in which they might be brought together, as assumed, to their unity. This is consequently the way leading the mind from the particular to the general (or, as termed by the *Enneads*, from the "lower" to the "higher") until it is believed to arrive at the ultimate unity which, understood as the "highest," cannot nevertheless dispense with the "lower" that ever remains posited outside it, and thus is thought to co-exist with its opposite.[9] Beginning with a distinction, this kind of dialectic keeps in fact resting upon the distinction as such and thus legitimizes it. Because of this, the *Enneads'* dialectic never brings the mind any closer to the knowledge of the real (all-embracing) unity, which is opposed to nothing outside itself and wherein all distinctions and dichotomies between the opposites are truly overcome. From this treatment of the opposites maintaining them immutable in their distinction, it is quite evident that—unlike Eriugena's understanding of the constructive role of contradiction (which makes his vision of dialectic akin to that of Hegel's)—Neoplatonism does not even imply to resort to *contradiction* as a means of breaking through to the true knowledge of unity by getting the opposites duality overcome. No speculations on Eriugena's indebtedness to Neoplatonic metaphysics could therefore be fair or justified in depth. As seen from the *Enneads'* conception of "dialectic," it suggests nothing other in fact than a mechanism of attaining the finite knowledge of "*what it is*" type; the infinite knowledge of "*that it is*" type, a possibility of which Eriugena's dialectic is entirely focused on,[10] remains beyond the Neoplatonic reach.

Rediscovery of Eriugena

Characterizing much of the interest in Eriugena among the Christian philosophers and theologians of post-Hegelian Germany,[11] Beierwaltes

8. Plotinus, *Six Enneads*, I. 3:4.

9. See ibid., I. 3:6.

10. On the distinction between the knowledge of '*what it is*' and '*that it is*' type see chapter 6 of the present work.

11. About the scholarly debate around the impact of Eriugena's thought on

writes as follows: "The philosophical preoccupation with Eriugena in the nineteenth century may be styled a rediscovery, since his ideas, having been obscure and silent for a long time, came to life again by virtue of new philosophical impulses and were questioned and discussed intensively."[12] "It was assumed," he continues regarding the reasons of this "rediscovery," "that Eriugena had overcome the opposition of the eternal and natural world, that he had justified his belief philosophically and had united insepara-bly philosophy and Christianity, faith and knowledge, and thus had first founded a speculative theology."[13] In particular, F. A. Staudenmaier, whom Beierwaltes calls "theologian and philosopher in one," was among the first who considered Eriugena "the father of speculative theology" and found in him "the germ of all present philosophy" (i.e., the idealism of the post-Hegelian age), largely focused on "the problem of the unity of philosophy and theology, faith and knowledge, reason and revelation."[14] And this is the point that struck German scholars most: what seemed in bringing philoso-phy and theology together an innovative breakthrough towards the cardinal reconsideration of the doctrines and practices of Christian faith, turned out in fact to be a thousand year old agenda articulately formulated by Eriugena in the ninth century. *Speculative theology* was thus reasonably understood by German thinkers to be the ground where all innovative tendencies in Christian scholarship and Eriugena encountered. As Werner Beierwaltes points out, this is the theology that "attains its end in constituting the unity of the divine and human spirit, in establishing the real oneness of revelation and reason in their deepest life and being, and in reconciling the incarna-tion (i.e., the second creation) with creation;" and this is how this theology understands salvation to be "fully achieved."[15]

The Neoplatonism Issue

Rightly acknowledging thereby the "epoch-making achievement" of the ninth-century thinker, Werner Beierwaltes however (erroneously, to my mind) finds it to result from Eriugena's adherence to a Neoplatonic model of the "hierarchical difference between modes of being or natures (*natu-rae*)." "This hierarchical difference," he insists, "is determined decisively by

philosophy and theology, both Catholic and Protestant, in post-Hegelian Germany see Brilliantov, *Влияние восточного богословия*, 16–45.

12. Beierwaltes, "Revaluation," 190.

13. Ibid.

14. Ibid., 191.

15. Ibid.

a Neoplatonic element: God is absolutely transcendent ("*supra omnia*," "*nihil omnium*"—nothingness of all), even if he must be thought in all, being the ground of all."[16] Moreover, Beierwaltes believes that Eriugena's system is constructed "according to a Neoplatonic ground-plan. The rhythm of the whole follows the triadic structure of μονή–πρόοδος–επιστροφή. The elements of the triad are conceived as concretions of God's cosmological operation and of the sacred history originated by him."[17] It is likely a certain resemblance seen from this between the Neoplatonic ἐριστροφή and Eriugena's *reditus* (not infrequently interpreted in the Eriugenian studies as a cosmological *reversio*[18]) that compels Beierwaltes to make a wrong assumption. According to him, the doctrine of *emanation* may not unfairly be found befitting Eriugena's doctrine of *creation*. Understood as the Word's incarnation in the world followed by the *reversion* of this world (for its "final perfection") "into its original state," emanation, the scholar thinks, may well match Eriugena's vision of creation, which is believed to squarely rest upon the "philosophical model" of *processio* followed by *reversio*—this is, the progression of all things from the source of their being *followed* by "the return of the effected into its efficient cause, or the reversion of the many into its origin, the One."[19]

Be it the case however that a judgment by appearance could lead us to a valid conclusion, would a certain resemblance between the two approaches really make any sense of Eriugena's conception? Would it be appropriate at all with regard to his dialectically coherent system to think of *processio* and *reversio* in terms of temporality? Finally, would it be fair to apply the *triadic* structure of the universe to the *fourfold* division of Nature offered by Eriugena? To my mind, the answer is quite obvious: no matter how attractive a metaphysical schematism might seem to be, it is in fact utterly irrelevant to a dialectically coherent way of thinking of the living *whole*, and for this reason can hardly be imposed upon Eriugena's discourse. Indeed, to the extent the triadic "rhythm of the whole," as the Neoplatonic metaphysics

16. Ibid., 193.

17. Ibid., 194.

18. Beginning his detailed analysis of "the structure of the return" in Eriugena's *Periphyseon*, Stephen Gersh defines *reditus* in a cosmological sense as "the motion of created things towards their Creator" (Gersh, "Structure of the Return," 109). Proceeding further through the consideration of a variety of possible meanings of the return, the researcher arrives however at the conclusion that there is no clear vision yet how *reditus* in Eriugena should be understood. "These metaphysical ideas regarding the levels of being, unity and multiplicity, and spatio-temporality," writes Gersh, "are not the subjects of special excurses in the text of *Periphyseon* but rather assumptions underlying the discussion of the return in general" (ibid., 117).

19. Beierwaltes, "Revaluation," 194.

suggests, is thought of in terms of temporality (so that *processio* and *reversio* are understood to follow one another), this scheme of succession proves to be inapplicable to the dialectic of unity developed by Eriugena.

According to this dialectic, the one Principle, that gives rise to everything, may only be truly known when understood as neither decreasing nor getting exhausted, but remaining ever identical to itself (i.e., to the proper nature of oneness). In other words, while bringing everything forth into existence, the Principle actually retains its all-embracing oneness (outside which there is nothing), and therefore cannot be abandoned by anything at all. In this sense, *processio* can only be coherently thought of as being *at the same time reversio*, since nothing alien to the one and self-identical Principle can ever be brought into being. As the true beginning of all, the absolute Principle is only conceivable as the one that unfolds *itself* and therefore *returns* to itself *at the same time*. For this reason, the true Principle is properly known (through a dialectical treatment of contradictories perfectly intrinsic to thinking of the whole) as the real Unity, which is not unfairly said to be simultaneously the Beginning and the Middle and the End.

Unlike this dialectically monistic view of unity, however, Neoplatonism tends to discriminate between unity and multiplicity by *setting them apart* (as appropriate to the dichotomy between eternity and temporality), and thus remains captive in fact to a metaphysically *dualistic* approach to what is only declared to be the One. "The transcendent 'One' of Neo-Platonists," says E. N. Trubetskoy,

> does not conquer the mundane reality, and the contemplative mysticism of their philosophy gets on with a deep dualism. Neoplatonism gets cleaved asunder by the contrast between the remote divine unity on the one side, which is transcendent, supersensual, and absolutely incorporeal, and the matter on the other, which is hostile and alien to the divine reality. As the principle of everything imperfect and evil in the world, this matter resists the Godhead. It is not made by Him, but is equally eternal and cannot be internally transformed or annihilated by Him. Between heaven and earth, the Divine and material there is irreconcilable enmity; discord of the conflicting principles, and strife and split lie there at the heart of the entire existence.[20]

As follows from the *Enneads*, the intelligible world of unity and the sensible world of multiplicity do not simply differ but oppose one another. Eternity and temporality are the opposite principles appropriate to each of the two worlds respectively, and thus (when metaphysically separated)

---

20. Trubetskoy, *Миросозерцание*, 17.

making them mutually confined or excluding. Understood like this, the eternal never leaves the One, the immovable and immutable,[21] whereas the temporal is by contrast associated with motion and change.[22] As Plotinus further clarifies, being "at rest within rest with the One" (or the Principle) is *eternity*.[23] To the everlasting Being understood as the absolute "rest" it is intrinsic, however, that it "can have no this and that," because "it cannot be treated in terms of intervals, unfoldings, progression, extension," and for this reason "there is no grasping any first or last in it."[24] Apart from this motionless and unchangeable Being, therefore, there must be something else that would host a variety of transient things understood as the world of flux, lying outside the Principle of being and, in this sense, found to be opposed to It. That is why what is assumed in the Neoplatonic system to oppose the eternal Principle is understood to belong to the temporal, and for this reason it is postulated to be nothing other than the "essential existence of generated things" that "seem to lie in their existing from the time of their generation to the ultimate of time after which they cease to be . . ."[25] As a result, along with the dichotomy between the eternal and temporal, being and non-being prove likewise to be rigidly set over against one another as the diametrically opposite entities. This inevitably means, however, that the absolute Unity, claimed by Neo-Platonists to constitute the focal point of their metaphysics, is put at risk by the very division of the entirety of existence into the mutually opposed realms of being. Deeply implanted in their reasoning, this division is actually taken on board by Neo-Platonists as almost a legitimate principle of their *complementative* (and therefore essentially *non-dialectical*) vision of the whole, according to which, as they assume, the supreme and indivisible One could occupy the "highest" level of being to reign over the "lowest" one, associated with the inferior status of manifold things.

As follows, in order to avoid apparent inconsistencies of their logic and to amend the substantial defects of their metaphysical construct of the universe (which turns out to be fraught with disruptions in the connection between the One, or the Prime Principle, and the world of generation), Neo-Platonists seek to secure the link between the opposite extremes of existence. This is why, as evident from the *Enneads*, a certain *intermediary* is to be placed in between. The intermediary element of this kind, additionally

21. See Plotinus, Эннеады, III. 7:6.
22. See ibid., III. 7:7–8.
23. Plotinus, *Six Enneads*, III. 7:6.
24. Ibid.
25. Ibid., III. 7:4.

postulated by the metaphysical system in support of the integrity of its hierarchical model of being, is assumed to promote the transmission of eternal forms to the world of transient things and thus to allow the latter, by receiving the orderly forms, to take definite shapes.[26]

This auxiliary agent of the cosmological process of generation introduced by Plotinus is what he calls "the Soul of the All."[27] It "holds mid-rank among the authentic existences"[28] and is supposed to connect the eternal and the temporal.[29] Nevertheless, instead of bringing the extremes together, as expected of its operation, the mediator—being *twofold* by its own nature (which is said to be engaged either in contemplating the superior Intellect or leaning to the inferior bodies[30])—comes in fact to bring about the dissemination of division across the entire universe. The final results of this quasi-mediation (actually maintaining the extremes in their mutual confinement) prove to be something opposite to what was there at the start of the Soul's downward movement and pertained to the Supreme Good— namely, such opposites of the absolute Principle as the formless matter and evil,[31] which remain beyond the Soul's reach at the periphery of existence. In consequence of this, the Neoplatonic conception of *emanation* becomes utterly incompatible with the biblical doctrine of *creation* and, accordingly, with Eriugena's dialectically coherent approach to it in attempt of building a consistently theological system, firmly based on the truth of Goodness lying—as conspicuously revealed by the opening chapter of the Book of Genesis—at the very heart of the whole of creation.

Indeed "aiming at the completion of the universe," the Soul gets involved, as Plotinus suggests, in a descent "to its own downward ultimate,"[32] gradually progressing further and further away from the Principle itself, and thus degrading towards the levels of being of lesser perfection.[33] And as the author of the *Enneads* further argues, "the movement of a being in abandoning its superior is running out to serve the needs of another: hence there is no inconsistency or untruth in saying that the soul is sent down by God . . . "[34] The dialectical approach to thinking consistently of

26. See Plotinus, Эннеады, III. 7:4.

27. Plotinus, Six Enneads, IV. 8:8.

28. Ibid., IV. 8:7.

29. See Plotinus, Эннеады, III. 7:13.

30. See Plotinus, Six Enneads, IV. 8:7.

31. See Plotinus, Эннеады, I. 8:14.

32. Plotinus, Six Enneads, IV. 8:7.

33. See Plotinus, Эннеады, V. 2:2.

34. Plotinus, Six Enneads, IV. 8:5.

the substantial unity of creation would however strongly disagree with Plotinus's understanding of "consistency" and "truth" implied here and, above
all, with the two constitutive ideas of his hierarchically-structured vision
of reality giving rise to the metaphysics of emanation itself, which may be
expressed as follows:

1. The generated things are meant in the course of emanation to *abandon*
   the Principle of all beings (so that "the Soul of the All" is understood to
   be sent down by God, as if *the One* could ever be transcended or there
   could be anything whatsoever beyond his reach);

2. The outgoing process of emanation is thought to be carried out
   through the *downward* movement of the Soul that complies—through
   a number of successive stages—with the decrease of the primal perfection, of which G. Reale fairly says as the exhaustion of Good.[35]

In other words, the dialectical view of creation (entirely focused on its
substantial unity) would strongly disagree with a metaphysical understanding of the generation of things as being started *from without*[36] and therefore brought about in defiance of the fundamental principle of *Goodness*
(or the absolute Self-Identity) constituting the very basis of creation, when
coherently seen in accordance with the Genesis account. In particular, as
a process of bringing the corporeal world into being (by giving an orderly
form to the matter), emanation is understood, according to the *Enneads*,
to proceed away from Good and, as a result, to approach Evil.[37] This scan-
dalous understanding of the process of generation as resulting in what is
opposed to its beginning is a direct implication of a non-dialectical treatment of contraries as equally substantial entities on which Plotinus builds
his argument. According to him, "Evil is of necessity, for there must be a
contrary to good." "To essential existence," he further argues, "would be opposed the non-existence; to the nature of Good, some principle and source
of evil." This particularly means that "to the content of the divine order, the
fixed quality, the measuredness and so forth—there is opposed the content
of the evil principle, its unfixedness, measurelessness and so forth: total is
opposed to total."[38] So that, apart from the absolute Good there must also
be acknowledged in accordance with this way of reasoning (metaphysically setting the contraries apart) the existence of the absolute Evil, which is

---

35. See Reale and Antiseri, Западная философия, 247.

36. See Plotinus, Эннеады, V. 9:3–5; II. 4: 8.

37. See ibid., I. 8:3.

38. Plotinus, *Six Enneads*, I. 8:6.

assumed to be manifest "together with the derived evil entering something" that is *not itself* (or devoid of good).[39]

Despite the apparent inconsistency of his thinking of the One, on account of which the Prime Principle (or the Supreme Good) proves actually to be opposed to the other (and therefore becomes confined and substituted in its operations by an auxiliary mediator), Plotinus does not seem however to be confused by the implications of his reasoning. Instead, he continues to insist on applicability of the metaphysical vision of the totality of existence (consisting, in his opinion, of the contraries added up) to the conception of the generation of the universe. "But why does the existence of the Principle of Good," the author of the *Enneads* argues,

> necessarily comport the existence of a Principle of Evil? Is it because the All necessarily comports the existence of Matter? Yes: for necessarily the All is made up of contraries: it could not exist if Matter did not. The nature of this Cosmos is, therefore, a blend; it is blended from the Intellectual-Principle and Necessity: what comes into it from Good is good; evil is from the Ancient Kind which . . . is underlying Matter not yet brought to order by the Ideal-Form.[40]

As a result, by the very logic of his reasoning Plotinus is compelled to admit that along with the Prime Principle of all there does co-exist another Principle, which is "Matter in its potency,"[41] the dwelling place of Evil.[42] And thus he has to acknowledge in fact nothing other than a failure of his attempt to deduce a coherent system of thought reflecting upon the absolute nature of the only Principle of all that is posited to be *the One*. That is why almost in despair, appreciable in his intention to introduce additional postulates to the constructed system (as it is the case with Matter as the eternally co-existing Principle), the father of Neoplatonism tries to save the situation (though making it even worse in fact) by suggesting what he calls "another consideration establishing the necessary existence of Evil." "Given that The Good is not the only existent thing," he says, "it is inevitable that, by the outgoing from it or, if the phrase be preferred, the continuous downgoing or away-going from it, there should be produced a Last, something after which nothing more can be produced: this will be Evil."[43] Thus the explicit strategy of a non-dialectical separation of the opposites (making

---

39. See ibid., I. 8:3.

40. Ibid., I. 8:7.

41. Plotinus, Эннеады, II. 5:5.

42. See ibid., II. 4:16.

43. Plotinus, *Six Enneads*, I. 8:7.

them co-exist or follow one another, as if they were appropriate to the reality of mutation) inevitably results in converting *processio* into the temporal cosmological movement, in which the beginning and the end are set apart as the polar extremes. "As necessarily as there is Something after the First," the *Enneads* read, "so necessarily there is a Last: this Last is Matter, the thing which has no residue of good in it: here is the necessity of Evil."[44]

It is clear from this that a process of generation, which begins from Good but ends with establishing Evil in existence (that happens on account of Good's deficiency, resulting from its exhaustion in the course of degrading towards the inferior levels of being), may have nothing in common with creation. For it is essential to creation that Good never decreases but dominates in it through and through, bringing the entire creature to greater perfection of the Image of God, so that no discrepancy between God's will and being is seen in what has been made by him. With regard to creation, therefore, the Beginning and the End may only be inseparably one, and *processio* and *reversio*, accordingly, may only be properly thought of as being simultaneous. In this sense, a coherently understood doctrine of creation is amenable to dialectic alone, and those who assume, as mentioned above, that Eriugena's thought adheres to the Neoplatonic vision of the hierarchically-ordered universe should be found falling into delusion. The metaphysical doctrine of emanation[45] befits neither the biblical account of creation nor Eriugena's dialectical view of it, developed, as the present inquiry will show, into a coherent system of theological thinking.

All this consequently means that the Neoplatonic *hierarchical* model is just inapplicable to Eriugena's system, simply because in the reality he is looking for there is no hierarchy at all. *Hierarchy* and *division*, as they occur in the *Periphyseon* (the thinker's *opus magnum*), are exactly what Eriugena seeks to overcome as categories appropriate to a *metaphysical* way of thinking, taking its departure from the assumption of what he calls

44. Ibid.

45. Following his reading of Plato's *Timaeus*, Plotinus suggests "the explanation of Plato's Triplicity" as being appropriate to "the order of generation—from the Good, the Intellectual-Principle; from the Intellectual-Principle, the Soul." In support of his view of generation as proceeding from the Primals (or "the Beings gathered about the King of All") to "a Secondary containing the Secondaries, and a Third containing the Tertaries," Plotinus appeals to a certain intellectual tradition coming down to Plato and his predecessors (such as Parmenides). "These teachings," writes the author of the *Enneads*, "are, therefore, no novelties, no inventions of mind, but long since stated, if not stressed; our doctrine here is the explanation of an earlier and can show the antiquity of these opinions on the testimony of Plato himself." Even "the Platonic Parmenides" is understood by Plotinus to make the distinction "between the Primal One, a strictly pure Unity, and a secondary One which is a One-Many and a third which is a One-and-many; thus he too is in accordance with our thesis of the Three Kinds" (ibid., V. 1:8).

the *fundamental division*. That is the division of the whole into opposites, beginning with those of *being* and *non-being*, which, in his conviction, is utterly incompatible with *infinity* of the true Being, solely appropriate to God in his Unity.

Anti-Hierarchy Argument

Despite its seeming resemblance to the *Periphyseon*'s doctrine of division of the universal reality into species of Nature, proceeding from the infinite God through the primordial causes to the finite things and coming back to God again, the Neoplatonic "hierarchical difference" between the levels of being as a model of universe is in fact essentially inappropriate to Eriugena's vision of creation. In the fourfold division of Nature developed in the *Periphyseon* there is implanted a dialectical "mechanism" of overcoming all division through the *integrity* of all the contraries, leading to affirmation of the indivisible unity of God's infinite being, as appropriate to the one and true God in whose reality there is no hierarchy or coercion (causation from without), but Love alone. As for the Neoplatonic idea of the "hierarchical difference," however, it is "decisively determined," as mentioned above, by God's *absolute transcendence*, which in fact is nothing more than just a *metaphysical* conception of God resulting from the mind's *divisive* attitude to reality. By no means therefore does it apply to the way Eriugena treats the infinity of God's being, of which Beierwaltes leniently says as "the apparent ambivalence of Eriugena's dialectical thought" concerning the immanence and transcendence of God.[46] "Eriugena's attempt," he admits, "to consider God at once both absolutely in and above world and man remains ambivalent."[47] But this "ambivalence" (or to be fair, the *dialectical* approach) is exactly the point where the Neoplatonic emanation significantly differs from Eriugena's vision of creation, according to which, as Baur points it out, "only in the unity with the finite could the infinite be truly infinite."[48]

To Eriugena, the universe of creation (i.e., reality as it substantially is) cannot be known otherwise than in a dialectically coherent way, when it is understood to proceed from the universal Principle of all and stay within it at the same time. Coming forth and back may only be truly known (i.e., known as being appropriate to the substantial reality of the universal Principle), when they are taken *simultaneously* (but not one after another) and therefore dialectically conceived by means of *contradiction*. *Processio* and

46. Beierwaltes, "Revaluation," 193.

47. Ibid., 194.

48. Ibid.

reversio should not be understood as *separate* motions, but as taking place in the reality of the infinite whole *at one and the same time*. Otherwise, they would be simply inapplicable to the reality coming forth from the universal Principle of all, understood by theology as that of creation. That is the reality which, as said, is inconceivable (and therefore unknown) *without contradiction* at all. Indeed, in its truth the universal may only be known as *giving rise to everything particular and remaining at the same time abandoned by nothing*. This is the cardinal contradiction lying at the heart of the theology of God's Oneness, an articulate expression of which constitutes the major objective of the project Eriugena undertakes in his *opus magnum*. The profoundly dialectical nature of Eriugena's discourse is consequently where his system fundamentally differs from any other attempts, like those of the Neoplatonists', to approach the same truth of God's Oneness by building up metaphysically structured models of reality. A proper understanding of dialectic as it works in the *Periphyseon*[49] should therefore safeguard Eriugena from any erroneous assumptions about (as well as false accusations of[50]) his allegiance to the Neoplatonic agenda. The hierarchical order of being, inherent in the Neoplatonic metaphysics, is utterly alien to Eriugena's dialectical approach to the reality of the whole; and this principal difference between the two systems of thought makes them altogether incompatible and irreconcilable.

A close reading of Eriugena's own text (regrettably not often used in Eriugenian studies as a tool for a better understanding of the speculative profundity of his thought) very quickly convinces us of the fairness of this conclusion. While discussing in particular his vision of creation, Eriugena finds it crucial to emphasize that nothing whatsoever may properly subsist in the created reality by abandoning the Principle of all beings. A *dialectical* reading of the Areopagite (whose thought likewise has often been

49. While discussing dialectic in Eriugena, Dermot Moran largely concentrates on the Neoplatonic dialectical elements and the Carolingian understanding of dialectic, but not on the dialectic as it actually works in the body of the *Periphyseon*'s text itself. In particular, under the influence of Cicero's and Boethius's use of dialectic as the art of discussion, Moran argues, the Carolingians were familiar with dialectic as a general method of proceeding in philosophical reasoning (see Moran, *Philosophy,* 125). "For the Carolingians," Moran says, "dialectic was the rational art of defining, arguing, and distinguishing truth from falsity" (ibid., 126). Despite a certain value of these observations, however, it would be fair to acknowledge that no comparison between Eastern (Neoplatonic) and Western (Carolingian) approaches to dialectic will ever bring us any closer to a better understanding of Eriugena's innovative contribution to it, unless the text of the *Periphyseon* itself is brought into focus of a careful analysis of the way dialectic is really implanted in it.

50. About A. Stöckl's contribution to a Neoplatonic misinterpretation of Eriugena's work see Brilliantov, *Влияние восточного богословия,* 27–28.

exposed to misinterpretation in the light of the Neoplatonic hierarchical metaphysics) does substantiate this truth, and Eriugena enthusiastically includes the thinker's own words in the *Periphyseon*'s text. Thus, as the text reads, "'when the theologians say that the Immutable goes forth into all things . . .,'" such a "'motion of His is to be piously understood not as carrying away, or as an alienation from oneself, or an exchanging, or as a turning round, or a motion in place . . ., but as God's bringing into essence and containing all things, and . . . as His self-identity holding together the middle and the extreme parts, the container and the contained, and as the return of those things which have come forth from Himself into Himself'" (523b–524a).[51] This means that, to Eriugena, it is of great importance to understand first of all that the universe of creation as a whole can by no means be opposed to the Creator,[52] because nothing whatsoever in it, unlike the Neoplatonic vision of emanation,[53] can actually be understood to subsist *outside* the One God. It would be utterly wrong therefore to assume concerning the infinite being of God, Eriugena argues, that there might be "another thing apart from Him and outside Him. For in Him are all things and outside Him is nothing" (517b). Not improperly should God be known for this reason as "the Limit of all things beyond which nothing proceeds" (516a). "For if another thing which is not Himself," the author of the *Periphyseon* further argues,

> is understood to be with Him, or if there is something acci-
> dental to Him, then surely He is neither infinite nor simple—a
> thing which the Catholic Faith and the reason must firmly deny.
> For they confess that God is infinite and more than infinite—
> for He is the Infinity of infinities—and simple and more than

51. Here and onwards fragments from the *Periphyseon* are quoted from *Iohannis Scotti Eriugenae Periphyseon*, as indicated in Bibliography.

52. As it will be clear from the ongoing inquiry undertaken in the present work, any attempts of interpretation of Eriugena's thought in a pantheistic sense are invalid for that simple reason that Eriugena has never meant to associate God's presence with the world of finite things. It is an axiom to him that the things participating in the substantial reality of creation are not finite; their finitude is only the way they appear to the sense (and the sense-dependent knowledge). That is why throughout the entire *Periphyseon* (and, above all, in Book 4) Eriugena diligently keeps distinguishing between the ways things only appear to be and are properly known as they truly are according to their infinite (self-identical) nature, coming forth from and staying within the universal Principle of all.

53. According to the Neoplatonic vision of emanation, as S. N. Bulgakov puts it, the world "is not made by the act of creation, but emerges from the One, as if pouring out of the Divine, similarly to the light out of the sun; the world is the Divine emanation subject to the law of decreasing perfection" (Bulgakov, *Свет невечерний, выпуск 1, книга IV*, 14).

simple—for He is the Simplicity of all simple things—and they believe and understand that there is nothing with Him, since He is the periphery of all things that are and that are not and that can be and that cannot be and that appear to be either contrary or opposite to Him . . . (517b).

From this holistic vision of the Divine being, it is clear therefore that in the reality of creation there is no room at all for anything to be affected *from without* or to be *subordinate* to any *outer* force (be it even the supreme power of the Sovereign). And the reason for that is very simple indeed: nothing external, as seen above, is allowed to co-exist with the totality of Being—neither outside nor within that which is believed and understood to be infinite and simple. Hence, it would be logically erroneous to impose a hierarchical order of being upon the reality of the infinite whole, where God never "moves beyond Himself, but from Himself in Himself towards Himself" (453a). Moreover, it would be wrong to try to ascribe a hierarchical perspective to Eriugena's vision of the infinite reality as it substantially is "by itself and through itself and in itself and for itself" (454d). Indeed, the author of the *Periphyseon* finds it entirely inappropriate to conceive of the Divine reality of creation in terms of higher or lower or intermediate places. According to him, "these names do not proceed out of the nature of things but from the point of view of one who observes them part by part. For there is no up and down in the universe, and therefore in the universe there is nothing either higher or lower or intermediate. These notions are rejected by a consideration of the whole, but introduced by attention to the parts . . . " (467a).

It follows then that, neither hierarchy nor coercion dominate in the reality of the absolute whole, but *Love* alone. "Love is a bond and chain," Eriugena holds, "by which the totality of all things is bound together in an ineffable friendship and indissoluble unity" (519b). *Love* is the fundamental principle of Christian faith; and Eriugena enthusiastically accepts it, applying the whole rigor of his philosophical reasoning to radically reconsider in accordance with this principle the way the entire universe appears to us. Thus he seeks to bring our vision of reality, and accordingly the mode of our existence, into perfect conformity with what has been revealed to us as the eternal Truth. In this sense, Eriugena is indeed a profoundly Christian thinker; and it is utterly unfair to mingle his system of thought with that of Neoplatonism, deeply rooted in a pre-Christian religious tradition and based on the fundamentally different methodological principles, appropriate to a non-Christian type of mentality.

After all these elucidations concerning the apparently hierarchy-averse dynamics of Eriugena's thought, I find it wholly inappropriate to associate his system with the Neoplatonic agenda and to keep considering it along the lines of the hierarchical metaphysics, which regrettably has become quite an archetypal tendency in Eriugenian studies since the foundation of SPES.[54] The statements erroneously acknowledging Eriugena's loyalty to a hierarchically structured approach to reality have long been accepted by Eriugenian scholars as almost a commonplace.[55] Thus, discussing the five modes of being offered by Eriugena in the opening part of the *Periphyseon* among the constitutive (and in many respects problematic) elements of his system, John O'Meara, deservedly reputed to be one of the leading founders of SPES, particularly suggests: "In the system of Eriugena the most important of these modes of being is the second, i.e., that according to a thing's place in a hierarchy."[56]

Such is the prevalent tendency in the Eriugenian studies up to the present and, perhaps, for many years onwards. As Hegel says, metaphysics, the genuine source of the hierarchical universe, has been overcome in the history of *thought* only, but not in the practice of everyday reasoning applied to all aspects of human activity including science.[57] And although Dermot Moran insists that the hierarchical order of being as it develops in the *Periphyseon* should rather be considered as a product of human mind than an outcome of the cosmological process, his appeal to mind-centered *subjectivism* as a way of dismantling the hierarchical division does not do justice to the real depth of the problem. "For Eriugena," Moran argues, "the hierarchical order of nature is in fact a product of mind, and is absorbed and transcended by the mind of the spiritually liberated person, the Pauline *homo spiritualis*."[58] By saying this, however, the scholar misses the point that if the mind's transcendence implemented by the "spiritually

54. "The whole of the *Division of Nature* is essentially an exercise in trying to follow the descent, or possibility of descent of creatures from One, and their return to the One up the hierarchy of being" (O'Meara, "Introduction," XII).

55. Among the solid monographs of the kind such may be mentioned, for example, as O'Meara, *Eriugena*; Moran, *Philosophy of John Scottus Eriugena*; and Otten, *Anthropology of Johannes Scottus Eriugena*.

56. O'Meara, "Introduction," XII.

57. In his *Logic*, Hegel says: "It is only in relation to the history of philosophy, however, that this metaphysics *belongs to the past*; for, on its own account, it is always present as the way in which the *mere understanding views* the objects of reason" (Hegel, *Encyclopaedia Logic*, 65, §27). And again: "All philosophy in its beginnings, all of the sciences, even the daily doing and dealing of consciousness, lives in this belief" (ibid., 65, §26).

58. Moran, *Philosophy*, 81–82.

liberated person" is understood in a purely subjective (apophatic-like) manner, then the very truth of infinity of the absolute being is put at risk, and the shortcomings of the hierarchical metaphysics as a paradigm of thinking remain insuperable.[59]

Indeed, in the above statement it remains unspecified whether the mind that *produces* "the hierarchical order of nature" and *transcends* it is one and the same or of different types (at least, in terms of methodology used). The readers' impression may therefore be that not the mind but the types of personality it is supposed to belong to are different, namely those of the spiritually "liberated" and "unliberated" ones. If so, and the mind mentioned is meant to pertain to different *subjects* (or types of personality), then this mind must simply be likewise *subjective*, no matter whether it is understood to produce or transcend the hierarchical order of being. It consequently means that the "transcendence" mentioned can only be a subjective procedure carried out by a subjective mind. The fact however is that nothing objective can be overcome (transcended) by the subjective, as well as the finite by the infinite, until both remain mutually countered and are not seen from the perspective of the absolute to be absorbed by it. By its very definition (and therefore proper nature), a *subjective* mind can be nothing else but a mere counterpart of the *objective* reality. Despite any claims, therefore, the subjective mind cannot actually pertain to "the spiritually liberated person," who is meant to be *the image and likeness* of God and whose independence is supposed to be in conformity with the absolute freedom of the infinite whole. Nevertheless, in spite of these dialectical subtleties of theological thinking, Dermot Moran believes that "Eriugena's system, while seeming to provide an *objective* hierarchical metaphysics of order, actually presents a *subjectivist* and *idealist* philosophy, in the sense that all spatiotemporal reality is understood as immaterial, mind dependent, and lacking an independent existence; and also in the Hegelian sense, whereby all finite reality is understood to require infinite reality for its full intelligibility and completion."[60]

Anti-Subjectivism Argument

Moran is not alone in looking at Eriugena's system from a *subjectivist* perspective. Ferdinand Christian Baur[61] likewise acknowledged the subjectivist

59. For a closer consideration of apophaticism as intrinsically metaphysical approach to being see chapter 2 of the present work.

60. Moran, *Philosophy,* 81.

61. Ferdinand Christian Baur, the founder and leader of the New Tübingen School

character of Eriugena's discourse, though, unlike Moran, he was very far from appreciating it as a merit of the system the medieval thinker developed. "According to F. Ch. Baur's critique of Eriugena," Beierwaltes says, "neither the process of incarnation and resurrection nor the creation takes place objectively, since Eriugena does not think them idealistically throughout. And thus the proceeding from God and the reversion into God cannot be taken as two different momenta. In the creation and self-incarnation God has not proceeded from himself, and the reversion is equally without result; both motions can only be distinguished by the thinking mind, and they are thus only distinguished subjectively."[62] Baur is confident that in Eriugena we are dealing with an explicit *subjectivism*; and it is this subjectivism that, according to him, does not allow Eriugena's system to be consistently idealistic. As Beierwaltes further elucidates Baur's position, it is resolutely critical of Eriugena's so-called subjectivism: "The process of God, expressed by Eriugena, is not an objective process . . . ; God's self-mediation and consequently the idea of the Son and the Spirit and the idea of the Trinity and the four natures also, belong merely to the subjective consciousness of the construing mind. God's being, described as process, remains abstract, unmediated in itself; the thinking mind fails to achieve for himself the mediation of the process."[63]

Similarly to Moran's, Baur's argument concerning Eriugena's "subjectivism" does not seem ungrounded. It is true that the stages of the "process" resulting in the hierarchical order of being are in fact nothing more to Eriugena than a product of the mind; because, and it is essential to his view of creation, no particular beings abandon *objectively* the universal Principle of all. It is the mind indeed that separates these *particular* beings from the source of their existence and—denying thus the very possibility of their participation in the infinite nature—places them *outside* the universal Principle, as if it is normal to them to leave their Creator. This is however the case when the mind, being *corrupted* (deceived and misled) by senses, develops a *wrong vision* of reality. The major task of theological thinking, as Eriugena sees it, consequently consists in the restoration of a *sound vision* of reality to be known as creation, and thus in bringing all things created (including human being) back to the original unity of the substantial reality that is said to be "by itself and through itself and in itself and for itself." The return to the pristine state of unity, lost in the result of the mind's corruption

---

of theology, is usually reckoned among the admirers of Hegel, although this admiration did not go that far in fact as the adoption of some of the basic ideas of Hegel's philosophy of history.

62. Beierwaltes, "Revaluation," 196.

63. Ibid., 194.

(symbolically expressed by the scriptural story of Fall), is therefore seen by Eriugena in the way of the restoration of the mind's dignity, attainable through the proper operations of *right reason*, perfectly fit for being in union with the substantial order of reality as it truly is.

This restoration of the mind is however not merely an *epistemological* (subjectivist) motion that simply contrasts with the historical or cosmological (objective) one, but is the restoration of the real wholeness, and in this sense is a purely *spiritual* act of being at one with the absolute whole. The *epistemological* agenda, as Eriugena understands it, is that of the mind's conformity to the *true being*. It goes therefore hand in hand with the *ontology* proper, the prime concern of which is *the way the true (infinite) being can be coherently thought of*[64] so as to let all humans, thus radically transformed, be actually at one with the true Being itself.[65] Not unfairly therefore is this return to the universal unity called by Werner Beierwaltes the "act of salvation or the soteriological return of the world," by which all beings return to the Principle not "'naturaliter,' i.e., by a cosmological process," but by *grace* (*gratia*),[66] when the whole of being finds itself in perfect union (or harmony) with God himself who, in Eriugena's words already mentioned, never "moves beyond Himself, but from Himself in Himself towards Himself."[67] These different types of the return are what Eriugena distinguishes as the *general* and *special* ones, meaning by them respectively the *cosmological* and *spiritual* motions; and it is apparently the latter one that is to be identified as the focal point of his systematic thought. This is the return that takes place not in the "objective" world of physical objects which are opposed to the *subjective* mind (claiming power of its sense-dependent experience over the rest of the world), but in *Spirit* as the living whole, in whose ubiquitous unity there are neither opposites nor division. The *cosmological* ("general") and *spiritual* ("special") types of return should therefore be properly understood as appropriate to different *perspectives* of reality. And these perspectives are

64. As Dermot Moran suggests, it was well known to Eriugena from his translation of Maximus the Confessor's *Ambigua* that God is *to auto einai* meaning *Being itself* (see Moran, *Philosophy,* 119).

65. The anthropological theme, evolving in Eriugena in the context of the return of human nature to the substantial state of unity of being, is closely considered by Willemien Otten in her *Anthropology of Johannes Scottus Eriugena.*

66. Beierwaltes, "Revaluation," 195.

67. It is important not to forget that God's being is only conceivable as the *infinite* one, beyond which there is nothing. So that, when God's "motion" is understood to proceed "from Himself in Himself towards Himself," it is meant to cover the whole of the infinite being. In this sense, strictly speaking, there can be no *cosmological* return in the reality of creation, because there is in fact no room for a spatio-temporal motion where God alone *infinitely* is.

directly related to *different types of mind*, which can perhaps be best distinguished after Kant as those of *Verstand* and *Vernunft*, or the *subjective* and *spiritual* mind. As a staunch Christian thinker who is immensely concerned about the way salvation (or the return to the substantial reality of the infinite whole) is brought about, Eriugena can therefore be best understood, to my mind, in the light of his intellectually thoroughgoing struggle for a cardinal change of the paradigms of thinking, without which the proper depth of the truth of Revelation remains hardly accessible.

So Baur is definitely right when he critically says of Eriugena that, according to him, "the proceeding from God and reversion into God cannot be taken as two different momenta." But the German theologian is profoundly wrong when says that Eriugena *subjectively* approaches these "objective" processes, and for this reason accuses him of *subjectivism*. In fact, Eriugena is not a subjectivist but a *dialectician*, and his approach to the infinity of God's being is not subjective but *dialectical*. Dialectic indeed does not permit us to treat contraries *separately*, in a "first-then" manner, but requires them to be taken *simultaneously*. Only thus, taken in their integrity, do the contraries prove to be appropriate to the reality of the whole as it truly is, while proceeding from the universal Principle of all and never abandoning it. Proceeding from himself, the infinite God never moves *beyond* himself, but only *unfolds* himself or manifests *himself*. And in this sense, God stays *within* himself, remaining *identical* to himself or, as it were, ever *returning* to himself. The "proceeding" and the "reversion," as far as they are considered with relation to the infinite being of the absolute whole, are *inseparable*, and can only be properly known therefore as taking place *simultaneously*.

This is how the infinite being is coherently thought of and becomes close to those who are prepared to be transformed by the renewing of their minds.[68] God moves nowhere; it is *us* who move in our integral (i.e., dialectically disciplined) mind that, like a living Spirit, brings us into conformity with the reality of the One. Just as in the Parmenidian ontology, so it is in the ongoing history of dialectic, passing through Eriugena up to Hegel, that thinking and being are understood to be not two different things but one and the same.[69] And this is the point that finds its conspicuous expression in Hegel's cardinal idea of unity of the historical and logical, that is, of the principle inseparability of temporality and eternity in *our*—as the patriarch of dialectic emphasizes—ascent to God. According to dialectic, *the Other* of God cannot be understood as subsisting "objectively," and

---

68. See Rom 12:2. As a Christian authority, St Paul is so much revered by Eriugena that throughout the *Periphyseon* is called simply *the Apostle*.

69. Parmenides's *Periphyseon* (3:3) reads: "To think and to be are one and the same" (Parmenides, *Эллинские поэты*, 179).

therefore remaining immediately given to the mind as something substantial. So that, as Hegel suggests in his *Logic*, although nature (or creation) can be considered as the Other posited by God, it does not mean however that both nature and God co-exist as substances. "When we say, 'Consider nature, for it will lead you to God, and you will find an absolute final purpose,'" Hegel explains,

> this does not mean that God is mediated, but only that *we* make the journey from an other to God, in the sense that God, being the consequence, is at the same time the absolute ground of what we started with, so that the position of the two is reversed: what appears as the consequence also shows itself to be the ground, while what presented itself as ground to start with is reduced to [the status of] consequence. And that is precisely the path of rational proof.[70]

The dialectical reformation of the mind or its restoration to the proper *rational motion*, as Eriugena calls it,[71] is actually what brings all human beings, according to him, to life of dignity in the reality they originally belonged to. A vision of this dialectical reformation of the mind—revolutionary by nature, scale, and implications—lies at the very heart of Eriugena's endeavor of approaching and rethinking the Christian theology of salvation; and I would like to show by the present inquiry into the meaning of the *Periphyseon*'s text where and how in Eriugena's discourse dialectic comes to work.

The Major and Minor Tasks

In the light of the above given arguments, it is not hard to see how crucial dialectic is to the entire of Eriugena's project. Yet, in my view, this dialectic is not sufficiently investigated in Eriugenian studies in terms of its centrality and innovative role for the doctrine developed by Eriugena. In particular, dialectic is not considered at all as a paradigm of thinking in contrast to metaphysical thinking. At best, endlessly repeating each other, scholars keep talking about Eriugena's "use of a sophisticated dialectic with moments of progression and recollection,"[72] though understanding these "moments" in a non-dialectical manner of the "mutually complementary" counterparts' temporal succession. They tend therefore to relegate Eriugena's dialectic to a

---

70. Hegel, *Encyclopaedia Logic*, 75, §36 ad.

71. As one of the fundamental notions of Eriugena's system, *rational motion* is closely considered in chapter 4 of the present work.

72. Moran, *Philosophy*, 123.

kind of *method* just applicable to the mind's "natural activity," "with its out-going and returning movements, its affirmative and negative capabilities."[73] And thus the scholars demonstrate no interest in *contradiction* as the fundamental principle of dialectic, which alone, when properly treated, allows us to consider the contraries in their unity.

As a result, dialectic comes to be interpreted by the Eriugenian scholars in line with certain presuppositions largely related to what Moran calls "a *negative* dimension" (developed by the Neoplatonist philosophy and apophatic theology),[74] but not in accordance with what is actually found at work in the whole of Eriugena's text itself. Not infrequently therefore do researchers' misunderstanding of his dialectic go as far as the assertion that it discovers "the divisions" as "the basic structure of nature herself."[75] Seen in the light of the so-called *negative dialectic* traditionally associated with the Neoplatonic-Dionysian apophaticism, the division of "nature" into the "essential" and "superessential" as its mutually contrasting (and even opposing) parts is normally understood by the metaphysically-oriented researchers to be the way of contemplating the entirety of reality. Aiming to cleave to the area of transcendence and, therefore, resting upon the divide between *being* and *non-being* as the contrary parts of existence (standing, as it were, for the alternative realities), such an expressly metaphysical vision of reality applies neither to a coherent approach to knowing God's Oneness as the absolute (all-embracing) unity nor to Eriugena's search for the way of thinking the infinite as the undivided and unconfined totality of being. When apophatically treated, the finite is supposed to be negated and overcome as something unsubstantial and incompatible with the infinite nature of the Supreme Principle of all. In fact, however, after being apophatically denied, the finite remains set over against the infinite as such and thus maintained in its independent existence as something consubstantial with its counterpart.

While trying to "see what transcends the sense-realm" (or the area of finite things) and, for this purpose, to lay aside "all the representations of sense" (appropriate to the immediate perception of the finite),[76] the apophatic "dialectic" remains captive, as seen above, to a *what*-type of knowledge since the principles of the *via negativa* were first formulated by the Neoplatonist thought. As a result, the negative "dialectic" has to recognise the transcendent (that surpasses the realm of finitude) to be ineffable and incomprehensible. By doing so, the apophatic thought proves therefore to

73. Ibid., 124.

74. See ibid., 123–124.

75. Sheldon-Williams, "Eriugena's Greek Sources," 4.

76. Plotinus, *Six Enneads*, V. 5:6.

be primarily concerned not as much about the way of thinking (and knowing) the infinite as about the way of speaking of it. As apophaticism in
general suggests with regard to our approach to the infinite, "we hold it not
so as to state it but so as to be able to speak about it. We can and do state
what it is not, while we are silent as to what it is . . . "[77] The apophatic definition, therefore, "could be only 'the indefinable,' what is not a thing is not
some definite thing. We are in agony for a true expression; we are talking of
untellable; we name, only to indicate for our own use as best we may. And
this name, The One, contains really no more than the negation of plurality
. . . "[78] The One and many are thus understood to be mutually countered,
in the result of which the Unity as such becomes in fact utterly unthinkable and unapproachable. All this, hence, makes the apophatic agenda
essentially irrelevant and inapplicable to the principal task of Eriugena's
anti-division project, and for this reason it should not be engaged in depth
within the framework of the present investigation of the *Periphyseon*'s dialectic as of the way of thinking coherently of God's Oneness. As *a paradigm
of thinking* constituting the very basis of Eriugena's speculative approach to
Christian theology, this dialectic, unlike the "negative" one, seems not to
draw the attention of the Eriugenian scholars at all, which is quite unfair
to his epoch-making achievements and counterproductive for any further
advanced studies of his legacy.

I find it very important therefore, and see it as the *major task* of the
present work, to uncover the dialectic which we are really dealing with in
Eriugena when closely and critically read his *Periphyseon*, and above all its
Book 4, the most difficult and perhaps least studied among all other parts
of the main treatise. This is a kind of approach which, I believe, allows us
to realise that at the basis of the dialectic sought there lies what might be
not improperly called the *cardinal contradiction*, for it really determines the
entire course of Eriugena's reasoning. This is undoubtedly the contradiction
that from the very outset of the *Periphyseon* is meant by its author to take
the shape of the unity of the first and fourth forms of Nature, and thus to
be articulated in the form of a paradoxical statement about God, according
to which he is understood to be the one who *does and does not create at the
same time*. And the reason why this contradiction is supposed to be cardinal
and determine Eriugena's train of thought is quite simple. By formulating
the contradiction, Eriugena has no intention to explain *how* God creates the
universe and dwells within himself. What Eriugena is really after and seeks
to achieve by thinking dialectically is an understanding of how *salvation* is

77. Ibid., V. 3:14.
78. Ibid., V. 5:6.

actually brought about or, in other words, how human beings return from their captivity in the world of finitude to the substantial reality of creation and union with God (i.e., how they can *truly be*).[79] In short, speaking in terms of the arguments presented above, it would be not unfair to conclude that the thing Eriugena is really interested in is not a *cosmological* but *spiritual* dimension of creation, where the spiritual liberation of the entire human being comes true.

Indeed, as it will be seen from the analysis of Eriugena's text and conception unfolding in chapters 3–7, it is a *radical transformation of the human mind* that secures its (and accordingly human being's) way back to the substantial reality of God's creation. Actually, it is the dialectic of the universal and particular that, according to Eriugena, provides the way of both tackling the ontological dichotomy (between being and non-being) and thinking consistently of the totality and infinity of God's being. From this perspective, it will also be clear therefore that, as a paradigm of thinking deeply implanted in Eriugena's discourse, dialectic effectively promotes the mind's progress towards knowing the truth of God's Oneness and, as a consequence, real adoption of the salvific truth revealed by Christ. That is why it will not be hard to understand how the dialectical conception of unity, as it evolves in the *Periphyseon*, gives Eriugena's readers an opportunity to radically reconsider the metaphysical view of creation that the theological reflection traditionally relies on. From a coherently dialectical point of view, God and creation cannot be set apart. Speaking more specifically, according to Eriugena's dialectic, the reality of creation cannot be conceived otherwise than in the way of being inseparable from the universal Principle that *gives rise to all things, but itself is abandoned by none*. This is a dialectical expression of the unshakable truth, and it is ignored solely by the mind corrupted by senses and therefore following the metaphysical pattern of the ontological dichotomy, called by Eriugena the *fundamental division*. Contradiction between the universal and the particular (like the one above) is absolutely essential to the dialectic coherently understood; and our analysis will show that Eriugena's discourse strongly appeals to dialectical contradictions and is actually based on their proper treatment.

---

79. The human *true being* is the focal point of the *fifth* mode of understanding of being offered by Eriugena, and as we shall see it later in chapter 3, the way human being *truly are* should be not inappropriately identified as the subject-matter of the final, *fifth*, book of the *Periphyseon*. In this sense, it is hard to agree with those by whom the fifth mode of being "was found to stand somewhat apart from the others, for instead of covering the complete realm of nature or created nature, it pertained to *humana natura* alone," due to which, they thought, it would be quite problematic "to fit man into the scheme laid down in Eriugena's overall *divisio naturae*" (Otten, *Anthropology*, 111).

This kind of inquiry into Eriugena's thought, the depth of which is only amenable to a methodological tool of close reading of the dense text of his voluminous Book, will definitely allow us to justify the validity of Noack's and Schlüter's vision of a striking affinity between Eriugena's system and Hegel's *dialectical monism*, as stated at the beginning of this *Introduction*. It will also help us to suggest some possible solutions to a variety of concomitant tasks of a minor sort, which however—when considered from the perspective of the promotion of a deeper understanding of Eriugena's legacy—prove in fact to be as important as the major one. Among these *minor tasks* that the present work deals with in addition to the major one, I would feature the following:

1. Recognition of a good deal of affinity between Eriugena's discourse and that of his Islamic contemporaries (notably, Allaf and al-Nazzam), who developed their dialectical ideas within the Mu'tazilah tradition of a philosophically disciplined approach to the truth of God's Oneness: making claim in connection with this that al-Nazzam's engagement with Parmenides's *Periphyseon* and his resistance to a possibility of a dualistic interpretation of its ontology might have provoked Eriugena's innovative approach to Christian theology with a view to suggesting a mode of overcoming dualism as the main obstacle on the way to the Truth revealed.

2. Suggestion of a possibility of having the *Periphyseon*'s structure reconsidered with reference to *five* modes of understanding of being (and not to the forms of Nature, as usually believed), which would allow us to associate these modes with the genuine subject-matter of each of the *five* books of the main treatise.

3. Reinterpretation of the fourfold division of Nature not in the sense of a basic structure of Eriugena's system, but as a means of the introduction of dialectic to the body of Christian theology by refutation of Augustine's metaphysical vision of a hierarchical threefold model of the universe.

4. Formulation of reasons for the necessity of reconsidering the entirety of Eriugena's system from the perspective of an *anti-division* project, by virtue of which it could be recognised as a historically significant step towards developing a coherent theology of God's Oneness, utterly incompatible with any attempts of its metaphysical interpretation in terms of division of the infinite being into opposites.

The Work Outline

From the account of the tasks that the thesis sets itself, it is clear that the research undertaken here aims to logically reconstruct the way in which Eriugena's thought seeks to provide a coherent theology of God's Oneness, as appropriate to the truth revealed by Christ and expressed in writing by St. Paul and St. John. According to this truth, God is really the One who is at one with the entire reality of his creation, for he never acts from beyond his being and produces nothing alien to himself. As a result, nothing whatsoever may be understood to fall out of God's creation (unless its substantial order is maliciously broken by a corrupt will going counter to it), because outside him who is the One nothing at all may subsist. All this consequently means that all human beings with no exception, as part of God's creation, may truly be known as his *children*, coming forth into being from the only Father of all. Essential to the theology following the truth revealed is, therefore, a new vision of creation, which is to be brought into conformity with a dialectical understanding of the *universality* of the Principle of all particular beings.

From the perspective of the truth revealed, creation should no longer be seen as the world in its appearance (i.e., as a conglomerate of finite things as they are immediately given to the senses), but as the substantial reality where the infinite and finite are not mutually countered, and the universal and particular are not separated from one another. The advanced and coherent theology, as Eriugena envisages it, should start not with God himself (i.e., with the assumptions concerning his being, which would simply reproduce the errors of metaphysics preoccupied with predicating attributes of the invisible essence), but with the way in which God's unity can be consistently thought of so as to allow the mind (and, hence, the entire human being) to actually be at one with the whole of the substantial reality. In other words, the new theology that Eriugena is concerned about would insist that the One God cannot be truly known unless humans are capable of being at one both with their genuine nature (where the essence and existence are inseparably one) and with him in whom there is no discrepancy between his will and being.

Not unreasonably, therefore, the agenda of the new theology, as it comes to the fore in Eriugena's discourse, might take up the shape of the following twofold expression:

> God can only be known from the perspective of the true reality;

> so to be able to know God, human beings should get into the true reality.

With regard to this expression (signifying that the ultimate knowledge and the true being are inseparably one), at least two interdependent questions arise to clarify the notions constituting the epistemological-ontological core of the advanced (or philosophically disciplined) theology, at the heart of which there should lie a strong appeal to what Eriugena calls a proper *rational motion* and understands as the most essential movement of human nature. The questions meant here may be formulated as follows: 1) Why knowledge? 2) How should the true reality be understood?

In its ultimate sense, *knowledge* is a clear vision of the invisible, which is, obviously, unattainable without thinking in paradox. God is not immediately present to the visible world of finite things and can therefore be only *known* (or thought of) as the infinite that comprises all things, being in and beyond them at the same time.

As for *the true reality* that ever is while remaining undivided from within and unconfined from without, it should be coherently understood as the absolute or self-identical Being that is neither preceded nor followed by non-being. This is, hence, the reality of self-disclosure (better known to the faithful mind as the reality of creation), where nothing external can subsist on its own, i.e., without being indivisibly whole (infinite in itself) or intimately connected to its innermost essence and thus determined by it.

To be part of the absolute whole (or belong to the infinite Being), human beings should, clearly, be whole in themselves (or restored to the self-identical integrity of their genuine nature), so that no discrepancy between their inner essence and outer existence (the mind and its visible manifestation or incarnation in flesh) could be found in them. This is the way to participate in the substantial order of creation and, hence, to really know the invisible God or to subsist indeed among what Eriugena calls "the Divine things." As the criterion of the profoundly understood unity of Knowledge and Being, Truth should therefore become the focal point in the mind of those who uncover the infinity of their self-identity and thus come close to the secrets of immortality and complete transformation of their life. This is the Truth that is understood to be the cornerstone of the coherent theology as it develops within Eriugena's discourse to lead the faithful to their salvation (or liberation from the captivity in the transient world of finitude) and their righteous life in the rightly-ordered reality of creation (or self-disclosure), in which the infinite God is adequately manifest and therefore really known.

Consideration of some of the central issues raised by Islamic philosophy (as seen in the context of the predestination controversy) and Cappadocian theology, Heidegger's and Parmenides's ontology, Plato and the dialectical approach to contradiction as such is not undertaken within the framework of the present project with reference to the *historical* evolution of their doctrines. As a matter of fact, it is undertaken for purely *logical* reasons and proceeds with a view to highlighting a number of crucial turns in the train of thought that leads us to resolving a methodological task of reconstruction of *the inner logic* of Eriugena's discourse and, along with this, to identifying *the cardinal contradiction* as the basic and formative principle of his system, in which philosophy and religion, as we shall see it later, are understood to be one and the same.

From the Mu'tazilah tenets of the Divine Unity and First Obligation (which seem to have immensely influenced Eriugena's views on freedom and predestination, good and evil), this consideration progresses towards a brief analysis of the *universalist approach* to the totality of God's being, suggested by Gregory the Theologian in continuity with the fundamentals of the Pauline theology. In particular, Gregory's interpretation of the Tetragrammaton brings us close to the problem of the interconnectedness of being and time and, as a consequence, to the point that Heidegger's hermeneutical ontology is largely focused on, which in turn convinces us that no profound and coherent ontology can avoid the issue of temporality. Moreover, a scrupulous analysis of the basic notions of this kind of ontology allows us to better understand that in so far as being and time are consistently thought of in their unity, the intimate connection of both transcends the horizon of the empirical existence and opens up a prospect of being beyond the limits of time. The dialectic of temporality and eternity, as it develops in Plato's thought, further deepens our understanding of the relationship between the universal and particular and proceeds towards a clearer vision of the non-dialectical character of Parmenides's approach to the totality of Being. The latter, and especially a danger of a dualistic misinterpretation of the ontology of the absolute whole, finally brings us to the agenda of Eriugena's *dialectical monism* (with its focus on the dialectical treatment of contradictions), which allows us to concentrate on reading his texts with a view to reconstructing a methodologically innovative approach to Christian theology. The dialectic of the universal and particular, deeply implanted in Eriugena's *Periphyseon*, turns out to be a methodological key to the whole of his system and, at the same time, an effective means of having it reconstructed as a coherent conception.

As a result of this logically determined consideration, it would be not improper, I think, to qualify the entire project as a work of *philosophical* theology. Such a status of the work would perfectly comply with the very substance of Eriugena's own discourse, theologically systematic and philosophically disciplined by nature. Largely stimulated—as the *Periphyseon* perspicuously shows—by his thoughtful interpretation of the first three chapters of the Book of Genesis, the novelty of Eriugena's approach to Christian theology apparently consists in its coherently philosophical integrity, essential to which is a strong appeal to thinking dialectically of the substantial unity of the entire reality of creation.

The inquiry undertaken in the present work is focused on such Eriugena's texts as:

1. *The Periphyseon*, Books 1–3;

2. *The Periphyseon*, Book 4;

3. *Treatise on Divine Predestination*;

4. *The Voice of the Eagle*.[80]

The work includes seven chapters bound up with one another by the following central ideas they are focused on:

1. God cannot be known as a *finite* being, and cannot therefore be thought of by means of *predicating attributes* of his essence.

2. The *infinite* is only conceivable by means of *contradiction* dialectically treated.

3. Understood as the universal Principle of all, God admits of nothing else *outside* his infinite being, so that the reality of creation can only be known as being *inseparably* one with its Creator.

4. The substantial order of the infinite reality is such that the particular proceeds from the universal, and not otherwise; this is the order that is manifest to the human mind in its proper *rational motion*, when conceived in a dialectical way, according to which the particular does not abandon the universal Principle while proceeding from it.

5. *Contradiction* becomes a means of thinking (and knowing) the universal unity when contradictories (that contradiction consists of) are considered as being *simultaneously true*.

6. Knowledge of the infinite, attainable solely through the mind's complete transformation in accordance with the dialectical discipline of thinking, gets the entire human nature restored to its integrity, and thus brings it to being at one with the universal reality as it truly (infinitely) is in its unity.

7. The infinite being of the One God is essentially indivisible within itself, and therefore is understood to be at once the Beginning and the Middle and the End; this consequently means that only that which

80. For the details of the sources listed see Bibliography

uncovers its true (infinite) nature, so as to actually become thereby the *image and likeness* of God, can *truly be*, that is, be perfectly at one with the universal reality of the One.

This sequence of ideas (appropriate to the order of the work's chapters) may not unfairly be suggested, to my mind, as an outline of the main stages through which develops a coherent theology of God's Oneness, as Eriugena understands it and presents by his *Periphyseon*'s conception.

CHAPTER 1

Eriugena: Personality and Origin

Vision

ERIUGENA IS A THINKER who said aloud that true philosophy and true religion are one.[1] And the world heard this in the mid-ninth century, when
Christendom was still in its infancy, and when a possibility of building
God's kingdom on earth was still believed to be a realistic social project
in the Carolingian Gall.[2]

Having found himself at the center of a new historical undertaking of
building up a Christian kingdom in the West of Europe (he appears in the
royal court of Charles the Bald around the year 847), Eriugena sought to
reconsider the way creation was traditionally understood. To him, it could
not be severed from the Creator and opposed to him, because it is the reality
that takes its origin from the Universal Principle which, due to its infinite
universality, can never be abandoned by anything coming forth from it. It
is the corrupt mind (the one subject to the irrational motion or entirely
captive to the dictates of senses) that makes things leave the Principle of
their being and take their place, as it were, outside it. Thus the corrupt mind
gives rise to the world of finite things which, like a veil made of sensible
fantasies, covers up the substantial reality that subsists in unity with the

1. From Eriugena's *Treatise on Divine Predestination* it is clear that although his view
of the relationship between philosophy and religion follows that of Augustine's (*De vera
religione*, 5:8), Eriugena is much more explicit and radical in his articulation of their
identity. "If, indeed, as Saint Augustine says, it is believed and taught as the fundamental principle of man's salvation that philosophy, that is study of wisdom, is not one thing
and religion another . . .," the author of the *Treatise* argues, "what else is the exercise of
philosophy but the exposition of the rules of true religion by which the supreme and
principal cause of all things, God, is worshipped with humility and rationality searched
for? It follows then that true philosophy is true religion and conversely that true religion
is true philosophy" (Eriugena, *Treatise*, 7).

2. On the Carolingians' attitude to Augustine's *On the City of God* as an authorita-
tive guideline for building a 'City of God' on earth see chapter 7 of the present work.

ultimate Principle of all. Finding themselves in such an illusory world, human beings have to lead a false life or search for the way back to where they truly belong by their genuine nature brought forth into being by one and the same Principle of all.

In this search for the way out, Religion and Philosophy, as Eriugena saw them, must go hand in hand, indeed, because they have one and the same subject of their interest—namely, the Ultimate Reality; and the objective, or the basic question they are both concerned about, is that of the way human beings can actually subsist in it. Thus Religion and Philosophy do meet together, while providing the proper goal for the human soul's aspiration and the tool for having this aspiration brought about, which, as Eriugena persistently convinces us, is all about the restoration of the human mind to its proper rational motion.

The articulation of this fundamental vision of the meaning of human life, profoundly religious and philosophical at the same time, must have sounded very revolutionary for the ninth century—at the dawn of a new era and new expectations of human life. Nevertheless, the most amazing thing about all this perhaps is that it sounds very much the same at the outset of the twenty-first century, when the human world is facing a dilemma of its further degradation and complete annihilation or spiritual regeneration and movement towards a new horizon of being. To be or not to be is the perennial dilemma of Hamlet, haunting humanity all the way through its historical drama. Does Eriugena bring us any closer to its solution? This is the question to be answered by those who feel call for searching the Truth.

Background

John Scottus Eriugena is undoubtedly a prominent and at the same time a mysterious figure in intellectual history. He appears in Gall (the territory of modern France), literally speaking, out of the blue around the year 847, and likewise suddenly disappears after the year 877. The height of his intellectual might, the depth of his thought, and the scope of his erudition are extraordinary. He is a philosopher and theologian, translator and commentator, poet and educator. His knowledge of Greek and Greek Fathers is quite unique in the West of those days. His monumental works *On Divine Predestination* and, above all, the voluminous *Periphyseon* are out of comparison with anything else of the kind. No one like him was ever known to the West between Augustine and Anselm, that is, for a span of about six hundred years. The brilliance of his mind strikes many, as much amongst his contemporaries as among the illustrious scholars of the following generations.

Like a rock, he is said to rise above the empty plain, surprisingly enough anticipating many of the crucial turns and developments of thought of later days, up to the post-Enlightenment and the age of Romanticism, which deservedly won him, as mentioned above, a reputation of the "Hegel of the ninth century." Despite all this, however, on the horizon of the ninth century Europe Eriugena, seen from the perspective of the magnitude of his system, remains a solitary and enigmatic figure. How he could suddenly emerge among the Carolingian scholars who were just taking some faltering steps on their intellectual path, where he did come from, from what intellectual background—remains a mystery.

Sources

For about two centuries (actually, since the post-Hegelian time in Germany) Eriugenian studies have been trying to shed light upon this mystery, upon the sources of Eriugena's thought and the intellectual tradition it might be associated with, but hardly anyone could say for sure nowadays that this riddle has been unraveled.

Perhaps, one of the misleading assumptions was and still is, since researchers have been gathered under the aegis of SPES, to approach this problematic issue from speculations upon the meaning of Eriugena's name. For some reason, it is strongly believed by many that his *nomen gentile* Scottus and *cognomen* Eriugena can explain much. In particular, it is assumed that these two parts of Eriugena's full name allow scholars to firmly bind up his fleshly and intellectual origin with both the Celtic area (Ireland or probably Scotland) and the Celtic spiritual tradition, normally associated with a network of Irish monasteries settled in mainland Hibernia and widely spread across the Continent.[3] The truth about all these speculations is however that the meaning of the *cognomen* "Eriugena" does not seem to be as clear as that of the *nomen gentile*. As John O'Meara suggests, it might indicate either Ireland (meaning then "the Irishman born in Ireland") or some other individual locations in the Celtic world. The meaning of the name is in fact so uncertain that the range of possible interpretations may go as far as Schaar Schmitt's solution to the riddle. "Schaar Schmitt," O'Meara admits, "took Eriugena to be equivalent to the Greek Erigenes, meaning "born in the East."[4] To my mind, the latter version of the name would sound quite plausible and relevant to what we are actually dealing with in Eriugena. Given his unique expertise in the Greek language and

3. See, for example, O'Meara, *Eriugena*, 1–4.
4. Ibid., 2.

Eastern thought that came not from the monastery schools in Ireland, why would it be illogical to assume that a young man could travel to the East, live there for some time and, when the time was ripe, come from over there to the Carolingian Gaul as a mature scholar? Should not the main name be proper to the experience of the second, spiritual, birth as an intellectually advanced personality comes through in the process of his or her formation? To me, this is precisely the case with the name of John Scottus Eriugena, the Irishman born in the East. If so, however, then the problematic issues of the origin of his thought as well as the way of his thinking and the objectives of his mission in the Carolingian Gaul should definitely be seen from a different perspective.

As for the "sources" of Eriugena's system, almost all key figures of Christian thought that flourished both in the Latin West and the Greek East prior to Eriugena are normally reckoned among them. Not much has actually changed in this area of Eriugenian studies since a solid inquiry into the matter by the Russian theologian and scholar A. I. Brilliantov, *The Influence of Eastern Theology on Western Theology in the Works of John Scottus Erigena,*[5] first came to light in St. Petersburg in 1898. Offering a profoundly systematic analysis of the theology of Gregory of Nyssa and Maximus the Confessor in comparison with the Augustinian elements of Eriugena's thought,[6] Brilliantov's book hitherto remains, in scholars' opinion, "perhaps the best research on the theological views and literary work of Erigena, one of the most intriguing religious thinkers of the Middle Ages."[7] The whole gallery of authorities—including, in addition to those mentioned, Ambrose, Epiphanius, Basil the Great, Gregory the Theologian and, of course, Dionysius the Areopagite—are fairly nominated by the prominent Russian scholar among Eriugena's predecessors,[8] whose impact on him who was well familiar with their writings is indisputable at all. Since then however it has become a norm in Eriugenian studies to treat these authors as the direct "sources" of Eriugena's own thought. And this tendency has turned in fact into a kind of preoccupation with identifying the ideas that seem to be "borrowed" by Eriugena from his predecessors, which, in my view, is wrong, unfair and counterproductive.

Eriugena appeared at the Carolingian royal court as a scholar of high reputation, who enjoyed the king's favour and was deeply respected by his

---

5. For the source details see Bibliography.

6. See Brilliantov, *Влияние восточного богословия,* 90–234.

7. Innokentiy, "Санкт-Петербургская духовная академия," 233.

8. For the full list of the Latin and Greek authorities that Eriugena refers to in his works see Brilliantov, *Влияние восточного богословия,* 119–23.

colleagues. He was certainly a person capable of making his own contribution to the Carolingian scholarship; his expertise in the subtleties of advanced thought undoubtedly allowed him to say something new indeed. In the situation Eriugena found himself in the Palace school (obviously not the major center of sophisticated learning), it was quite natural for him, I believe, to refer to as many Christian authorities as possible to elucidate and substantiate his position, especially for those who might find it unfamiliar and challenging.[9] No wonder therefore that the Christian authors, particularly those whom he carefully read while translating, at the king's request, from Greek into Latin, could be broadly quoted by him for this purpose. In this sense, I assume, any attempts to underestimate the originality and innovative character of Eriugena's thinking can result in diminishing the magnitude of his system and, as a consequence, discourage any further development of Eriugenian studies. It would be likely more constructive therefore to look at the evolution of Eriugena's thought from the perspective of a possible *direct* influence on it—namely, from the perspective of the *intellectual climate* in which Eriugena could really grow up as a profound thinker, skilled both in theology and philosophy. Such an environment, or a scholarly community, could, clearly, be formed by the *contemporaries* of a similar intellectual might, who likewise set themselves the task of acquisition of the highest truth of faith. Surprisingly or not, but on the fringes of Christendom, where perhaps the Nestorians settled next to the Muslims,[10] such an environment did exist, precisely when a gifted young man called John Scottus could have some good reason to appear there.[11]

The Eastern Turn

"In broader cultural terms," Dermot Moran writes, "the ninth century in fact marks the beginning of several centuries of Islamic dominance in the fields of philosophy and science. The centers of intellectual learning and the heritage of Greek thought moves from Alexandria to Baghdad, where Al-Kindi

9. For example, Eriugena's first big treatise, *On Divine Predestination*, written at the Court was to some extent a failure, since, despite the author's extensive quotations from Augustine, it was little understood and received quite unfriendly, both by the opponents and the superiors.

10. "In Caliphate Christians could take very high position." Especially Christian scholars were favoured. "Thus Abu Zakharia Juhanna, a devoted Christian, was appointed the Head of the first House of Wisdom ("Academy of sciences")" (Amangaliev, "Несторианство," par. 16).

11. For the cultural situation in Baghdad of those days see Peters, *Aristotle and Arabs*, 7–55.

(c. 800–877) developed the first major Neoplatonic metaphysics, adapted to Islam."[12] Meaning furthermore a certain affinity between al-Kindi's and Eriugena's thought, Moran also suggests that a comparative analysis of the two systems could bear good fruit. "It would be interesting," he argues, "to compare the two Neoplatonic systems of Eriugena and Al-Kindi, as they were almost exact contemporaries."[13]

In continuity with this, I would suggest however that the results of such a comparison of the two systems[14] could be more than "interesting:" they will completely change our understanding of the origin of Eriugena's thought. Indeed, even the overall impression of the *First Philosophy*, al-Kindi's major work on the "knowledge of the First Truth Who is the cause of all truth,"[15] is absolutely striking. The central themes discussed in the treatise are essentially congenial to those of Eriugena. The universality of the Principle outside which there is nothing; the alternative kinds of perception and accordingly the alternative perspectives of the mind; the "eye" of intellect and search for a "non-representational perception" overcoming the "blindness" of intellect; "possible" and "impossible" contradictions; principle incompatibility of the order of the universe, its rest and motion, with the "first/then" pattern[16]—all these notions of al-Kindi are likewise the basic ideas constituting the very structure of Eriugena's discourse displayed in his *Periphyseon*.

How could it happen that the Islamic and Christian thinkers could stand so close to one another? The answer, I think, is very simple—it is to be found in the very circumstances that stimulated an active intellectual interaction between members of different religious traditions present in the cultural environment of Baghdad of the ninth and the following centuries. Lack of dogmatic pressure and ecclesiastical hierarchy in Islam helped a great deal to those who believed in the universal truth common to all faiths and esoteric teachings to develop contacts between Muslims, Christians,

12. Moran, *Philosophy*, 2.

13. Ibid.

14. Taking into account how passionate al-Kindi was in his belief in the creation *ex nihilo* doctrine as well as what is said in Introduction about the "Neoplatonic" flavour of Eriugena's system, we may fairly acknowledge that a certain "ism" ascribed to both thinkers in the quotation above is not necessarily relevant to what they are actually doing in their systems. "It is therefore surprising to find," Alfred Ivry admits, "that al-Kindi borrows so little explicit doctrine from the major work of Neoplatonism, Plotinus's *Enneads*" (Al-Kindi, *First Philosophy*, 15). In particular, quite "apparently he rejects Neoplatonic ontology but is drawn to its view of the transcendent One Who is, nevertheless, the Creator" (ibid., 15–16).

15. Ibid., 12.

16. See ibid., 35–40.

and Jews and treat them as equals.[17] Search for "the inner meaning of the Sacred Scripture," lying at the heart of all religious traditions, brought them all together.[18] Representatives of all religions and philosophical schools were, for example, warmly welcomed at the scholarly debates regularly held in Baghdad by the Mu'tazilites, who were famous in those days for their strong appeal in the search for truth not to authorities but to reason alone[19] (meaning by this that even sacred writings should be read with the mind's "eye").

It is this attitude of reason to truth and authority that, in his *Crisis of Western Philosophy*, Vladimir Soloviev takes for the starting point of Eriugena's thought. Its central postulate can be formulated, according to the Russian philosopher, as follows: if reason is right, it cannot contradict truth; so that if the church doctrine (*auctoritas*) is true, it cannot disagree with right reason (*recta ratio*); otherwise, the *auctoritas* is false and needless.[20] From this point of view, reason alone cannot disagree with authority, and in this sense it is responsible for both its own *rectitudo* and *veritas auctoritatis*; otherwise the latter, that is supposed to communicate truth, would be simply meaningless. Therefore, according to Eriugena, *auctoritas* can only derive from *recta ratio*, but not *recta ratio* from *auctoritas*; for the *auctoritas* unjustified by *recta ratio* proves to be impotent.[21] This finally means that the religious dogmas can neither be regardless of reason nor alien to it. And Eriugena, as Soloviev sees him, was a passionate exponent of this belief. But how he came to it, whether through the debates organized by the Mu'tazilites or through his careful reading of the Christian authors, we do not know for sure. What we do know is that he suddenly, as if out of the blue, appeared in Carolingian Gaul about the year 847 and likewise suddenly disappeared about the year 877. And these are precisely the dates of the beginning and the end of persecutions of the Mu'tazilites. The persecutions began under Caliph Mu'tawakkil, after he assumed power in 847,[22] but came to a halt after the death of Ya'qub ibn Ishaq al-Kindi in 877.

17. See Sagadeev, "Статус философии," 23.

18. See ibid., 24.

19. See ibid., 26. For a story about a Spanish Arab, who took part in those meetings, see also Guzel, *Мутазилиты*, 264–65.

20. "Vera enim auctoritas rectae rationi non obsistit, neque recta ratio verae auctoritati: Ambo siquidem ex una fonte, divina videlicet sapientia, manare, dubium non est" (*Ioanni Scoti Opera Omnia*, edited by Floss, quoted in Soloviev, "Кризис," 511).

21. See ibid., 513.

22. Soon after Caliph al-Mu'tawakkil assumed power (847–861), persecutions of the Mu'tazilites began: "Al-Mutawakkil was not inclined in favour of the Mu'tazilah, and also most of the people were opposed to them. As a result the Mu'tazilah and their admirers suffered a reverse, nay, a reprisal. In the purges that followed much blood was shed and homes were ruined. The period is remembered by Muslims as the time of "mihnah"—times of adversity and trial." (Mutahhari, "Introduction," §19).

To my mind, it cannot be just a miraculous coincidence that these two crucial dates perfectly match the intellectual biography of Eriugena. Rather they shed light upon the genuine background to his evolution and thus allow us to understand better how and why in the body of his system philosophy and theology come together. This means that after almost fifty years of enthusiastic studies under the aegis of SPES we come at last to realise that a vast *terra incognita* still lies ahead of us. Perhaps, over all these years we had been moving in a wrong direction while trying to explain the origin and evolution of Eriugena's thought solely by the conditions of the Carolingian cultural context. A broader view of the cultural history, spreading well beyond the boundaries of the Carolingian West, gives us an opportunity not only to better understand the reasons for his knowledge of the Greek sources, but also to come closer to the point where we could turn round and, facing East, begin a new journey to *the Eriugena unknown*. The first step on this way should then, clearly, be an insight into what the Mu'tazilah doctrine was all about and how it might help a young Christian from the Celtic West to find his way to the truth of God's Oneness.

The Falsafah Agenda

The *philosophical approach* to the matters of religion, as found at work in Eriugena, allows its upholders to succeed, as they assume, in overcoming the *contingency* and *particularity* of the religious experience. This is the experience which largely rests upon the senses—that is, sensible images and representations that always take the shape of individual, separate things, as they are borrowed from the transient world of appearance immediately given to the mind in perception, and therefore are used as metaphors (or symbols) of something sublime and hidden, normally treated by those involved in the religious experience as something mysterious, ineffable and incomprehensible. To philosophical inquiry, deeply concerned about finding the way of approaching the ultimate reality, this is a problematic issue to decide how far the sensible images and representations claimed to be metaphors and symbols of the infinite reality are actually compatible with it. On this decision it further depends how far the truths conveyed through the sensible images and representations generated in the religious experience and transmitted through it can be understood to match the Divine revelation. This is the approach which lies at the very heart of Eriugena's discourse and can be well discerned throughout the major of his works written in Gaul.

The first big project Eriugena found himself involved in on the Caro-lingian soil was his treatise *On Divine Predestination*, written in response to the debate that broke out in the circles close to the royal court. Though requested by those in charge of the intellectual climate in the kingdom to defeat their opponents, Eriugena produced a text which made many feel puzzled, for it was found by them to challenge some of the central beliefs adopted by the Carolingian church and society. These discrepancies with the official beliefs, nevertheless, appear to us to be of great importance, since they, firstly, give reason to assume that the author's views on the matter (and it may well be, the entire outlook) might have been not of the Carolingian origin. Secondly, in many respects these discrepancies with the Carolingian church beliefs turn out to be, surprisingly enough, congenial to something else that had been developed by then quite far away from the Carolingian Gaul—namely, in Baghdad under Muslim caliphs. And those religious and philosophical views, the close affinity with which Eriugena so unexpectedly reveals in his attitude to a complex of issues related to the debate on free will and fate, were successfully developing in quite a systematic way within the framework of the so-called Mu'tazilah tradition that flourished in the Middle East in the period of the second half of the eighth and the first half of the ninth centuries, reaching its climax by 830s–40s, during the reign of caliphs al-Mamun and al-Mu'tasim.

Mu'tazilah was a school of Islamic theology where reason and philo-sophical learning were warmly welcomed, and where reflection on ortho-dox beliefs developed in close cooperation with rational inquiry, for to the Mu'tazilites reason and revelation did not counter but complemented one another.[23] Wasil ibn'Ata (699–748) is unanimously considered to be the founder of this movement,[24] who strongly believed that theological thought should primarily focus on the truth of the Divine Unity, so as to let its pious adherents hold to this focal point as that of departure in their intellectual journey, the nearest destination of which is the infallible truth of the Divine Justice.[25] God is unconditional Good, and cannot be held responsible for the existence of evil in the world. It is the human being who is the author of all wrongdoings, and is therefore to blame for any evil stemming from the er-rors of his acts. As al-Shahrastani put it, "The Mu'tazilis unanimously main-tain that man decides upon and creates his acts, both good and evil; that he deserves reward or punishment in the next world for what he does. In this

23. See Valiuddin, *Muslim Philosophy*, "Mu'tazilism," sec. A.

24. See ibid., sec. B, §1.

25. Among the five basic principles of the Mu'tazilah teaching the first most fun-damental two are those of the Divine unity (al-Tawhid) and justice (al-Adil) (see ibid., sec. A).

way the Lord is safeguarded from association with any evil or wrong or any act of unbelief or transgression. For if He creates the wrong, He would be wrong, and if He created justice, He would be just."[26]

A strong appeal to reason, so much characteristic of the Mu'tazilites' teaching since the beginning of the movement, became a thoroughgoing turn in the development of Islamic theology that gave a new impetus to the ongoing scholarly debate. At the heart of the Mu'tazilites' standpoint, out of which the whole spectrum of their views derived, there lay the doctrine of *the first obligation*: "Mu'tazilites believed that the first obligation of humans, especially adults, in full possession of their mental faculties, is to use their intellectual power to ascertain the existence of God, and become knowledgeable of His attributes."[27] It is vital for those who really accept the truth of the Divine Unity (and adhere to it in their practical life) that the essence of their nature, which has no other source of its origin save God alone who is the One, cannot be neglected:

> One must wonder about the whole existence, that is, about why something exists rather than nothing. If one comes to know that there is a being who caused this universe to exist, not reliant on anything else and absolutely free from any type of need, then one realises that this being is all-wise and morally perfect. If this being is all-wise, then His very act of creation cannot be haphazard or in vain. One must then be motivated to ascertain what this being wants from humans, for one may harm oneself by simply ignoring the whole mystery of existence and, consequently, the plan of the Creator.[28]

In Islamic theology the doctrine of *the first obligation* that Mu'tazilites so resolutely entrenched in debates with their opponents[29] is known as *wujub al-nazar*—that is, the obligation to use one's speculative reasoning to attain ontological truths, essential for a mature attitude to faith in the One God.[30] Such faith, in so far as it is conscious and consistent, cannot dispense with a deep understanding (or abundantly clear contemplation) of the Divine unity, the universal scope and distinctness of which are provided

26. Al-Shahrastani, *Kitab al-Milaa wal-Nihal*, quoted in Wensinek, *Muslim Creed*, 62.

27. Mutahhari, "Introduction," §6

28. Ibid.

29. The doctrines that Mu'tazilites hated most were *anthropomorphism* in interpreting the divine matters (emerging from the sacred scripture) and *fatalism* (see ibid., §§6–10).

30. See ibid., §6.

by the vigour and coherence of *speculative* thinking[31] of the infinity of being, free from its dichotomy into opposing extremes of being and non-being. "It is speculative reasoning (*al-nazar*)," R. C. Martin points out, "which leads to knowledge of God, because He is not known by the way of necessity (*daruratan*) nor by the senses (*bi l-mushahada*). Thus He must be known by reflection and speculation."[32]

The Mu'tazilah Key Concepts

The views of Mu'tazilah were being formed and articulated in the course of theological debates they found themselves directly involved in from the very outset of their movement. One of the central issues of those ongoing debates was that of *predestination* and *free will*,[33] which also entailed such closely related issues as whether evil is created by God and whether the attributes of God given in Qur'an are to be interpreted literally or allegorically.

The Mu'tazilites in particular insisted that the doctrine of the freedom of human will may well be referred to the Prophet Muhammad himself, since they upheld to the belief that man is to be judged by his deeds. Their opponents (the school called *jabaria*) in turn insisted on the entire predestination as a contrary vision of the relationship between human beings and God, and held their fatalistic views by arguing that man is not responsible for his actions, for they ultimately proceed from God. Surprisingly enough, these opposite views and the problematic dilemma they posed may have derived from one and the same source, namely, the Qur'an itself: "That is, the Qur'an refers to this issue in a manner which stimulates thought on the subject. Because some verses clearly indicate that man is free, not coerced in any of his acts. On the other hand, there are verses which, with equal clarity, indicate that all things depend on the Divine Will."[34]

The content of these debates was later summed up by Allaf (748–840)[35] in a number of key notions, including justice, unity, promise, threat,

---

31. The Latin *speculare*, to contemplate, gives us to understand that "speculative thinking" should ultimately refer to a way of thinking that makes thought capable of *seeing* the reality hidden from bodily senses.

32. Martin, *Defenders of Reason*, 57.

33. The "oldest problem was that of free will and determinism, in which the Mu'tazilah, of course, sided with free will" (Mutahhari, "Introduction," §6).

34. Ibid., §13. With regard to the contradictory ways of reading the Qur'an, it is for example believed that the meaning conveyed in verses 4:78 and 57:22 implies total predestination, whereas those of 4:79 and 18:29 explicitly support the idea of human freedom.

35. Abu al-Hundhail Allaf "received instruction from 'Uthman bin Khalid Tawil, a pupil of Wasil" (Valiuddin, *Muslim Philosophy*, sec. B, §2).

and the middle position, which he termed as the "Five Principles" of the Mu'tazilah.[36] These principles, giving an outline of the whole scope of the Mu'tazilah teaching, are usually listed as follows:

1. Divine Unity (al-Tawhid);

2. Divine Justice (al-Adil);

3. The Promise and Warning (al-Wa'd wa al-Wa'id);

4. The Intermediate Position (al-Manzilah Bauna al-Manzilatayn);

5. Advocating the Good and Forbidding the Evil (al-amr bil ma'ruf wa al-nahy'an al munkar).[37]

The first, and therefore the most fundamental, of these principles points to the very heart of the Mu'tazilites' belief, which is, as obvious for Muslims, all about their strong conviction of *the absolute unity* of God. What is however distinctive of this central Mu'tazilites' belief is the emphasis they make in their particular vision of the Divine Unity. As a matter of fact, it is understood by them not as much as God's uniqueness or singularity (when in contrast to polytheistic beliefs, out of many gods only one is chosen for the true one, while others are rejected as being false), but as his *oneness*. In other words, according to the Mu'tazilah principle of the Divine Unity, God is believed to be one not because he is assumed to be a solitary being, but because he is understood to be all-embracing absolute being, *apart from whom nothing else at all can be permitted to exist outside and alongside him*, be it considered as proceeded out of him or eternally co-existing with him.

This specific Mu'tazilah vision of the Divine Unity, which apparently sought to bridge the gap between God and the creature and was therefore conducive to having cardinally reconsidered the relationship between the two, did challenge popular sentiments about God and his creation, for which it seemed quite normal to set them apart and thus, by setting them over against each other, to keep believing in the supreme, utterly matchless and immutable God Almighty.[38] So the Mu'tazilah thinkers were fortunate enough that the complexity of the problem of unity required of them a great deal of profundity and consistency of reflection and made them strictly follow the lines of the philosophical discourse. This, at least for the time being, safeguarded them from a breakout of popular discontent and allowed

36. See ibid., sec. A.

37. See ibid.

38. See Mutahhari, "Introduction," §19.

to develop their views within the framework of Islamic theology until the implications of their beliefs[39] became clear, both to the rulers and public.[40]

The way the Mu'tazilites approached the issue of Divine Unity took the shape of speculative investigations into the nature of the divine attributes, the existence of which was found to be logically illegitimate on account of their distinction from the Divine essence and thus was subsequently denied. Thus, Allaf, an outstanding dialectician who is said to have effectively used dialectical arguments while converting people to Islam from the grip of old religions,[41] sought to overcome any dualism in the views of divinity, and with regard to this argued that the divine qualities "are none other than the divine essence and cannot be separated from it."[42] In particular, while tackling the pre-Islamic eastern beliefs, according to which Light and Darkness are "the ultimate principles of the universe," Allaf refuted any attempts to undermine in theory the totality of the Divine Unity by dividing the ultimate reality in two and inaugurating the opposite principles as mutually dependent ontological entities to be imposed upon what in reality is whole and indivisible. A non-dialectical vision of the opposites set over against each other, he believes, is utterly incompatible with the truth of the Unity of divinity.

The One God, according to Allaf, may only be known, when dialectically approached, as the "Necessary Existent" to be thought of as the Self-determined Being that is caused to being by nothing else, apart from itself, and therefore is opposed by nothing or, in other words, has no competing rivals.[43] Accordingly, he is also the One who admits of no dichotomy within himself, which might be conceived as a discrepancy between his will and acts,[44] or as qualities found separated from his essence, when associated with its manifestations among finite things.

39. Understood in the absolute sense, the principle of Divine Unity facilitates establishing the truth of human freedom; and this truth, when consciously adopted, might pose threat to faith politically engaged, of which submissiveness to authorities resulting in docility of entire society would be most wanted effect.

40. Even al-Kindi, despite his unsurpassed fame and authority in philosophy among all the Arabs, fell victim to severe persecutions along with other Mu'tazilites in the time of Caliph Mu'tawakkil: "his large private library was confiscated and he was apparently beaten" (Al-Kindi, *First Philosophy,* 3).

41. "The story does that by his dialectics three thousand persons embraced Islam at his hand" (Valiuddin, "Mutazilism," sec B, §2).

42. Ibid.

43. See ibid.

44. The lack of discrepancy between God's will and acts does comply not only with a general vision of creation, shared by all believers, but also with what may be identified as the *third principle* of the Mu'tazilah teaching concerning the Promise and the Warning, according to which God never acts contrary to his Promise.

As a result, in his vision of the Divine unity Allaf "accepts such attributes as are one with the essence of God, or one may say, accepts such an essence as is identified with the attributes."[45] The two are not separated but regarded as one. So that, as Mir Valiuddin argues, when God is said to be the knower, it does not mean that knowledge is found in the essence of God, but that *knowledge is his essence*. Likewise power and life, when applied as attributes to powerful and living God, should be understood as his very essence. In the same way, al-Shahrastani interpreted the identity of divine essence and attributes in terms of the perfect adequacy of the latter to the former, and went even further to having attributes denied altogether. For when, according to him, God's knowledge is understood to be his very essence, it can in fact signify only one thing—namely, that God knows with his *essence* and not with his knowledge (i.e., *through* his essence only and not *through* knowledge, that might be understood as something accidental or ascribed from without).

It is therefore this denial of attributes considered as accidental qualities that allows us to conclude that the *existence* of what Allaf called "the Necessary Existent" must be understood as none other but *its very essence*. Accordingly, knowledge and any other attributes whatsoever should properly be understood not as those just applicable to God's being (as if the properties either accidental to or even inherent in it), but as precisely *the way* God actually *is* while making his innermost essence adequately manifest. And this lack of discrepancy between essence and existence, as ascertained by the Mu'tazilites, is where they believed the real ground for the true unity is.[46] Among the nearest implications of this Mu'tazilites' understanding of one of the central tenets of their belief there can easily be seen such doctrines as those of *advocating the Good* and the so-called *first obligation*, both of which were already mentioned as a hallmark of the Mu'tazilah. That explains a great deal concerning the extraordinariness and prominence of their teaching.

In the light of their vision of the Divine Unity, according to which nothing whatsoever can be understood to subsist *outside* the Divine being (i.e., in the way contrary to that of the Divine subsistence), it seemed to be clear to the Mu'tazilites, and they tried to convince others of this,[47] that in order to truly serve God so as to really please him, human beings are to strive for being at one with him, and for this are obliged to do actually

45. Valiuddin, "Mutazilism," sec. B, §2.

46. See ibid.

47. See, for example, ibid. about the debates between Allaf and Salih, the Magian, a staunch upholder of dualism of a Manichaean type who went that far as to assert that there were two Gods.

nothing else but to make sure that–in consonance with the way the Divine reality is—*the innermost essence of their nature comes to be adequately manifest.* This is what allows all human beings to live in reality as it truly is, where everything goes on while remaining one with its proper nature originating from the sole source of all beings, and thus to lead the true life of those who belong to God's creation. This is consequently what was exactly expected by the Mutazilah of human beings when serving God, in so far as they are supposed to be faithful indeed and remain consistent in their faith in the One God. For in him who is the One there is no discrepancy between essence and existence (i.e., the hidden and the manifest). Furthermore, along with him, as mentioned above with respect to the Mu'tazilites' view of God's Oneness, nothing contrary to his nature can ever subsist, nor can it proceed out of him.

From this it is not hard to see how crucial was the denial of subsistence outside God for the conclusions the Mu'tazilites drew from it. First, it allowed them to establish the futility of any dualistic attempts to challenge the unity of God's self-determined being by introducing illegitimately a variety of auxiliary or complementary principles, be they simply intermediary agents or adversary rivals. Above all, however, this denial was true about the entire creation, with no exception for human beings: humans do not subsist outside God's being unless the senses, deceiving and misleading the mind, succeed in convincing them of the contrary. The mind purified (i.e., liberated from the dictates of senses) is where human beings and God meet. For it is not senses but the mind, when recovered from its latent and suppressed state, that allows all humans to embrace the infinity of being and thus to become fit for receiving the truth of God's Unity.

Moreover, it is exactly a proper attitude to the mind inherent in human beings that, unlike the senses that see God nowhere, allows them to occupy the right place *within* the reality of God's creation, and not *outside* it, so as to conform to the truth of God's being countered by nothing.[48] In fact, as the essence of their nature that makes all humans distinct among the whole creature, the intellectual power cannot be understood otherwise than being a God-given gift, that is, the essence originating from the source of all essences. Therefore, to be part of God's creation, this essence must be adequately manifest, as the very order of creation would require it.[49]

48. It would be immensely unfair to forget that the principle of the Divine Unity, as the Mu'tazilah understood it, does necessitate that nothing at all can ever be admitted of its subsistence outside God who is truly believed to be *the One.*

49. As seen above, the debates about the relationship between divine attributes and divine essence did result for the Mu'tazilah in the denial of discrepancy between the two, which in turn let them admit, as confirmed both by Allaf and al-Shahrastani, that the divine essence and existence are one.

Otherwise, as long as the essence remains just a potential hidden in the secret recesses of human nature, it will be merely neglected and nipped in the bud. The Mu'tazilites' doctrine of *the first obligation* (*wujub al-nazar*), derived from their understanding of the Divine Unity, aims to remind human beings about their duty to really follow the truth of faith accepted, and for this purpose to get the hidden potential of their nature fully realized. The "full possession of their mental faculties" crowned by speculative reason (*al-nazar*), capable, as said before, of attaining ontological truths (i.e., those of absolute being and unity communicated by the sacred scripture) is consequently where the Mu'tazilah saw the way for all humans to conform to the Divine subsistence. The actual existence of human beings must be fully adequate to the essence inherent in them and hidden deep inside their nature. Their existence, in other words, must be fully determined *from within*, by their essence. This is the way things go in the reality of the Divine Unity. All efforts human beings make to let the essence of their nature manifest itself is actually what enables them to live righteously and, hence, to please God indeed.[50]

From all this it is also clear how the doctrines of the Divine unity and first obligation come to be bound up with another aspect crucial for the Mu'tazilites' teaching and counted among its fundamental Five Principles, namely, the doctrine of advocating the Good. As the absolute Good and Justice, God cannot be, according to Mu'tazilah, the author of evil; evil is of human origin. It is precisely the deviation from the essence of their nature that makes human beings go astray, that is, contrary to the way things go in the God-centred reality. This deviation, when it is falsely assumed that existence can dispense with essence, becomes therefore the cause of all wrongdoings and, hence, of the existence of evil in the world. All this gives the Mu'tazilites reason to maintain–as mentioned at the beginning of this brief survey–that all evil existing in the world is produced by human deeds when they, as the acts of "unbelief or transgression," break God's will. What else becomes furthermore clear in the light of the Mu'tazilites' understanding of humans' first obligation to the One God is that evil as such proves in fact to be rooted in a wrong assumption that humans make about a possibility of living in defiance of their essential nature. That is the assumption about a possibility to live while neglecting the essence that lies at the very heart of their nature, and remains hidden there unless manifest in the mind rigorously applied, as said above, to attaining the ontological truths communicated through the sacred scripture.

50. As we shall see it later, this way of subsistence in conformity with God's being is one of the central themes of Eriugena's *Periphyseon*.

Advocating thus the absoluteness of Goodness of Divinity, some Mu'tazilites, like al-Nazzam (d. 845),[51] found this principle so cardinal for their beliefs that resolutely went that far as to assert that God has no power over evil. In particular, he said that "when evil or sin is the attribute or essence of a thing, then the possibility of occurrence of evil or the *power to create* it will *itself be evil*. Therefore, it cannot be attributed to God who is the doer of justice and good." Moreover, he continues to argue, "if God has power over evil, it will necessary follow that He is ignorant and indigent. But this is impossible . . . "[52] When closely examined, the argument that brings al-Nazzam to this conclusion develops as follows: "If God has power over evil, then the occurrence of evil is possible . . . Now, God might or might not have had knowledge of the evil which occurred. If we say that He did not have the knowledge of it, it would necessarily follow that He was ignorant; and if we say that He did have it, it would necessarily follow that He was in need of this evil; for had He not been in need of it, He would not have created it. . . . It is definitely true that God is all-wise; so when any evil is caused by Him, it necessarily follows that He needed it, otherwise He would have never produced it." The conclusion consequently is that "since it is impossible to think that God needs evil, it is impossible to think that He creates it."[53]

Thus, though the Five Principles of their teaching and especially through al-Nazzam's radical denial of God's power over evil, the Mu'tazilites expressed in a thoroughgoing manner their firm belief in the Divine Unity. According to this belief, the absolute, self-sufficient, being of God does not admit of the existence of anything else apart from him who is the One, and speculative thinking (al-nazar) is the only means (or gateway) through which it is given to human beings to know this truth.

The Predestination Controversy

Al-Nazzam's argument, as seen above, brings us close to understanding how Eriugena might have found himself involved in the predestination controversy that broke out some time later amongst the Carolingians.

51. Abu Istiaq Ibrahim ibn Sayyar called al-Nazzam was Allaf's pupil. He is said to have "studied Greek philosophy well and made full use of it in his works" (Valiuddin, "Mutazilism," sec. B, §3). As we shall see it later in chapter 3, al-Nazzam is a crucial figure for the present inquiry into Eriugena's thought, for he is likely the one who had made a significant impact on Eriugena's argument against dualism in ontology central to the entire of his system.

52. Ibid.

53. Ibid.

This controversy sheds light upon the unique (in terms of the Carolingian scholarship) approach of Eriugena to the complex of problems raised by the debates. "It is from the surviving texts of the predestination debate," writes Dermot Moran, "that we gain the most *testimonia* concerning Eriugena, and the overall picture emerges of a *rationalist scholar*, well equipped in the liberal arts and also in Scripture, willing to follow *his own mind* on the great theological problems of the day" (italics mine).[54]

Eriugena's treatise *De divina praedestinatione*[55] (followed by his contemporaries' criticism) is his first appearance on the historical stage from nowhere: "The predestination controversy marks the first written evidence we have of Eriugena's life and activity."[56] Showing in terms of argumentation a sort of theoretical supremacy over the contemporaries, this treatise also provides a clue to a better understanding of Eriugena's background.

Though the circumstances that encouraged the predestination debates breakout remain unclear,[57] it is known for certain that it was monk called Gottschalk who triggered the controversy. A troublemaker in the eyes of many, Gottschalk was dedicated to studies of Augustine (the indisputable authority for the Carolingians), and brought to the fore what he thought to be found in *De civitate dei* as Augustine's doctrine of *double predestination*, the preliminary principles of which were assumed to have first been formulated in the course of dispute with the Donatists and Pelagius in *De libero arbitrio* (AD 395). The polemical origin of Augustine's doctrine retained in itself many traces of ambiguity,[58] however, which could only stimulate further strife, when its key notions were uncritically used in the context of the ninth-century theological debates.[59] As an expert in theology and the liberal arts, Eriugena was requested to oppose Gottschalk (and others, like Prudentius, Lupus, Florus, and Ratramnus, who supported him and

54. Moran, *Philosophy*, 34.

55. For the source details see Bibliography.

56. Moran, *Philosophy*, 35.

57. Perhaps, a tension between the rivalry political parties within the kingdom provoked the debates. "In part, the predestination issue was a pretext for a political power struggle between Hincmar and the northern bishops, against Florus and the southern bishops of Gaul" (ibid., 33). It is also important to note here that king Charlse the Bald sided with the "northern" party, whose position Eriugena was supposed to entrench. Being not enmeshed in politics, however, Eriugena paid little attention to anything else apart from the theoretical aspect of the debates, which obviously could not win him many friends.

58. On the general ambiguity of Augustine's teaching see, for example, Trubetskoy, Миросозерцание, 6–7.

59. See Moran, *Philosophy*, 28–30.

maintained that Augustine did actually teach a double predestination) and to write a work clarifying the problem.[60]

According to Devisse, Eriugena "had no impact at all on his contemporaries because his arguments were so removed from them as to be incomprehensible."[61] As a result, Hincmar, who employed Eriugena for the task of refuting the opponents, "was unhappy with this intervention on his behalf and was quick to disown it. Others—Prudentius and Florus—attacked Eriugena severely."[62] This criticism, however, could hardly be found to be constructive, since it did not go any further than conceited accusations of Eriugena of being *vaniloquus et garrulous*. All this means that both the premises and argumentation presented by Eriugena in the treatise were completely unfamiliar and even alien to the Carolingians, who saw in his work nothing more than just *pultes Scottorum* (Jerome's phrase used against Pelagius),[63] admitting thereby in fact their failure to understand it.

Why however were the views conveyed in Eriugena's treatise contrary to what was expected of him, on the one hand, and so unusual that they caused a great deal of fury among his opponents, on the other? Among the "remarkable and unusual features in Eriugena's tract" Moran identifies the following three: "First of all, his argument is based on careful metaphysical and dialectical reasoning about the nature of God, good and evil. Second, he argues that the superiority of his own position is based on his more thorough understanding of the liberal arts, which gives him a better basis for the correct interpretation of the authorities. Third, Eriugena's position offers an assessment of the human place in the universe, seeing this world as an opportunity given to human nature to perfect itself."[64] As a result, by contrast to the position of those upholding a double predestination theory, Eriugena's vision turns out to be, as Moran puts it, "extremely *optimistic*: Salvation is available to all. Even if our flawed moral judgment fails us, grace is available. Furthermore, Eriugena's God does not merely not know evil, He did not create hell. Human sinfulness is responsible for creating its own hell."[65]

This belief in God's "lack of knowledge" concerning evil is quite remarkable for Eriugena's standpoint. This is likely one of the major things which made the Carolingians, both sponsors and opponents, especially

60. See ibid., 27–28.

61. Jean Devisse, *Hincmar*, vol. 1, 150–51, quoted in Moran, *Philosophy*, 34.

62. Moran, *Philosophy*, 33.

63. See ibid.

64. Ibid., 32.

65. Ibid.

furious with Eriugena. It is however this belief, utterly alien to the Carolingian theology, that reveals a close affinity between Eriugena's convictions and those of Mu'tazilah, and al-Nazzam's in particular.

While denying Gottschalk's views on double predestination (which he borrows, to the amazement of many leaders of the Frankish church, from Augustine himself), Eriugena is aware of the *novelty* of his own approach and "apologises in advance to those who think he is being heretical by denying God's knowledge in this area."[66] He does not seem to care much about a possible shock that his views might cause. To him, it is much more important "to demonstrate, using his own citations from Augustine, that there is no predestination towards evil, because in the strictest sense God could not be said to know evil at all."[67]

The roots of the predestination controversy are believed to go back to *De libero arbitrio*, where Augustine attacked Pelagius, who thought that human free will was directly involved in salvation.[68] By contrast to Pelagius's views, Augustine is said to have tended "to overemphasize the total human dependence on God's grace, thus supporting the view that we are predestined by God and are not free to act otherwise."[69] And though this was the prevalent tendency in Augustine's views on predestination (that might be not unfairly explained by the extremities of any polemics), in fact they were not as simple as that. As Moran admits, in the same *De libero arbitrio* (II. XX. 54), "Augustine had argued that human will can choose either higher or lower things. Owing, however, to the weakness of fallen nature, it generally tends towards lower things, that is, towards the pleasures of the body rather than the goods of the soul."[70] Moreover, it was not easy either for Augustine to decide whether the inclination to the lower was natural (and therefore inevitable) or voluntary. Despite these uncertainties of his beliefs, however, Augustine gradually "moved to the more extreme position that human beings were totally dependent on divine grace for every action and decision. In this sense, some are predestined by God's will to be saved, other are predestined to be damned. The individual cannot save himself, since his nature is essentially flawed . . . "[71]

This is exactly what Gottschalk articulates in his writings (later, in 849, burned on condemnation by the synod of Quierzy) and presents as

66. Ibid., 31.
67. Ibid.
68. See ibid., 29.
69. Ibid.
70. Ibid., 30.
71. Ibid.

his explication of Augustine. In particular, he argues that "predestination is in fact twofold"—that is, *ad vitam* and *ad mortem*, to beatitude in heaven or damnation in hell, "and there is nothing they can do to change this."[72] The impact of this twofold predestination on humanity—and here Gott-schalk follows what he explicates from *De civitate Dei*, where the evolution of Augustine's views on the matter reached its climax—is that it comes to be divided "into two groups, *civitates*: the elect, led by Christ, and the damned, led by the Devil."[73]

Eriugena, the dialectician and theologian of God's Oneness, could, clearly, by no means agree with a theory challenging the truth of the divine unity. All the more he was requested by bishops Hincmar and Pardulus (the party that the king himself sided with) "to oppose Gottschalk," whose influence grew so fast among the church leaders that many of them came to support his views. Thus, for example, bishop Prudentius argued in his *Epistola ad Hincmarum et Pardulum* (PL CXV. 971–1010) that Augustine "did actually teach a double predestination."[74] So Eriugena came to the fore, as bishop Pardulus of Laon explains in his letter to the church at Lyon, "to write a work clarifying the problem."[75]

Vehemently rejecting the doctrine of *double predestination* put for-ward by Gottschalk in his explication of Augustine's views, Eriugena finds it to be a mere misunderstanding of what is in fact there in Augustine and explains Gottschalk's error by his "lack of education in the liberal arts."[76] An apparent subtlety of the distinction that Augustine draws between the two kinds of freedom available to human beings—that is, *libertas* (freedom proper) and *liberum arbitrium* (freedom of choice)—eludes Gottschalk,[77] which inevitably results in making him fall into delusion and offer a theory that in effect was largely based on an erroneous interpretation of Augus-tine's actual views, sometimes ambiguous and problematic. That is why to

72. Ibid.

73. Ibid.

74. See ibid., 27–28.

75. Ibid., 27.

76. Ibid., 31.

77. Generally speaking, any distinction subtlety is only amenable to *dialectic* as a type of logic that treats distinction as a principle of self-identity. As a teacher of the Pal-ace school, Eriugena had kept making a strong emphasis on the importance of studying dialectic and including it in the curriculum as one of the most essential disciplines of the liberal arts. So he likely had good reason to rebuke Gottschalk of lacking proper education in the liberal arts: dialectic could obviously not be reckoned among the intel-lectual skills of him who demonstrated his inclination to setting contraries apart, as it is the case with a choice between good and evil, or division into those that are saved or damned.

pursue the task of refutation of what had in fact become the upshot of misreading the authority, Eriugena tries—along with the articulation of his coherent vision of the Divine Unity—to clarify the profundity and complexity of Augustine's thought of the matter. This is the approach which, he believes, enables him to arrive at a clear conclusion—put in the Epilogue to the treatise and revealing therefore the genuine objective of the whole undertaking—that there is "no double destination or two destinations or one divided into two parts . . ."[78]

The premise Eriugena chooses to proceed from in his argument against Gottschalk's theory of double predestination is the statement of God's Unity, pivotal for his understanding of God's being: God is *una substantia*.[79] This is actually the basic vision, the development of which in the course of his argument does allow Eriugena not only to reject as illegitimate an appeal to division, be it applied to an understanding of God's being or his selective attitude to the creature. It also allows him to articulate his optimistic understanding of salvation as being available to all humans on account of their freedom, thoroughly concurrent with that of the absolute self-determined being.

The freedom of the absolute being of *una substantia* that depends upon nothing apart from itself (since nothing is there beyond it) is where love alone, not coercion affecting it from without, reigns through and through, being in fact a specific type of causality, universal to the entire reality of creation and operating as the power of interaction and interconnection, making everything bound together from within. To be saved, therefore (i.e., to live in harmony and union with him who is absolute freedom and all-embracing love), *one is to be free*—that is, liberated from captivity to the world of appearance, which is thought to be sustained by forces external to it. Indeed, nothing whatsoever can be free when governed *from without*; likewise, understood as sustained by external forces, the realm of appearance has nothing to do with the reality of creation as it truly is while being at one with him who is the One. As a wrong vision of the surrounding reality, the world of appearance is imposed upon the creation by the corrupt mind like a veil that covers up its true face. Spiritual liberty thus is where and how God exercises his power over the whole creation and lets all humans become awakened from illusions of the mind misled by exterior senses. This is consequently where and how all human beings become able to return to the reality where they originally belonged and where life ever-lasting is. This is finally the reality that lies just at hand, but is hidden until those misguided

78. Moran, *Philosophy*, 31.

79. See ibid.

by the dictates of senses (i.e., remaining in bondage to sin) turn their back on it and lead a life of the flawed nature, finding themselves confined among the things divided and the opposites set apart.

As mentioned before, Eriugena was well aware of the *novelty* of his approach to the predestination issue, so that he even found it reasonable to apologize in advance to those Carolingians who might suspect him of heresy. What that *novelty* was about may easily be understood from what has just been said above with regard to the premise of his argument, and therefore not unfairly be defined as the *ontological* approach. In consonance with this, while commenting on 390c and 394c of Eriugena's treatise *On Divine Predestination*, Dermot Moran admits that since the language we employ to speak of God cannot be used literally "because He is incorporeal and corporeal signs cannot adequately express His nature," the latter can be "best referred to by the single word *esse*," which allows us to realise that God "*is* existence," whereas "evil, by contrast, does not exist."[80]

---

80. Ibid., 31–32.

CHAPTER 2

Parmenides's Ontology: The Cradle of Dialectic

The Ontological Approach

THE DIRECT ENGAGEMENT WITH *ontology* in the course of debates over the divine matters, especially those going so far as the denial of God's knowledge of evil and even its existence in his presence, seemed to be really a new development in the Carolingian West. But this was not the case in the culturally and doctrinally more advanced East, both Christian and Muslim, where Cappadocians and Mu'tazilites have equally made considerable progress on the way to a deeper and more consistent understanding of God's Oneness. An *ontological* approach to God's nature, so much a characteristic of both schools of religious thought, is consequently where the Eastern influence on Eriugena's discourse comes to light. As a matter of fact, this influence can easily be traced back not only to his immediate contemporaries within the Mu'tazilah movement, particularly to Allaf and al-Nazzam (whose prime ideas are explicitly present in Eriugena's view on predestination), but also to the Christian tradition as it must have been found at work in the Middle East of his time. Two Gregories, *Nazianzenes* and *Nyssenes*, appear to be those key figures through whom the Cappadocian legacy had reached Eriugena, making an immense impact on the principles of his speculative theology.[1]

Gregory Nazianzus (the Theologian) was one of the Christian theologians of the East who first inaugurated the *ontological* approach as the most appropriate to a coherent treatment of God's nature. In his later works

---

1. A tendency to exclude evil from being was quite common to the Eastern intellectual tradition and can be found for certain as in Mu'tazilites (al-Nazzam), as in Cappadocians. Thus Gregory of Nyssa particularly maintained that evil "possesses its being in non-being" (Gregorius Nyssenes, *De anima et resurrection*, PG 46 Col. 93B. Quoted in Gaginsky, "Онтологический статус Бога," 35).

of 380–383 (*Oratio* 30, 38, and 45) he holds God to comprise "the whole being," because he is himself being of the whole.[2] In *Oratio* 30 (18:14–18), he says in particular: "We are seeking the nature to which being as it is on its own pertains and has nothing to do with anything else; this being as a whole is what indeed is specific to God, and it is neither confined nor disrupted by anything else, neither prior to Him nor after, for it neither was nor will be."[3] In *The Word on Epiphany* (Oratio 31.23:10–11), Gregory further expounds the meaning of *being the whole*:

> Always God was and is and will be or, better to say, has always been. For "was" and "will be" are segments of our time and transient nature, but Being always *is*. And this is how He calls Himself while talking to Moses on the mount, for He comprises in Himself the whole of being, which neither began nor will end up, like a limitless and unconfined sea of being that exceeds any notion of time and nature, but is slightly outlined by mind alone—though quite uncertainly and insufficiently—not from what He is in Himself but what is there around Him, approaching the truth by shedding representations alien to it.[4]

Thus, according to Gregory, God's nature may not improperly be approached from the perspective of *being as a whole* (λοόν τò εἶναι), which also means that all being may only be understood as subsisting *in* God (ἐν αὐτῷ). For Christian theology this is quite a thoroughgoing vision of God's being which promotes the truth that there is no ontological abyss separating God from his creation. In other words, this is the vision that allows us in fact to heal the illicit (merely imaginative) chasm between the two and to understand the reality of creation as included (though not in the form of its immediate appearance to senses) in him who is the universal Principle of all. And this is very much so, and cannot be otherwise, because *nothing particular can ever abandon the universal nor subsist outside it*. What is however even more extraordinary about this overtly *universalist* approach is that it comes down not only to the Cappadocians, the first systematizers of Christian orthodoxy in whose writings the very foundations of Christian theology were being laid down, but also to St. Paul's legacy, where a coherent explication of Christ's unique teaching first came to light.

Indeed, the basic statement of Gregory's universalist approach, "All things are possessed by God inside Himself,"[5] does comply with those of the

---

2. See Gaginsky, "Онтологический статус Бога," 36, 40.

3. Ibid., 37.

4. Ibid., 41.

5. Ibid., 43.

Pauline theology, to which universalism and the total inclusiveness of God's being are out of the question. As Paul puts it in particular, God "is not far from each one of us. For 'In him we live and move and have our being' . . . " (Acts 17: 27–28). It is hard to imagine therefore that Gregory could ignore Paul as the source of his thought and inspiration–that very Paul, for whom "there is no God but one" (1 Cor 8:4). In his *Word on the Holy Light* (*Oratio* 39, 12: 2–3), the Theologian quotes one of the key passages from Paul's writings, claiming thereby his direct indebtedness to the tenets articulated by the Apostle: " . . . for us there is one God, the Father, from whom are all things and for whom we exist, and one Lord, Jesus Christ, through whom are all things and through whom we exist" (1 Cor 8:6).

It is undoubtedly the Pauline theology therefore from which Gregory deduces the fundamental principle of a system of theology to be raised up– that is, the *ontological* approach to God, whose absolute nature is only susceptible of knowledge when consistently conceived in terms of all-embracing being that ever is from itself and through itself and for itself. "For from him and through him and to him are all things," says Paul (Rom 11:36), whom Eriugena, a spiritual heir to the Eastern theological tradition, will later persistently call *the* Apostle. Thus he certainly recognised the centrality of the figure of Paul to Christian thought and paid a tribute to the bundle of ideas pivotal to the Pauline theology. Among those prime things, taken by Eriugena on board his speculative theology, there no doubt was a far reaching *universalist insight* into being that unceasingly is from itself and by itself and through itself and for itself, as well as an *anthropological optimism* following from this insight. On account of the existence of all things inside the universal being, this optimistic view allowed the faithful to actually claim the humanity's kinship to God as that of his offspring (Acts 17:28–29). To Eriugena, this was the theology that opened to human beings a prospect of *theosis* and being at one with God the Father through the cardinal change of the way of perception of reality they live in. "Do not be conformed to this world," says the Apostle, "but be transformed by the renewing of your minds, so that you may discern what is the will of God–what is good and acceptable and perfect" (Rom 12:2).

Along with this, the compliance of the *ontological* approach to God with the biblical tradition goes even much deeper and is perfectly evident in Gregory's interpretation of the *Tetragrammaton*. Like many other Byzantine theologians, the Cappadocian father did not know Hebrew, and for this reason in his scriptural studies referred to the Septuagint, where God's name is conveyed at Exod. 3:14 as ὁ ὤν, which he understood as "He who was and is and will be or, better to say, has always been."[6]

6. Ibid., 41. The same reference to God as him who *was and is and will be* is scattered throughout the whole of Eriugena's *Periphyseon*.

Being and Time

Due to this interpretation of the Tetragrammaton, the *ontological* approach renders even more concrete by acquiring a new dimension that the senses (by focusing on things that come and go) perceive as *temporality*, but reason—while enjoying the holistic view of being that expands to the utmost of its capacity—understands as *eternity* which never ceases to be. This furthermore means that in its fundamental sense the ontological approach to divine matters would hardly be conceivable at all when dispensing with the idea of interconnectedness of being and time. It is the understanding which has survived throughout the intellectual history from Plato and Greek Fathers until the present day as something cardinally intrinsic to any profound ontology, coming up anew in the focus of Heidegger's philosophy known as one of the most recent ontologies of the kind "possible only as phenomenology."[7] Similarly to the Cappadocian view of the all-embracing being outside which there is nothing, Heidegger's ontology sets up, though within the limits of human reality, the perspective of being that can only be seen *from within* and therefore understood as self-assertion in the world or, better to say, *self-disclosure*, termed as *Dasein*.[8] Understood like this, *Dasein* appears to Heidegger as a kind of *transition from the state of concealment to that of unconcealment*. This is an understanding which, in a broader view transcending the constraints of the anthropocentric world, can also quite perfectly match the truth that in the reality of creation—when seen from the midst of its wholeness—there should be no transition from non-being to being. And this is rightly so, in so far as the creation is consistently understood to be the reality of God's *self-disclosure*, and not of making out of an uncertain *nihil*, as if subsisting alongside God as something substantially different and even alien to him. In other words, creation is the reality where everything comes into being *ex Deo*, that is, from him who ever and everywhere *is*, so that nothing else is there apart from him.[9]

Thus in their sharing of both the same pattern of self-disclosure and the inner perspective of their being self-determined, *Dasein* and Creation agree however mutually they differ by their scale: whereas the latter conforms to the infinity of God's being, the former is correlated with the finitude of human existence. Due to this considerable distinction, they acquire, respectively to each, essentially different dimensions of their length—that is, *eternity* and *temporality*. It is consequently here, in the difference between

7. Heidegger, *Basic Writings*, 84.

8. See ibid., 75.

9. The issue of *creatio ex nililo* and *ex deo* is considered closer in chapter 3.

these two dimensions of reality, that the fundamental difference between humanity and divinity is convincingly evident. If however a belief in the One, ubiquitous and indivisible, God is true so as to constitute the foundations of the civilized world, it would be not unfair to call into question the chasm between humanity and divinity. A number of challenging questions, addressing the principle impossibility of finding anything else subsisting on its own outside One God, would be quite inevitable then: How do these extremes of endlessness and termination, indivisibility and fragmentation, continuity and disruption, unity and disparity, rest and motion occur? Are they mutually complementary or exclusive? Can they be reconciled or there is nothing in common between them?

Following the logic of *Sein und Zeit*, one may rightly conclude that its author's answer to the questions like these would be rather positive than negative. To overcome the chasm in question (which ultimately is the one between temporality and eternity), human being should, as follows from what Heidegger suggests, be brought to conformity with the order of creation, where Logos precedes anything whatsoever coming into being; for it is through him that all things, according to the Scripture, are brought into existence from God. "He was," the Scripture says, "in the beginning with God. All things came into being through him, and without him not one thing came into being" (John 1:2–3). Not unfairly should the creation be understood therefore as both the embodiment and revelation of him who *was* in the Beginning and *will be* in the End, because he always is *with* him who ever *is*, remaining inseparably the Beginning and the Middle and the End that, as the wholeness subsisting immutably in and for itself, is neither transcended nor abandoned by anything whatsoever. For again, as the Scripture puts it, the light—God's first utterance in the Genesis account (Gen 1:3), and therefore the very foundational manifestation of Logos, giving, so to speak, shape to the absolute Being that ever is in and for itself— "shines in the darkness, and the darkness did not overcome it" (John 1:5). The entire creation thus proves simultaneously to be the embodiment and manifestation of Logos, clearly seen in the light of the unity of Being, where light is not mingled with darkness. So that the movements of embodiment and revelation may not improperly be described in Heidegger's terms as those of concealment and unconcealment, bringing thus together again the reality of creation and that of *Dasein*, where self-disclosure equally takes place, filling up the realm of primary light with life and meaning. "What has come into being in him" (Logos), says the Scripture, "was life, and the life was the light of all people" (John 1:3–4).

In this way, Heidegger, who in his discourse seems to deliberately avoid any influence of dogmatic thinking overloaded with a pre-given content of systematic theology, brings the readers of *Sein und Zeit* close to a vision that it is self-disclosure of Logos where the Logocentric reality of creation and *Dasein*, the area of human existence, can tally with one another. Being in fact the element of language where Logos is found at work while arising from the secret recesses of human nature, *Dasein* actually proves to reproduce the same self-disclosure pattern of creation. In accordance with this concealment-unconcealment pattern, Logos, inherent in human being as the innermost word, passes the same way from its embodiment (concealment) to its full and adequate manifestation (unconcealment), when nothing hidden remains in the light of the Logos revealed, so that even "the things in themselves" break open, shining with their meaning.[10] *Dasein* is, as it were, a closed area, where no knowledge *from without* is let in. This is where the inner perspective of being develops, and the only kind of knowledge available here is that of seeing *from within*. Logos, in the words of Heidegger, is "a specific mode of letting something be seen."[11] Accordingly, the knowledge appropriate to this mode of vision from within but cardinally different from the conventional type of knowledge, when it is believed to be delivered by the senses from without, is *interpretation*.[12] As a matter of fact, it is by interpretation, not by empirical experience, that the Logos concealed in the innermost depths of Being is brought to light so as to be clearly seen in the meaning of beings.

Thus, as a mode of being perfectly conformed to the pattern of self-disclosure (that may only be properly understood, when consistently conceived, as ultimately belonging to the substantial reality of creation), *Dasein* proves to transcend the empirical existence as such, which human beings find themselves immediately enveloped in while trusting their sensual perceptions as a source of reliable knowledge. Moreover, it actually proves to be opposed to empirical existence, not as to something substantially existing, but as to being in fact *a product of vision*. As the world is packed with finite things, the empirical existence does not take its origin from the infinite Being of beings.[13] Despite any attempts to take it for the reality of creation (which is normally the case with those uncritical beliefs that tend to separate God from his creation by placing the ontological abyss between them), the world of finitude turns out to be simply produced by a certain *mode of vision*—namely, the vision *from without*, to which things only appear to come into being from nothing and pass away into nothing again. A great deal of imagination,

10. See Heidegger, *Basic Writings*, 82.
11. Ibid., 81.
12. See ibid., 86.
13. See ibid., 83.

therefore, comes to be involved in building up such a world: in order to be completed, it needs, paradoxically enough, to be divided by imagination in two—be it counterbalanced by "the next-worldly" realm or that of "nothing." In this way, the existence of this world immediately given to the senses is self-assuredly found to look justified and rooted in some unknown principles, merely hidden beyond the boundaries of appearance.

Hence, the inner perspective of *Dasein* is where the human mind is allowed to break through the illusory construct of the world and to see it *anew*—namely, as the totality of the indivisible Being that comprises all particular beings. This is the Being seen in the light of Logos that is said, as mentioned above, to be a specific mode of letting something be truly seen. In the perspective of Logos arising from the depths of Being, the reality does come to be seen, in Heidegger's words, as "the pure transcendence."[14] No externals can exist in it on their own (i.e., apart from their connection with the internal, or in other words, from what is there inside themselves). The truth of the substantial being revealed in the Tetragrammaton would simply not allow that: the innermost essence and its manifest existence, as follows from Exod 3:14, are one and can by no means be separated. This is the very foundation of the true infinity of God's being, outside which nothing else can subsist.

This fundamental unity is consequently where the meaning of all existence is brought to light: in the absolute being there is no discrepancy between the inner and its adequate manifestation, so that the existence itself and the meaning of what it exists for are in it inseparably one. No particulars of the empirical world are therefore excluded from the absolute reality of "pure transcendence" that substantially is and has nothing to do with the abstract identity or sterile indifference; they simply shed their hard shells of the sensibles, becoming thereby, so to speak, transparent to the light of Logos and a new type of knowledge appropriate to it. That is why Logos is rightly understood by the phenomenological ontology (as it is proposed by Heidegger) to penetrate as deep as "the things in themselves":[15] *interpretation*, as suggested above, proves to be that type of knowledge which allows human mind to see things really anew—that is, from the perspective of their meaning or, better to say, the meaning of their existence.

This is the knowledge that is further defined by Heidegger's ontology as the *transcendental* one, which is meant to replace the conventional understanding of knowledge as such, referring to the external experience as the source of its origin. Indeed, while pivoting about what is not unreasonably

14. Ibid., 87.
15. See ibid., 82.

called *veritas transcendentalis*,[16] it not only exceeds the limits of the empirical experience, but also drastically changes the entire vision of reality by getting itself concurrent with the perspective of Creation, taking its departure from the Being of beings, where any beings can adequately be seen through the Meaning of the Word only. This is consequently not the knowledge that deduces the universal Being from all particular beings, making it into an overall sum of all particulars. On the contrary, in line with what has been established by the Kantian *apriorism*, it follows the order where—by contrast to the evidence provided by empirical observation—the universal precedes the particular. In this way, the perspective of the mind proves cardinally changed or, to be precise, *inverted*,[17] when compared to the sensual experience with its straightforward engagement with the particulars. *Veritas transcendentalis* thus becomes a means of amending the mind that goes as far as bringing it into conformity with the substantial order of creation as the reality of self-disclosure, where all particular beings are brought to light from the universal Principle of being and, for this reason, acquire the meaning of their existence to the extent they remain within the totality of the universal and indivisible Being as the means of its manifestation.

Thus, what Heidegger calls "universal phenomenological ontology" should not improperly be understood as "taking its departure from the hermeneutics of Dasein . . . "[18] This hermeneutics, aimed at "an analysis of the existentiality of existence," is in fact nothing else but "the interpretation

16. Ibid., 87.

17. The *inverted perspective*, directly associated by Pavel Florensky with the fundamental principles of the Russian iconography and closely discussed by him with regard to the problem of the mind's attitude to the reality of the absolute whole, is one of the well-known themes from his philosophical legacy (see Florensky, "Обратная перспектива," 46–98). To Florensky, the *inverted perspective* is the one that conforms to the right order of creation (when seen, as it were, by God's "eye") and contrasts with the linear perspective of the empirical individual. The linear perspective (that Florensky finds both in the Euclidian geometry and the Renaissance art and Neokantian philosophy) is nothing more in fact than just a scheme that the mind uses to interpret the world given through the sensual perception. This perspective therefore is only appropriate to a faulty vision of the one and indivisible reality, available solely to the mind following the inverted perspective as it is presented, in Florensky's view, in icons. From the linear perspective, things look "realistic" and "natural"; from the inverted perspective, as the Russian philosopher suggests, they appear "spiritually meaningful." The linear and inverted perspectives are thus appropriate to different types of mentality in their attitude to reality—namely, *subjectivism* and *substantial realism*. "To the extent the cognition of the world was mediated by contemplation," B. V. Raushenbach points out, "icons appealed to reason. Unlike canvases of the modern art that appeal to senses and emotions, icons called for meditation and comprehension of the world" (Rauschenbach, "Икона как средство," 316).

18. Heidegger, *Basic Writings*, 87.

of the Being of Dasein," since—he argues—"as a being that has the possibility of existence," "Dasein has ontologically priority over all other beings . . . "[19]

As a "science" that by its very nature always aims to search for the universal by studying the particular, the "universal" ontology likewise resorts to purely cognitive means of approaching the particular phenomena while trying to find the universal Being behind them. This ontology is not at all a kind of imaginative knowledge of the transcendent that seeks to look beyond the immediacy of perceptions by simply defying their validity and introducing a fictitious world of new imagery, which would prove in fact, when carefully considered, to be nothing other than just an extrapolation of the sensible beyond its legitimate boundaries. On the contrary, while aiming to break through into the universal Being unavailable to the senses or, in other words, to restore cognitively the missing links in the invisible chain of the substantial order of the reality of self-disclosure (where the universal always has priority over all particular beings), ontology is said to appeal to "an analysis of the existentiality of existence," defined by Heidegger as the major means and objective of hermeneutics.[20] Thus by virtue of *analysis* why something exists rather than nothing, ontology and hermeneutics are brought together into a single whole to promote insight into the true nature of both, which is likewise the case with Eriugena's approach (as it should be with any other ontology proper) to the biblical interpretation with its characteristic appeal to ἀναλυτική as a cognitive means of following the order of creation and bringing about the *return* of human being to the reality as it truly is.[21]

This choice of "analysis" for a decisive methodological tool appropriate, as Heidegger understood it, to the task that the ontology of the universal sets itself does not seem accidental. Indeed, in terms of the transcendental knowledge again, this is a mode of cognitive approach which, in contrast to what Kant called a "synthetic judgment,"[22] does not expand the knowledge of things by adding to it something new that is borrowed from an external experience, but does simply explicate what is already latently present in the notions of things involved in the mind's cognitive attitude to them. So that, when applied to "the interpretation of the Being of Dasein," this kind of analysis allows hermeneutics to discern behind the phenomena

19. Ibid., 86.

20 See ibid., 87.

21. On Eriugena's notion of ἀναλυτική, understood by him in both logical and ontological sense as analysis, recollection or return, see, for example, the *Periphyseon* 526a–b (for the details of the *Periphyseon's* Book 2, see Bibliorgaphy).

22. On Kant's distinction between the "analytic" and "synthetic" propositions see Kant, *Критика чистого разума*, 37–38.

the meaning of notions that bring things into the focus of its cognitive approach. In this way, looking for the meaning inherent in the notions of things *a priori* present to the cognitive experience, hermeneutical analysis does take an opportunity to ascertain what precedes the presence of existents and what subsequently they exist for, so as to disclose thereby nothing else in fact but the meaning of their existence. This is, furthermore, how—through the knowledge subject to *veritas transcendentalis* and focused on what ontologically has "priority over all other beings"—the Logos itself, that is believed to precede all particular beings while giving rise to them, eventually comes to light in the space of *Dasein* opened from within. And along with it, the proper order of existence, in accordance with which the universal precedes the particular, gets restored and revealed, letting thereby the Being, previously hidden behind the appearance of particular things, become unconcealed and present to the coherently religious mind, to which nothing can come into existence (or to the fore of presence) otherwise than from the universal Principle of all.

Not unfairly therefore is ontology qualified by Heidegger as "the science of the Being of beings,"[23] and hermeneutics, that lies at the heart of this ontology, is understood to be a "historical interpretation."[24] Indeed, as clearly seen above, it is similar to science as such that ontology starts out by studying the particular as it is given at present. Unlike conventional science, however, it searches for the universal not in line with a *temporal sequence*, as empirical knowledge by contrast would most likely do while associating the idea of exceeding the limits of transient being with a spurious infinity of duration. By doing so, the empirical knowledge would try to reconstruct a full history of the particular present at a given moment, extending the immediacy of its appearance by investigating the antecedent past and forecasting the nearest and following future. In its pursuit of the universal that transcends the constraints of all confined beings, ontology instead, as said before, resorts to hermeneutics to secure—through the contrast between the present and the past that is always fraught with loss of immediacy—a short cut to its chief objective of finding the universal by disclosing the meaning of existence.

In short, what empirical knowledge seeks to get from extending the limits of the particular through the historical reconstruction perfectly conformed with the temporal dimension of reality, ontology achieves in an analysis of *the meaning* through a historically inverted view of the particular exercised by an interpretive approach to it. Differentiation between the

---

23. Heidegger, *Basic Writings*, 86.
24. Ibid., 87.

present and the past does allow hermeneutics to look into the meaning of existence (and, hence, into the substantial order of the reality) in which both the antecedence of the universal and the whole of its progression to the particular is preserved: from what is unconcealed at present, it is clear to the interpretive view what was there concealed in the past and what it actually existed for. As susceptible of *interpretation* (i.e., that kind of knowledge which in contrast to the conventional one perfectly conforms, as discussed above, to the reality of self-disclosure), this meaning of existence proves to manifest itself through the meaning of things that is conveyed by their generic notions and borne throughout the whole of their existence, from its very beginning up to the end. This is consequently the meaning that first shines forth through the contrast the "historical interpretation" ascertains between the present and the past so as to further bring through it, as the ground of their identity, both the present and the past and the future into a single and inseparable whole.

Thus in the ontology primarily concerned about the conformity to the substantial reality where the universal precedes the particular, which alone enables it to tackle the questions why something exists (comes to exist) and what is the prospect (possibility) of its existence, temporality as such gets overcome. Moreover, it is in the ontology of this kind that the fundamental truth articulated by the Tetragrammaton comes to be thoroughly apprehended—namely, the truth that the true infinity of the reality of self-disclosure, according to which the innermost essence and its adequate manifestation are inseparably one, cannot be conceived otherwise than in the way of *transcending the temporality*, appropriate to transient beings only. Both temporality, with its division of existence into separate segments of time, and infinity spuriously understood as an endless duration prove here to be irrelevant to the substantial reality of self-disclosure, where Logos brings all things to the light of being.

Indeed, in the light of the universal meaning this ontology uncovers, neither past nor future are any longer hidden behind the horizon of empirical existence as something remote from the present; for no contingencies of the flux of things seen from without matter any more to the transcendental knowledge. And it cannot be otherwise, unless the perspective of sensual perception is taken for granted as the only true perspective of reality. In so far as the reality is properly conceived of as that of self-disclosure (that is solely amenable to the mind liberated from the dictates of the senses and therefore restored to its capacity of cognitive thinking[25]), nothing particular

---

25. The role of proper thinking comes into focus of one of the later works of Heidegger, *What is Called Thinking* (for the source details see Bibliography).

in it can ever be understood to subsist on its own, independently of the universal. The very pattern of self-disclosure implies that the universal never moves *away* from itself while giving rise to anything particular: preceding all particular things, the universal actually moves nowhere else apart from itself, that is, to its own manifestation through the particular; for it is undeniably true that nothing else can ever subsist outside the universal, genuinely absolute and infinite. This consequently means that nothing particular can actually subsist apart from or alongside the universal. It can truly subsist only when staying *in* and *with* the universal, being intimately connected with it; and this connection is what is realized in the meaning of existence, through which the universal itself comes true.

As a result, the universal ontology of self-disclosure (which not unfairly should also be understood as the ontology of Creation) safely arrives at *paradox* that has always been implicitly present in its approach to the absolute self-identical Being, but only at this point of discourse renders fully explicit and can no longer be avoided. As a matter of fact, overcoming temporality does not mean its substitution by the opposite, eternity. Neither of them can properly be conceived as remaining merely opposed to one another (i.e., as *only* temporal and *only* eternal). As the mutually excluding extremes, they would simply turn into *abstract categories* applicable only to rationally abstract constructs of reality. Nor can they however be treated in a *metaphysical* manner as the complimentary counterparts that make up a single whole, when added together. They are the opposites that are to be treated *dialectically*—that is, by means of *paradox* dialectically understood. In accordance with this treatment, both opposites are considered to be simultaneously true so as to let them be completely transformed into a single whole freed from the one-sidedness of mutually confined extremes and available only to a new vision of reality as it truly, infinitely, *is.* Temporality and eternity, according to this vision, may only be truly known when conceived in their unity: the universal *precedes* the particular and at the same time *stays* within itself. Time and eternity are inconceivable as being separated from and opposed to one another. Likewise, change and immutability, motion and rest are mutually inseparable in a coherent vision of Being as a whole. So that, what is there in the Beginning, may only be truly known as being at the same time in the Middle and in the End. Nothing whatsoever falls out of the reality of the absolute self-identity, unless the mind's misconception of being (understood as rigidly opposed to non-being) forces human beings to let things leave it, making thus humans themselves live an illusory life in a fictitious world.

Temporality and Eternity

Quite unsurprisingly therefore does Heidegger refer to Plato's ontology at the very outset of his *Sein und Zeit*, finding in it a good example of ontology being essentially dialectical with a view to approaching the substantial order of the Logos-based reality. "That is why," he admits in the opening part of the monumental work, "the ancient ontology developed by Plato becomes 'dialectic.'"[26] Indeed, temporality and eternity dialectically seen in their unity may easily be found to lie in the focus of Plato's ontology, as it is likewise the case with Gregory's ontological approach to God and his interpretation of the Tetragrammaton considered above.

Thus, for instance, in the *Timaeus* Plato articulates the truth that the eternal being cannot be conceived in terms of duration only, when time is understood to be divided into separate segments. According to him, a coherent view of the whole also implies that of the ever-lasting presence, making the opposite perspectives actually into the modes of vision of *one and the same* infinite reality, unless they are illegitimately set apart to be applicable to different and separate realms of existence—namely, those of becoming and immutability. "These are all parts of time," Plato writes, "and the past and future are created species of time, which we unconsciously but wrongly transfer to the eternal essence; for we say that he" (i.e., God) "'was', he 'is', he 'will be', but the truth is that 'is' alone is properly attributed to him, and that 'was' and 'will be' only to be spoken of becoming in time, for they are motions, but that which is immovably the same cannot become older or younger by time, nor ever did or has become, or hereafter will be, older or younger, nor is subject at all to any of those states which affect moving and sensible things and of which generation is the cause. These are the forms of time, which imitates eternity . . ." (*Timaeus*, 37c–38a).[27]

This distinction between the duration and presence does not mean however that temporality and eternity should be treated as the principles of the two different realities mutually countered. They should rather be considered as the different dimensions or, better to say (as suggested above), the modes of vision of one and the same reality which need to be reconciled. And the ever-lasting presence, as follows from Plato's train of thought, may come to be the meeting point, where they do not simply encounter or mingle, but become reconciled in a single and indivisible whole. Eternity is not merely the opposite of time, its negation or absence. Nor is it time simply brought to a complete halt. Neither of them defies the other or prevails

26. Heidegger, *Basic Writings*, 71.

27. For the details of Plato's *Timaeus*, see Bibliography.

over it; rather both, when available to a dialectically coherent vision of the whole, transform into something of a new quality of their unity, which alone is compatible with the infinite reality as it truly, unceasingly, is.

Indeed, as the patriarch of all philosophers keeps arguing in the *Parmenides*[28] in line with a dialectical view of the universal whole (that precedes the particular and at the same time never moves away from itself), the absolute wholeness may only be truly known as being simultaneously in itself and in the other. And this is not unfairly so; since comprising all parts with no exception, the whole yet remains fully present in none of them, being thus at the same time in all parts and beyond them (see *Parmenides*, 152c–e).[29] The eternal whole therefore cannot be known otherwise than in the way of being *simultaneously* identical to itself and different from itself (*Parmenides*, 146a). So that, according to the profoundly dialectical view of the universal being developed by the "ancient ontology" of Plato, time and eternity can never be set over against one another. In so far as the universal whole is seen as being *simultaneously* in itself and in the other, it is fairly understood to be *in time and beyond it*. If the whole however, being divided into parts, is assumed to be separated from the other and thus seen as being *successively* in itself and in the other as two different states, then it is understood to change and be *in time only*, which would be appropriate to finite things alone that come into being and pass away. Temporality and

28. Although Plato uses the name of the real Parmenides both for giving the title to the dialogue and indicating one of its leading interlocutors, the dialogue's character should not be confused with the historical figure of Parmenides, and his statements should not be taken for the quotations from the Eleatic teaching itself. Indeed, many of the dialectical ideas proposed by Parmenides of the dialogue (as those of the absolute wholeness or the universal understood as *being simultaneously in itself and in the other*) do not actually comply with an apparently non-dialectical ontology of the *Periphyseon*'s Parmenides. According to the latter, the way in which the totality of Being (or the unchangeable and indivisible One) is conceived does not imply its simultaneous distinction from anything other. As A. F. Losev suggests, in the dialogue in question Plato is focused on the argument concerning the dichotomy between "ideas" and "things" rather than a presentation of the authentic teaching of the Eleatic school (see Plato, *Сочинения, Т.* 2, 586). It means that Plato refers to Parmenides's thesis that *all is one* to develop his own conception of *identity in distinction*, which he appears to contrast, according to Losev, to the ideas of the School of Megara. It seems more important to Plato to argue (by virtue of the statements he ascribes to Parmenides) against the Megarian approach to understanding the "ideas" by setting them apart from the contraries (the world of particular things) than to convey a coherent doctrine of Parmenides himself. ". . . what is new in the *Parmenides*," says Losev, "consists in the way in which *the dialectic of ideas and matter* is systematically presented" (ibid., 592). In this sense, in the *Parmenides* (bringing forth, by contrast to Parmenides's *Periphyseon*, the conception of the contraries unity) we deal in fact with the evolution of Plato's own ideas (see ibid.).

29. For the details of Plato's *Parmenides* see Bibliography.

eternity are, no doubt, always at one and hence, once the whole of being is really concerned, should never be set apart and over against one another (*Parmenides*, 152a). As separated and mutually opposed, they are equally false and irrelevant to the reality of the absolute whole. This latter may only be known as ever subsisting at present—not the present which lies between the past and future, but the present through which everything involved in becoming does pass (*Parmenides*, 152e).[30]

The Totality of Being

The dialectical vision of wholeness of being offered by Plato was historically a considerable step ahead in developing ontology. Among his immediate predecessors who had also made a substantial contribution to the development of ontology, and even initiated it as an area of philosophical expertise, was another Greek genius Parmenides, an illustrious founder of the Eleatic school, not unreasonably associated with the beginnings of metaphysics in what will later become a European intellectual landscape. Discussing his importance to the history of thought, Hegel in particular points out in the *Vorlesungen über die Geschichte der Philosophie*: "Seeing in it an ascent to the realm of the ideal, we have to admit that it is from Parmenides that philosophy in a proper sense of the word takes its departure."[31]

What gives Hegel reason to estimate so highly the role of Parmenides for the subsequent evolution of philosophical thought is undoubtedly his attempt to articulate the truth of the *universality* of Being, in a sense that "being alone does exist, whereas nonbeing does not at all."[32] Being, according to Parmenides, is really absolute,[33] ubiquitous and unceasingly present. It "neither was nor will be but is," says he, "has always been wholly now and indivisibly one" (*Periphyseon* 8: 5-6).[34] From this, it is to be recognised as

---

30. It would be a big blunder to confuse a dialectical approach of this sort with a pantheistic view of reality. To a dialectically coherent vision, reality is not at all a conglomerate of finite things exposed to a contingent flux. Dialectic actually defies such an empirical view of things and at the same time reveals the irrelevance of charges against those who, like Eriugena or Spinoza, were often suspected of their sympathy with pantheism. Thus Plato's understanding of ever-lasting presence makes it much clearer what Spinoza, for example, means when saying that God may "only be conceivable as existing" (Spinoza, *Избранные произведения*, 361).

31. Hegel, *Лекции по истории философии*, Кн. 1, 265. See also his *Encyclopaedia Logic*, § 86 ad. 2.

32. Ibid., 264.

33. In his *Commentaries to Physics*, Simplicius calls Parmenides's Being "the absolute being" (Lebedev, *Фрагменты*, 289).

34. For the details of Parmenides's *Periphyseon* see "О природе," in Bibliography.

a firm truth that *beyond being there is nothing*,[35] meaning that outside one and indivisible being nothing else can ever be recognised to subsist. By this categorical denial of the substantiality of "nothing" in favour of the totality of "being," Parmenides means to suggest, in Hegel's view, that—regardless of the shape the negative as such may take—it would be a big blunder to assume that the opposite of being could actually subsist or, speaking plainly, nothing could be taken for something. The delusion concerning the dichotomy between being and nonbeing therefore consists, as Hegel holds, in having both counterparts mutually differed or mingled up, as though they were of the same value as something equally substantial.[36] "Never shall this prevail, that Unbeing is,"[37] says Parmenides in his *Periphyseon*.[38]

No wonder therefore that Parmenides finds it immensely important for the explication of his philosophical standpoint to clearly distinguish two different views of the totality of Being, which he calls the *Way of Truth* and the *Way of Delusion*, actually meaning by them the opposite ways of approaching the reality as such.[39] The totality of Being cannot be really understood, according to him, to result from its full distinction from nonbeing or, as it were, from a sum of being and nonbeing. By contrast to such a delusion when being is assumed to co-exist with nonbeing, the truth requires that by no means can the latter be admitted of lying alongside the former; for the total Being, as Parmenides sees it, allows no rival to co-exist with itself and challenge its totality. In other words, the undeniable truth Parmenides wishes to insist on requires that the totality of Being cannot be reduced to that of the multitude of finite things, simply because nonbeing (that makes things confined and torn out of the wholeness of being, as if placing them outside it) is utterly not.[40]

Despite this truth, however, those whom the Greek philosopher calls "mortals" (i.e., the ones who find themselves living among finite things that come and go, and therefore conform their lives to the pattern of transient

35. See Parmenides, "О природе," 297.

36. See Hegel, *Лекции по истории философии*, Кн. 1, 264.

37. Parmenides, "On the Nature." Quoted in Kenny, *Brief History*, 10.

38. As Plutarch points it out, Parmenides's Φύσιζ stands for "reality," the meaning of which should certainly be understood as being much broader than that of "nature," often unconsciously reduced to a conglomerate of "natural" phenomena (see Plutarch, *Против Колота 15: 116a*, quoted in Lebedev, 296). Likewise Eriugena, while discussing the way of grasping the *fundamental division* of all things into those that are and are not, identifies Φύσιζ with the whole of reality understood, as we shall see it later, as the *totality* of Being (*Periphyseon* 441a).

39. See Parmenides, "О Природе," 295–96.

40. In his *Metaphysics* (1089a), Aristotle formulates Parmenides's thesis in the following way: "Never is that which is not" (Aristotle, *Сочинения*, 354).

nature) tend to divide everything into contraries such as light and darkness, life and death (see *Periphyseon* 8: 53–54), putting thereby the very existence of theirs at risk of negation and taking the multitude of finite things (limited by nonbeing) for the being as it really is. They keep setting apart the opposites found in the surrounding world that is immediately given to them through their senses, falsely ascribing an ontological status to the opposites relevant to the empirical (sensually experienced) dimension of existence only. And so doing, these "mortals" go so far as to divide even the principle of all things into competing agents (like those of "earth" and "fire"), which, they believe, allows them to attain the knowledge of what they call "natural phenomena"[41] and thus to take an allegedly proper place in the world resulting in fact from their own faulty assumptions. Following this *Way of Delusion*, the "mortals" eventually arrive at a vision of the Universe, in the middle of which "they place a goddess who governs all things."[42]

Thus the two ways of approaching the reality, being in effect the two different perspectives of the mind in its cognitive attitude to what may be understood as "real," do legitimise rival visions of one and the same reality, giving rise to alternative world pictures: one is infinitely one and indivisible, unceasingly remaining everywhere within itself; the other is split up into opposite principles and is identified with the flux of finite things. The first is exposed to thought, for, as Parmenides puts it, "to be" and "to be thought of" are one and the same (*Periphyseon* 2: 3);[43] the second is produced by senses or, to be precise, by the mind misled by senses. And many prominent classics of antiquity, while commenting on Parmenides's understanding of the origin of the alternative visions of reality, do agree about the epistemological nature of this distinction. Particularly, Aristotle holds in his *Metaphysics* (987b) that the unity of being, as Parmenides understood it, is known to reason alone, whereas the multitude of things may only be perceived through the senses. And rightly so; for, as Diogenes Laertius suggests, Parmenides liberated thought from "the deceptive imagination"[44]: "He called reason to be the criterion of truth; in the senses, he said, there is no accuracy."[45] Not unfairly does Sextus Empiricus conclude therefore

---

41. See Parmenides, "О природе," 297.

42. Ibid., 298.

43. To some extent, Descartes's "cogito ergo sum" may not unfairly be understood to be in continuity with the idea of identity between being and thought, first articulated by Parmenides.

44. Laertius, *О жизни*, 366.

45. Ibid.

that, according to the author of the *Periphyseon*, "one should trust not the senses but reason alone."[46]

By all these testimonies to the respective discernment of reason and the senses lying at the heart of Parmenides's discourse, we are given to understand in fact that the essential difference between the rival world pictures central to his ontology may be thoroughly explained by different types of epistemology involved in making them up. For the distinction of the alternative visions of reality, it is crucial to understand whether reason or senses are chosen for the means of a cognitive attitude to it and, consequently, whether it is universality of thought or contingency of sensual perception that are to be taken for the prime source of knowledge. Accordingly, it is also important to decide whether the knowledge itself should be focused on particulars of the empirical existence or aimed at the infinity of wholeness (where even the particulars are seen anew in the context of their integrity), without which a coherent faith in One God (but not a deity of imagination, like the "goddess" mentioned above) is hardly possible at all.

It is needless to say which of the two sides of this dilemma Parmenides chooses. Following the logic of the twofold structure of the *Periphyseon*, it is not hard to discern his critical attitude to the mind's reliance on senses and subjection to their dictates. To him, the prevalence of senses over reason can only be understood as "the way of non-being" leading to nowhere else but dispersion of the unity of being in the flux of transient things. This is what he calls "the Way of Delusion," "the illusory way" upon which, as M. Wolf puts it, "people enter under the pressure of their habit to rely on sensual perception."[47] And if Parmenides speaks of this illusory way in detail, he undoubtedly does so with the only intention of having it resolutely rejected as the erroneous one. His genuine aim is to establish *the Way of Truth* as the only proper way of approaching the true Being that opens up before the mind a panorama of the infinite and immutable whole, where no room for the opposite (that *is not*) can ever be found. The simplicity of this approach, as seen in the *Periphyseon*, is abundantly clear: "The solution is there—whether it is or is not."[48] By this unambiguous manner of articulating the truth, Parmenides means to suggest that it is possible indeed to affirm the totality of Being by categorically denying the existence of anything else apart from it: Being is, but non-being (i.e., the opposite or the other as such) is not.

---

46. Sextus Empiricus, *Сочинения*, 83.

47. Wolf, "К вопросу интерпретации," 7.

48. Parmenides, "О природе," 297.

Thanks to Simplicius however, who wrote about Parmenides's attitude to the opposites and contradictions they form, it is fairly easy to understand that the way of treating "the absolute being" cannot be as simple as that. Indeed, its totality, required by the Way of Truth, cannot be merely postulated in an "either-or" manner; it should rather be properly conceived. This implies that the opposite of the total should neither be merely discarded nor forbidden but dialectically overcome. It further means that the totality of Being can only be affirmed when its opposite is found by dialectical thought (fearless of contradictions resulting from metaphysical dichotomies) to be appropriate to the reality of finite things but utterly irrelevant to the infinity of the totality, when the latter is consistently thought of (and therefore beheld by the mind's eye, as Eriugena calls it) as the absolute whole. No truth can simply be declared; it can only be known, and therefore neither received nor imposed from without but attained from within the free mind (or, speaking in terms of Diogenes, reason *liberated* from the sway of senses) through being properly conceived. Truth is neither a precept to be adhered to nor a dogma to be taken for granted; it is a cornerstone of freedom (John 8:32), and as a cardinal epistemological-ontological category it firmly stands for the unity of knowledge and being.

The Opposites and Contradiction

In his commentary on Aristotle's *Physics*, Simplicius describes Parmenides's attitude to the opposites and contradictions they give rise to as follows: "That contradictory statements cannot be simultaneously true, he says in the verses where he reproaches those who identify the opposites . . . "[49] From this impossibility of treating contradictory statements *as being simultaneously true* (which alone constitutes the very nature of contradiction as such), it follows of necessity that on the Way of Truth—that is, the way of approaching the totality of Being which truly (everywhere and always) is— contradiction is utterly unacceptable to Parmenides. And this further means that the ontology he offers, though majestically philosophical by nature, is nevertheless apparently non-dialectical in its method, which considerably diminishes its validity.

A profoundly philosophical approach to Truth, being an attempt at establishing the unity between thought and the whole of existence, cannot actually dispense with dialectic as a specific discipline of the mind, which is in fact responsible for nurturing this unity and therefore intrinsic to philosophy as a type of knowledge. By embracing the diametrical opposites of

49. Lebedev, *Фрагменты*, 288.

existence (being and non-being), dialectic seeks the way of bringing them together so as—through overcoming their collision—to consistently conceive the totality of Being and thus to know it. On this way to Truth (or perfect conformity of both human mind and life to the infinite Being that unceasingly is), an appeal to contradiction and its proper treatment—with a view to overcoming the finitude of existence split into the opposites of being and non-being mutually confined—becomes therefore altogether unavoidable. Thus Hegel, the unsurpassed authority in dialectic who deeply saw both the merits and weakness of philosophical thought in its infancy (and yet highly appreciated, as said before, Parmenides's contribution to its birth), conspicuously admits in the very first of all theses to his doctoral work: "Contradiction is the criterion of truth; lack of contradiction is the criterion of delusion."[50]

As an effective tool to bring opposites to collision and revealing thereby their irrelevance to the reality of the whole (where nothing one-sided and confined can actually subsist), contradiction gives in fact an opportunity to reconsider the relationship between the polar (finite) opposites and find the way to the infinite hidden behind them. It may thus become an epistemological means of breaking through the finitude of the world of appearance into the true Being, which alone the universal (ontologically valid) truth is appropriate to. Not unfairly therefore should contradiction be understood as a mode of overcoming any division into opposites (like that into being and non-being, qualified by Eriugena as the *fundamental* one), illegitimately imposed upon the reality by the mind following a non-dialectical (non-contradictory) way of thinking. In this sense, contradiction promotes the mind's progression towards the knowledge of Truth, which is basically the truth of the absolute wholeness and, hence, of the perfect conformity of human mind (and being) to the unity of the whole. Accordingly, dialectic proves to be a paradigm of thinking where the way of bringing everything back to the unity of the original wholeness goes through; for it is in dialectic that the constructive role of contradiction is fully realized to put to an end the sway of the corrupt mind inclined to destructive dichotomies resulting from setting the opposites apart. As such, dialectic is consequently none other but a discipline of thinking, by virtue of which not only the mentality itself but also the whole of human life (of which the mind's operation is the most essential and distinctive part) becomes transformed, becoming inseparably one with the universal whole—that is to say, brought in effect to conformity with the perspective and the very order of reality that comes forth into being from the one and universal Principle of all. This is the vision

---

50. Hegel, *Работы*, 265.

of dialectic which really helps us to understand what Eriugena means when he identifies dialectic, as we shall see it later, with being both the order that *right reasons*, as he calls it, adheres to and the *art* of living. And it is exactly by contrast with the Parmenidian attitude to contradiction that Eriugena's coherent understanding of dialectic can be effectively explicated as lying at the very heart of his deeply theological discourse.

As it is clear from the aforesaid, remaining a staunch upholder of the holistic view of Being, Parmenides is nevertheless convinced that its total-ity can be unproblematically affirmed in a non-contradictory way, as if its truth might simply be established by the denial of what is contrary to being and on this account is classified as false. And he actually does so when he suggests that "Being is" but "Non-being is not," assuming thereby—as Sim-plicius testifies to it—that by no means can two contradictory statements be admitted of being simultaneously true. This means that, according to a non-contradictory approach, of the two contradictory statements—such as "Being is" and "Non-being is"—only one can be chosen for true, whereas the other is found to be utterly irrelevant to any sort of relation with being and therefore invalid or false. But does such an approach to the opposites in an "either-or" manner, according to which one of the contraries is just pre-ferred to the other, really lead to an affirmation of the all-embracing totality of Being or, instead of this, leave it merely confined? Is it possible indeed to hold anything whole when one of the opposites is simply neglected but not superseded? Does such an apparently non-dialectical treatment really open, as Parmenides believed, the way to Truth, which, as said before, can only be known but not merely postulated or appointed?

From the dialectical point of view, utterly intolerant to any incon-sistencies in approaching the whole, the simplest and the clearest answer to all these questions is obviously "No." The entire ontology from Plato to Heidegger convinces us of this. While insisting on the interconnectedness of time and eternity (ever-lasting presence), both ancient and contemporary ontology, as previously considered, are perfectly explicit about the principle impossibility of treating these two visions of reality (appropriate in fact to its different dimensions) either in a rationally abstract or metaphysical way, when they are respectively misunderstood to be either the mutually opposed extremes or complementary counterparts that, in like manner to constitu-tive components, are allegedly assumed to make up a single whole. Being as a whole (that unceasingly is) and its negation (non-being) that makes the ever-lasting presence disrupted and confined, should not be accord-ingly understood as something separate and set over against one another, as if either could subsist on its own. Otherwise, both time and eternity, and along with them being and non-being, will prove to be equally untrue (i.e., irrelevant to the substantial reality as it truly is in its absolute wholeness). Being as a whole, outside which nothing else does subsist, is not the one that comes and goes; it, as Parmenides rightly says, ever *is*. And in this sense indeed, non-being is not. However, to really adopt the truth of the totality and eternity of Being conveyed thereby, it must be comprehended. And for this purpose, cognitive thought must resort to contradiction, by virtue of which, when properly treated, temporality is not merely forbidden but dialectically overcome as being solely appropriate to finite existence resulting from a sensual perception of reality. Truth is revealed in and through the mind—through its right attitude to the infinite reality of the absolute whole. And it is the dialectical contradiction alone which opens the Way of Truth and allows the mind in effect to restore its proper relation with the reality as it truly is behind its sensible appearance.

All this gives us to understand that it is not actually enough for ontology as a profoundly coherent discipline of philosophical knowledge simply to establish the truth of the totality and eternity of Being, as Parmenides did. Nor is it important for it to know *what* Being as such is, for that would be appropriate to knowing external objects only. What really matters to ontology is *how* this totality and eternity of Being can be consistently thought of and thus become known, so as to bring human beings to conformity to it and let them thereby participate in it. So when proposing that "Being is" but "Non-being is not," and thus deliberately trying to avoid contradiction as being incompatible, in his view, with Truth, Parmenides, alas, is missing the point: in this way the truth claimed is not actually approached. In order to really know two crucial things about the truth stated by the Greek philosopher—that is, to know the true Being as the totality and eternity—it is important to understand not *what* totality and eternity are as abstract objects given to a knower in perception and therefore seen by him or her from afar; but *how* they can be conceived so close to their true nature that a knower might find him-or herself involved in (and embraced by) the real totality and real eternity.

As a matter of fact, it is impossible to know *what* the totality is or, to be precise, what it consists of and how many things it should include to be total; for, as it was seen in Plato's *Parmenides*, no matter how great the number of particular things included in it, the totality is fully present in none of them and therefore always remains beyond them. Likewise, it is impossible to know *what* eternity is—whether it is a state of immutability and complete rest or an endless duration or anything else. What is really possible to know, by contrast to all this, is *how* the totality uncovers itself in all its depth and breadth when fully distinguished from the opposite, which is to be "nothing" (that is, non-being understood as nothing); for the totality may only be truly known as the one outside which nothing whatsoever is found to subsist, because beyond it, as total in the truest sense of the word, there is utterly nothing. Likewise, the eternity of Being may be properly known as completely different from temporality (and hence confinement and mutation), when in its distinction from all finitude (where it is confronted by the opposite) being is found not liable to transition into non-being.

The truth of Being, identical in its totality to itself, is inconceivable (and consequently unknowable) therefore apart from being distinguished from the other, which further means—as Plato suggested in the *Parmenides* (146a) examined above—that, since outside the totality nothing else does subsist, the eternal whole cannot be truly known otherwise than in the way of being identical to itself and different from itself at the same time. Only thus can that be properly approached which ought to be known as the totality that precedes any particular things and at the same time, comprising them all, stays within itself, ever remaining identical to itself and irreducible to the multitude of the particulars that never can abandon it. When in contrast to this holistic view, however, the contraries are simply torn apart, as it is the case with Being that is and Non-being that is not, then nothing actually happens to the knowledge of Truth: puzzled by this division and squeezed between the confronting opposites, thought comes to a complete halt on the threshold of Truth, admiring its magnificence but never entering under its dome.

In order for thought to be enabled to step into the dwelling of Truth, the confronting opposites must be brought together so close that their collision would spark new light of a new perspective of the mind, which shines through the darkness of ignorance. This means that, formulated as contradictory statements, they must be presented to the mind in the form of contradiction. Hence, if the primary thesis inviting the truth is "Being is," then the opposite statement should be related to being as well and take shape of a negative proposition (antithesis) "Non-being is." Only as such, can thesis and antithesis, when taken together, make up a contradiction, which looks as simple as follows:

Being is;

Non-being is.

The immensity of the problem expressed by this contradiction is, however, hidden behind its deceptive simplicity, for it holds the keys to the narrow gate leading to the realm of eternal Truth. The way this contradiction is treated is indeed of tremendous importance for the entire evolution of thought and, as a consequence, of human condition. This is the point on which it depends whether thought, rejecting contradictions as sheer nonsense or signs of delusion, goes astray along the broad way of fantasies, producing a fictitious world of the man-made reality apt for illusory life only; or—recognizing in contradictions a critical point the paradigm of linear (non-contradictory) thinking may reach—it dares to press ahead to fearlessly face challenges of dialectical thinking, clearing the way of all stumbling-blocks of antinomies that used to be seen (and finally classified since Kant's first *Critique*) as insoluble and prohibitive to any further progress of knowledge.

The Dialectical Understanding of Contradiction

One of the first challenges on the way ahead that the mind has to face in its pursuit of the infinite whole (which alone truly, i.e., unceasingly, is) consists in a *dialectical* understanding of contradiction. From an instrument of strict prohibition of exceeding the limits of empirical evidence, contradiction must be turned into a means of embracing the opposite extremes of existence, by virtue of which thought is enabled to break through all-dividing temporality to eternity of the real whole and thus to bring the entire human being to living in conformity with it. The key to this cardinal revaluation of the role of contradiction is in the way its constituent elements, that is, contradictory statements, are considered. Unlike the Parmenidian approach that Simplicius, as indicated above, testifies to, according to which contradiction as such is diligently eliminated by setting the contradictory statements apart, the dialectical view implies that both thesis and antithesis are to be *simultaneously* taken into consideration. All the more, they are implied to be considered not in, so to speak, "either-or" manner, when of the two contradictory statements only one is chosen for true whereas the other is rejected as being false; but in "both-and" manner, when both statements are recognised to be *simultaneously true*. To thought, that has accustomed itself to adhere to a straightforward principle of non-contradiction, such a bizarre way of treating the mutually excluding statements must look too extraordinary to be true. Nevertheless, it is this dialectical view that does allow thought to coherently conceive the totality of the eternal Being, and thus—by overcoming the gravity of temporality that makes the unity of being dispersed in the flux of finite things—to liberate human beings, whom Parmenides calls "mortals" from their bondage to finitude and, hence, the illicit form of existence (the corrupt life) among the transient things of the world of appearance.

When—in contrast to Parmenides's attempt to avoid contradiction by formulating, as seen in Hegel, two tautological statements "Being is" and

"Non-being is not"—dialectic gets focused on the contradictories taken in their unity, it seeks to realise the truth of the totality of Being, in accordance with which the latter is only conceivable as being at the same time identical to itself and different from itself. For this reason, the flattening tautology "Being is," expressing the totality's identity, needs to be deepened as far as to let it articulate its truth in a more adequate and perfect way as that of *self*-identity. Not unreasonably, therefore, it needs to be counterbalanced by such a paradoxical statement as "Non-being is." By this paradoxical expression breaking up all linear connections between thought and reality, the tautological thesis is challenged by the contradictory antithesis and, as a result of this, the whole contradiction is set in motion. Thus thought is allowed indeed to concentrate on the truth of identity plainly conveyed in the form of tautology and, proceeding in this way, to conceive (and know) this truth not as an empty abstraction (rationally extracted and therefore severed from reality), but as the profoundly ontological truth, utterly inseparable from the being itself.

From this it is clear that in order that the true identity of the whole might be really grasped *as that outside which nothing else may subsist*, the notion of "non-being" should be let into play, but in a very cautious and subtle way. And this is actually what a dialectical treatment of the contradiction is all about. In particular, in so far as the contradiction is sought to be resolved (so as to let the mind step forward towards a new dimension of reality altogether incompatible with the finitude resulting from the mutual confrontation of the opposites), "non-being" should not be simply excluded from being, when forbidden to exist or understood to oppose it. The "non-being" should rather be conceived in such a manner that, when assumed to be included in the whole (since nothing at all is supposed to remain outside it), the self-identical wholeness would neither be shattered nor defied. By no means should its enclosure into the whole of being therefore be confused with an attempt to assign an ontological status to it. Like Parmenides, who reproaches those trying to identify being and non-being, Hegel as well warns those inconsistent in their thinking against falling into error of taking "nothing" for "something" when being and its counterpart, as said before, are intended to be mutually differed or mingled up, as if they were something con-substantial. Like a fatal virus, such an error infects thought, bringing it to a parochial vision of reality through the finite definitions appropriate to finite things only and based on the clear divide between being and non-being, which may solely result from the assumption of their equal con-substantiality. In contrast to this, dialectic with its subtle treatment of these fundamental opposites safeguards thought from making the pernicious blunder of reducing the infinite whole to a finite being (countered by non-being) and provides a remedy for restoration of a sound vision of reality as it truly (unceasingly) is while taking its origin from the universal Principle of all and never leaving it.

That is why it is crucial for dialectic as a paradigm of thinking that brings the human mind into conformity with the totality of the eternal Being to insist on considering the contradiction as consisting of the contradictory statements that are *simultaneously true*. Otherwise, if only one of the contradictories is true (i.e., meaningfully correlated with the being coherently thought of in its unconfined totality), then contradiction does not occur. On the other hand, if the contradictories are considered not simultaneously but separately (e.g., in succession to one another), as it might appear to be the case with being's transition into non-being in the course of its mutation, then neither of them proves to be meaningful and therefore relevant to the truth of the eternal totality of Being, though they may seem true with regard to the finite existence in which things are understood to come into being and pass away. Such a separation of the opposites (and the appropriate contradictories), leading to the loss of truth and to seeming alone, instead of clear vision of reality in the light of the true knowledge of it, proves in fact to be nothing other than *the Way of Delusion* at work that Parmenides so vehemently warns us against. This is actually the way by which the senses—as his Greek commentators quoted above remind us— deceive the mind; and while doing so, they mislead the mind so far as to make it believe that being can be followed by non-being as quite a legitimate phase of the changing existence. Following this way, the mind goes far away indeed from the true Being as it unceasingly is in its totality. Guided by a distorted vision fitting the confined beings only, this mind is inevitably brought to its wrong assumptions concerning the transient nature of reality, which it readily imposes upon the surrounding world perceived through the dictates of senses, making it into the realm of temporality packed with finite sensible objects.

Self-Identical Being

By no means, therefore, should the basic principle of the simultaneous truth of contradictories be disregarded once any cognitive contradiction (and above all the cardinal one about which dialectical ontology pivots) is meant to be properly tackled and resolved. This is how the self-identical Being can truly be known when conceived to be *distinct* from the other (non-being) but not *confined* by it. Indeed, as the all-embracing totality, Being cannot be identical to itself as being unless it is distinct from its other (non-being).

In fact, however, it can be distinct from nothing apart from itself, since its totality is confronted by nothing else. Hence, Being is self-identical in so far as it is at the same time different from itself only, so that nothing whatsoever alien (or opposite) to it can be found at all within or outside its totality. Accordingly, being and non-being cannot be truly known as lying *alongside* one another, be they assumed to stay within or outside the whole; for the whole can neither be divided from within nor confined from without.

All this gives us to clearly understand that the principle of the simultaneous truth of contradictories, when applied to the dialectical resolution of the ontological contradiction, should not allow us to misinterpret the relationship between being and non-being by virtue of their separation. In particular, neither of them should be understood as *followed* by the other, which complies, as seen above, with a temporal sequence in the course of mutation only. Nor should they furthermore be understood as being posited *alongside* one another, as would, for instance, be the case with the application of the *via negativa* in theology that—despite the apophatic affirmation of the supremacy of the infinite over the finite—actually results in having both counterparts (as if appropriate to different *levels* of being) mutually confined and, therefore, inadequate to the true infinity of the real whole. The infinite cannot be properly understood as consisting of the opposites added up in like manner to the complementary components, nor can it be truly known as simply exalted over the finite that remains, as it were, to co-exist with it. The infinite whole, as said above, is neither divided from within nor confined from without. It means that the true Being, infinite in its totality, does not contain being and non-being, but is a single and indivisible whole.

This is true, however, unless the mind comes to trust the senses as reliable sources of knowledge and, for this reason, finds it legitimate to reduce the whole of being to a conglomerate of finite things as they appear to the mind when immediately given to it through the sensual perception. Should it be the case that the mind falls victim to the dictates of the senses and, as a consequence, to a parochial vision of being, it has to erroneously associate the infinity of the divine with pure negativity of the transcendent. Apophatically approaching it however by *negating* the immanence of "all existence"[51] (relegated, as mentioned, under the pressure of sensible evidence to the existence of finite things), the mind is actually compelled to locate the infinite of the divine nowhere else but *beyond the limits of being*. As a matter of fact, gradually denying all finite definitions (and along with them the existence of *all* finite beings) as incompatible with the divine infinity, it cannot finally

---

51. See V. Lossky, "Очерк мистического богословия," 18.

arrive anywhere else except a sterile abstraction of what is supposed to be an alternative to *a* being, but proves nonetheless to be nothing more than just a complete negation of being as such. So that, when led in this way to pure negativity of existence that can only be known as non-being (and therefore unknown, in any positive sense of knowledge), the apophatically oriented mind does nothing other in fact but calls into question the ontological status and the very reality of what is believed to be ineffable and incomprehensible. But negative theology, so outspokenly enthusiastic about the apophatic approach to being, remains tacit about this unwanted implication of its efforts. Instead, it keeps insisting on complete lack of knowledge as the only true way to the highest form of being. "By virtue of ἀγνόσια alone," says Vladimir Lossky about the apophaticism of the Dionysian mystical theology, "can one know Him Who is above all possible objects of knowledge. Following the way of negation, we ascend from the lower levels of being to the highest, gradually discarding anything knowable so as in the darkness of complete ignorance to approach Him Who is unknowable."[52]

Regarding this, however, the haunting question in fact is whether the *via negativa* really helps the mind to move away from the "bottom" of being and come any closer to its very "top," where the incomprehensible infinite is expected to be encountered. In other words, does it really mean that it is nothing else but the lack of knowledge that brings the mind to conformity with him who is unknowable? Does it not rather mean that the ascent to the infinite One, inaccessible to finite knowledge, simply requires a completely new type of knowledge, essentially different from the finite one but thoroughly appropriate to infinity? Perhaps, it is the very all-consuming darkness of ἀγνόσια that does not allow the upholders of apophaticism to see clearly enough that the infinite understood *as negativity only* can actually have nothing in common with being at all. Moreover, as *incomprehensible*, this negative infinity can only be found, so to speak, on the other side of the divide that separates it from everything finite and comprehensible. To be recognised at all, the negative infinity needs therefore to be contrasted with the positive so as to become fully distinguished from it. This would make the infinite, however, continuously dependent on its opposite and illegitimately turn the latter, finite and transient by nature, into something substantial (constantly present), as if it could always remain there beyond the infinite and be retained as unchangeable and sufficient in itself. Should it be the case, the opposite of the substantial would be the *unsubstantial* alone. But as a vision of reality, the unsubstantial infinity placed elsewhere above the substantial finitude would inevitably prove to be a mere construct of the

52. Ibid.

faulty mind, highly inappropriate to the real whole, both indivisible from within and unconfined from without.

Thus standing up for ἀγνόσια that forsakes the ground of sensible evidence (which is fairly justified by its incompatibility with the divine infinity), the apophatic mind, alas, arrives not at the highest level of being, as mystical theology on the whole would claim, but at that stage of ascent where it finds itself set over against the initial point of its departure anchored among finite things and associated with being or its lower levels. Indeed, as far as the infinite is found to be *above* all beings, it proves in fact to be *confined* by them and therefore irrelevant to being as such. By no means should the ascent to the highest and infinite being be understood as a kind of *flight* from the lower and finite. No finite things should simply be abandoned and neglected by the ascending mind (i.e., left to their own so as to remain as they seem to be in the inferior state of their immediacy), as though they could co-exist with something superior and be outside of what is assumed to be infinite. The infinite as such can only be truly known as *embracing* all finite things, which, being *inside* the infinite, cardinally change or, better to say, lose their finite form appropriate solely to the exterior perceptions of the mind.[53] So that, as long as the true knowledge of the infinite escapes the mind whose perspective remains conformed to a wrong vision of infinity, the finite things—although discarded as inappropriate to the highest being—can only be understood as being exterior to the infinite and therefore con-substantial with it. If this is the case, the apophatic mind, despite its loftiest expectations, can actually ascend to nowhere, but can easily become guilty of imposing a fictitious hierarchy-like construct upon the entire reality by merely adhering to a *metaphysical* paradigm of thinking and reproducing its major prejudice. According to this prejudice deeply inherent in metaphysics as a type of mentality, the mind may deal with no other reality in fact apart from the one *divided in two* between the finite and infinite, where both counterparts (also distinguished as the immanent and transcendent) ever remain set over against one another and appear to be improperly associated with being and non-being respectively.

---

53. In this sense, the ontology of infinity may not unfairly be understood as implying a cardinal change of the mind's perspective. Accordingly, when finite things are supposed to be found *inside* the infinite, they are meant to be seen *anew*—that is to say, not as subsisting on their own but as being intimately bound up with the infinite or participating in it. Seen in the light of a new perspective of the mind fitting the scope of infinity, the finite things may come to be known as, say, Plato's *ideas*, Hegel's *notions* or, as follows from the above analysis of Heidegger's hermeneutical ontology, *meanings*, appropriate to the meaning of their existence.

Dialectic Versus Metaphysics

To summarize the above scrutiny of the possible ways of understanding of the relationship between being and non-being (which, as it will be seen in the following chapter, is crucial to the entire of Eriugena's system of philosophical theology), some distinct features should be highlighted as follows.

Non-being may be either:

a. metaphysically understood to be excluded from being or

b. dialectically thought of as an aspect of negativity, indispensable for knowing the totality of being as neither divided from within nor confined from without.

Furthermore, as excluded from being, non-being may not unfairly be understood at least in three possible ways:

1. as forbidden to exist for that simple reason that nothing whatsoever, as required by Parmenides's *Way of Truth*, can ever be found there outside the total being;

2. as following *after* being, as meant by Parmenides's *Way of Delusion*, according to which the mind deceived by senses tends to mistake a temporal sequence of changing things for the reality as it truly is;

3. as posited *alongside* (or "above") being, as apophaticism in general does acknowledge while denying definitions of all finite beings, but leaving these transient beings as they are in their immanent existence.

As indicated in the above *points a and b*, in contrast to this one-sidedly *metaphysical* approach to non-being the alternative, *dialectical*, way of understanding of the relationship between being and non-being seeks to get the latter "absorbed," so to speak, in the former, where no opposites—as required by the universality of the Principle of all beings and the order of reality it gives rise to—can subsist *after* or *alongside* one another and thus divide the whole of being from within or confine it from without. As appropriate to the universal Principle of all, the whole of being may only be truly known as *infinite* that is ever unconfined and therefore irreducible to the multitude of finite things, regardless of their number included in it. The totality of Being that unceasingly is admits of nothing other (or *non aliud*, as Eriugena puts it) within or alongside itself; it is solely conceivable indeed, as ascertained before, in the way of being *simultaneously* self-identical and different from *itself*.

This contrast between metaphysics and dialectic in their understanding of what being and non-being are further means that, while inclined to metaphysical divisions, apophaticism would be prepared to consider the ontological contraries as being simultaneously *con-substantial* and therefore relevant to truth, as if they might refer to different realms of existence. However, unlike this faulty approach leading to an apparent misconception of infinity, the dialectical vision of the same contraries from the perspective of contradiction (where they take shape of the contradictory statements) does not imply at all that their *simultaneous truth* could ever be *equally* distributed, so to speak, among the contradictories, as far as they remained mutually countered. In other words, the *simultaneous truth* of the contradictories dialectically understood is applicable to their *unity* only, since they cannot be known as being con-substantial and therefore *equally* true.

Resolution of the Contradiction

All this subsequently means that the only effective resolution of the contradiction that allows the mind to overcome the opposition of the contraries, tearing the infinite reality of the whole into pieces, may be provided by *dialectic*[54] alone. In particular, the resolution comes to be brought about in the way of knowing "being" and "non-being" not as remaining mutually opposed and confined in their distinction (when they would be appropriate to the world of finitude only), but as belonging to the totality of all-pervasive Being—though not as its constitutive components, but as the aspects of its absolute self-identity, known solely through its self-distinction. Hence, in the contradiction

Being is;

Non-being is,

where the unity of the contraries is expressed by the predicate *is*, both "being" and "non-being" are understood to be simultaneously referred to the all-embracing Being, so that neither of them is meant to be set over against the other. As a result, in conformity with the dialectical vision of the contradiction (but in contrast to the metaphysically apophatic attitude to the transient things), "being" can neither be opposed to nor confined by the contrary "non-being." Indeed, from the dialectical point of view, "being" cannot be known as a mere *immediacy* or *appearance* of existence, relevant only to the phenomenal world of finite things that are always present to the

---

54. Eriugena's understanding of dialectic is more closely considered in chapters 4 and 5. At this point of our discourse, it is important to clearly understand that to Eriugena dialectic is a paradigm of thinking perfectly appropriate for the task of approaching the theological truth of Christian faith.

mind "here" and "now," but never "after" or "before." As a bare *appearance* of transient things as they are immediately given to the mind through the exterior senses, a confined "being" would therefore turn out to be nothing other than just a kind of *improper* or *false* being. This is the "being" which—in accordance with the *fourth mode* of Eriugena's understanding of being and non-being—should not unreasonably be qualified as the *untrue* one or, in fact, *non-being*, inasmuch as found irrelevant to the infinite whole of Being which alone truly is while remaining in its unconfined and indivisible totality.

Thus within the contradiction dialectically understood, the contraries of "being" and "non-being" become, as it were, mutually replaced while changing *semantically* (i.e., acquiring the opposite meaning). As Hegel would explain it, any contrary, when contrasted with its counterpart and as such taken on its own to be extended to the utmost of its extremity, inevitably turns into the opposite and thus smooths away the divide of their distinction, giving the mind an opportunity to reconsider the relationship between the two from the perspective of their unity. As a result, what was previously found appropriate to the semantics of the metaphysically apophatic approach to existence, now comes up in the light of a completely new understanding. In particular, as seen before, apophaticism as such seeks to associate being with the immediacy of finite existence, and non-being with infinity as bare negativity that is supposed to exceed the limits of the immanent presence. By contrast with this merely alleged overcoming of finitude (where infinity as negativity only seems to surpass the finite but in fact remains opposed to it and therefore confined), the dialectical treatment of the ontological contraries seeks to embrace being in its entirety, so as to leave no room for anything opposite, neither within nor outside, and thus to know it as the infinite one. In this way, dialectic aims to overcome indeed the insubstantiality of the opposites mutually confined in their opposition, and thus to bring the whole of being to conformity with the absolute Being, which alone truly is (and therefore is true) while ever remaining at one with the universal Principle of all things that come forth from it but never leave the totality of it. Little wonder, therefore, that within such a holistic approach of dialectic (coming to the fore, as we shall see it later, in the *fourth mode* of Eriugena's understanding of being) non-being can only be acknowledged as a mere *appearance* of the true (infinite) being or its *false vision*. For it is from the perspective of this sort of vision that the entire existence is erroneously found identified with a multitude of contingent things which seem to come and go at random, while being exposed to the mind through the exterior senses and the experience based on their dictates.

All this convinces us that in truth there is no reality divided into being and non-being, where things would come into existence and pass away.
In this sense, resolution of the contradiction may not improperly be understood from the dialectical point of view as being all about the cardinal
change of the meaning of being, when the latter is found by the mind to be
embraced in its infinite (self-identical) totality through overcoming in full
its distinction from the opposite. Consequently, the contradiction

Being is;

Non-being is

comes to be resolved in so far as the contradictory statements it consists of
are known as being *simultaneously true*, because:

- there is nothing *external* or *alien* (opposite) in the true being of the
  absolute self-identity;

- so that no appearance nor pure negativity of the immediate should
  ever be identified with the being itself;

- for nothing else can be known as the true being apart from the one
  unconfined (opposed by nothing other) that unceasingly is.

A Blueprint for Eriugena's Discourse

With regard to this, therefore, it would be not unfair to suggest that the dialectical treatment and resolution of the ultimate ontological contradiction
provides the mind with a means of restoration of the sound vision of reality
as it truly is while coming forth from the universal Principle of all and never
leaving it. This is the reality known to faith and theology as that of creation,
and the vision of it is available not to senses or the corrupt mind subject
to their dictates, but to the reason which, being dialectically disciplined,
deservedly acquires the name of *recta ratio*, as Eriugena calls it. It is this
recta ratio restored to its proper *rational motion* (where senses with their
contingent contents borrowed from without do not go ahead of the general
notions of reason) that is capable of following the right order of the reality
of God's creation, where the universal precedes the particular, and not *vice
versa*. Thus by reason alone those who, unlike Pilate, find the truth (and,
above all, the one of God's ever-lasting kingdom) to be valid are enabled to
see through the "mind's eye," as Eriugena puts it, the unconfined reality as
it truly is in all its magnificence. And they are doing so, as it is abundantly
clear from what is suggested by the Philosopher, while breaking through the

sensible appearance which—like a veil woven by the perverse (irrational or sense-dependent) motions of the corrupt mind—covers up the glorious face of God's creation.[55] In this way, and in accordance with the doctrine of *return* (*reditus*) central to the whole of Eriugena's system, the entire human being comes to be brought back to the original conformity with the substantial reality of creation, as appropriate to the pre-fallen state of human mind, unseduced by the senses and therefore not guilty of setting the opposites apart. This is consequently the way in which all humans come to live in perfect communion with him who truly is the real source of all life.

55. It would be perhaps not irrelevant to note here that in the Christian orthodox iconography God's Mother (*Theotokos*) is always portrayed with an uncovered face, which may not unreasonably be understood to symbolize the truth revealed. The shroud, traditionally present in all the icons of God's Mother, is depicted to cover her head only, whereas, say, Isis, the Egyptian patroness of all mysteries, was often meant to hide her face behind the shroud.

CHAPTER 3

The Keys to Eriugena's System

The Ladder of Notions

FROM THE PRECEDING ANALYSIS it follows that the dialectical ontology, which alone is appropriate to the conception Eriugena develops in the *Periphyseon*, is the one that is focused on the proper treatment of the ultimate ontological contradiction and the implications of its resolution. This kind of ontology proves to bind up the key links of Eriugena's discourse into a coherent train of thought, resulting in a majestic conception of a philosophically rigorous approach to the theologically profound truth of God's Oneness, which is revealed to all humans through the salvific message of Christ's teaching. Not improperly therefore these links of the Philosopher's discourse could be summed up in the form of the following sequence of notions progressing towards realization of the truth of salvation, understood as the return of human beings from the illusory world of sensible things to the true reality of God's creation:

- *Sound vision* of the reality provided by the dialectical resolution of the ontological contradiction;

- *Reality* (Φῦσιζ or *Natura*) as it truly is while coming forth from the universal Principle of all;

- *Availability* of the true reality, not to the senses but to *recta ratio* (right reason);

- *Recta ratio* as reason capable of following the substantial order of creation that proceeds from the universal to the particular;

- *Appearance* as the corrupt mind's construct imposed upon the true reality, hidden thereby from senses but not from *recta ratio*;

- *Return* (*reditus*) of human beings (or bringing human life) to conformity with the substantial order of creation, resulting in the cardinal change of the prospect of human existence within the reality ever-lasting.

Such is the "ladder" of notions which, as Eriugena's discourse suggests, brings all human beings (in their ascent from the abstract to the concrete that dialectic in its proper Hegelian sense is all about) to the knowledge of the One God as the infinite Being that unceasingly is in and through and for itself, ever remaining "All in All." In this sense, the whole sequence of the above notions could be fairly crowned (as appropriate to the agenda of the *Periphyseon*'s doctrine) with the idea of:

- *God's Oneness* known as a single (indivisible) whole of God's infinite (undivided) being, outside or within which nothing alien (opposite) does subsist.

Overcoming of Dualism

As a coherent conception of the absolute unity of God's being, to which it is essential not to allow the creature to subsist outside the One God, Eriugena's philosophical theology may not unreasonably be considered as a systematic attempt to overcome the *dualism* of religious thought. That is the dualism which the mind inevitably faces as soon as the metaphysical dichotomy between God's being and that of the creature is taken by common belief for granted. Furthermore, as it is clear from the emphasis on the availability of the true being to *reason alone* that, in unison with Parmenides, the author of the *Periphyseon* unambiguously makes in the *fourth mode* of understanding of being and non-being, it is not unlikely that his system developed in response to some unfair misreading of Parmenides. In particular, it could respond to the possibility of a dualistic interpretation of the Parmenidian approach to the totality of Being, well discussed by Islamic scholars at the time of Eriugena–namely, the possibility of a regrettable misinterpretation of the Greek philosopher largely conditioned by deep deficiencies in the non-dialectical character of his approach. In this sense, it does not seem implausible that Parmenides's *Periphyseon*, with its strong appeal to the *Way of Truth* as that of approaching the true Being, immensely encouraged Eriugena, who was greatly concerned about the way of thinking of the infinity of God's being, and thus gave impetus to his *opus magnum*, accidentally or not called likewise the *Periphyseon*.[1] Moreover, since there is no compel-

---

1. Should it be the case, it has to be acknowledged then that, apart from a successful reconsideration of Parmenides's non-dialectical stance, Eriugena has also succeeded in making an intellectual journey from the uncertainties of poetic symbolism, that

ling evidence that the Carolingians, among whom this monumental work of Eriugena's first came to light, were familiar with writings of Parmenides, it can be fairly assumed that Eriugena might have been acquainted with Parmenides's ideas through his Eastern contemporaries. Had it been the case, a key figure among the latter would certainly be al-Nazzam, a disciple of the dialectician Allaf and a prominent member of the Mu'tazilah movement, who was well read in Greek philosophy and in Parmenides in particular.

In his close studies of Parmenides's writings and other works of the School of Elea (and, above all, those of Zeno), al-Nazzam was particularly interested in the way of knowing the reality as it truly is, lying beyond any sensible images and sense-based assumptions. Both Parmenides and his pupil Zeno were known to al-Nazzam (as they are to all students of philosophy nowadays) as those who, on account of the principle divisibility of space (distance) and time (duration) *ad infinitum*, denied a possibility of movement[2] or, to be precise, its susceptibility of being thought of. This further meant to them that the true reality, amenable to thought alone, must be immovable; since movement as such is unthinkable. Enthusiastic about the prevalent role of thought in approaching the true reality as it was exercised by these thinkers, al-Nazzam yet remained greatly puzzled by a prospect of a dualistic understanding of reality it seemed to lead to. To these doubts of al-Nazzam concerning the status of sensible world, that threatened to cleave its reality asunder, Mir Valiuddin gives quite an explicit characteristic:

> Among the Greek philosophers, Parmenides and Zeno had denied movement itself. They could not declare untrue the movement which is observable and is a fact, so they claimed that perception cannot reveal reality. They maintained that senses are not the instruments of real knowledge and are deceptive, and the phenomenal world is illusory, a mirage. The real world is the rational world, the knowledge of which is gained by reason alone in which there is neither plurality nor multiplicity,

---

Parmenides often resorts to in his philosophical poem, to the philosophical clarity of notions fundamental to the theology of God's unity constituting the body of his own *Periphyseon*.

2. According to Mir Valiuddin, the Eleatic denial of movement on the ground of division of any part of space and time *ad infinitum* can be described as follows: If divisibility is true, it does progress to an unlimited extent. This means that "every half of a half goes on becoming half of the other half. During the process of divisions, we never reach a limit after which we may be able to say that it cannot be further divided into halves." "Now, to traverse a distance, which is composed of infinite points," he continues, "an infinite period of time would necessarily be required. Is, then, the traversing of a distance impossible? Does it not necessitate the denial of the existence of the movement itself?" (Valiuddin, "Mu'tazilism," sec. B, § 3, 14–15).

neither movement nor change. It is an immutable and immovable reality. But they could not explain how this illusory and deceptive world was born out of the real world. Thus their system of philosophy, in spite of their claiming it to be monism, ended in dualism.[3]

As a consistent dialectician, Eriugena would, clearly, disagree with such a conclusion and strongly object to a dualistic misinterpretation of the Parmenidian ontology; although at the same time he would hardly be able to deny that this kind of misreading might easily result from those uncertainties of Parmenides's thought with which a mere *postulation* of the totality of Being (and not a coherent thinking of it) was largely fraught. As seen perspicuously enough from the inner logic of the entire *Periphyseon*, Eriugena is very determined to offer an effective antidote to any temptations of the mind to cleave asunder the reality of the infinite whole by placing outside it an "extra" world consisting of sensible things. And in the profound meaning of Book 4, where the collision between the proper *rational motion* of human nature and the deceptive affect of senses upon the mind is brought into focus, this major concern of Eriugena's is especially evident. To him, it does not seem terribly difficult to explain how the "illusory and deceptive world," the presence of which al-Nazzam was much puzzled by, could emerge. In the first place, it could not be *born out of the real one* so as to be located, as if something substantial, elsewhere outside it. The sensible world simply comes as an *illusion* indeed from a wrong vision of reality in the result of *deception* of the mind by the senses, when its pure judgment, in Eriugena's plain words, is "clouded by sense-bound thinking."[4] As a matter of fact, this world cannot exist elsewhere outside the true reality; it can only be an *appearance* of the latter one when immediately given to the mind through the exterior senses. It appears to come to the mind *from without* and therefore proves to be nothing more than just a wrong perspective of reality, where in truth nothing whatsoever can come into being otherwise than *from within*.

As a Christian scholar who thinks theologically and in a dialectically coherent manner, it is obvious to Eriugena that this *coming from within* is the way things go in reality as it substantially is—that is, *the reality of creation* which comes into being from the One God, beyond the infinity of whom there is nothing other where else things can come from. Anything whatsoever, when genuinely believed to be *created*, may only be understood to subsist not otherwise than by coming from God and staying within

3. Ibid., 15.
4. Eriugena, *Voice of the Eagle*, 72.

him who is the universal Principle of all, which, as *the universal* indeed, may be transcended by none. For as Eriugena suggests in his *Homily* on the Prologue to St. John's Gospel, the Evangelist gives us to understand that "through the Son all things were made and that nothing subsisted outside of him."[5] "All things, therefore, that were made by the Word," the author of the *Homily* continues, "live in him unchangeably and are life. In him all things exist neither by temporal intervals or places, nor as what is to come; but all are one in him, above all times and places, subsist in him eternally." And further he concludes: "Visible, invisible, corporeal, incorporeal, rational, ir-rational—heaven and earth, the abyss, and whatever is therein—in him all live and are life and subsist eternally. Even what seems to us to be without all vital movement lives in the Word."[6] To Eriugena, this is the soundest theological view well-grounded in the heritage of him whom he keeps call-ing throughout all his writings the Apostle: "For in him" (the Word), as the Sacred Scripture says, "we live and move and have our being."[7]

So in order that the reality as it truly is might be seen and thus "the countenance of the universal nature" be restored, as Eriugena puts it, "to its former glory" and beauty (748c), the mind should no longer be con-formed to the world of things that are seen *from without*. Instead, the mind must be transformed by its renewing, as St. Paul reminds us in Rom 12:2. And in accordance with the aforesaid, this renewing of the mind should mean only one thing indeed—namely, that the mind must bring itself to conformity to the way things truly are so as to properly contemplate them all *from within itself*. This is the vision of reality that becomes available to the mind, as shown above, through the contradiction dialectically treated. For it is in contradiction that metaphysics and dialectic as the two paradigms of thinking, appropriate to different perspectives of reality, come to collision as those appealing to senses or thought and starting from the particular or the universal respectively. It is consequently here, in the contradiction dialecti-cally resolved, that the perverse motion of the corrupt mind, inclined under the dictates of senses to make things leave God and therefore responsible for placing them outside him, gets overcome. And along with it, the very misconception of God is overcome as well.[8]

5. Ibid., 84.

6. Ibid., 86.

7. Ibid., 87.

8. The overcoming of this cardinal misconception proves to be extremely important to Eriugena, for it allows, as evident from the very logic of his discourse, to give way to a new prospect of human life. Moreover, it is the latter that may not unfairly be understood as the ultimate goal of his intellectually passionate quest. Indeed, it is the discussion of human true being that constitutes the *fifth mode* of understanding of the

Indeed, God cannot be properly known as a remote and superior being that is simply located elsewhere above (or alongside) the inferior world of finite things; nor can he be known as present to the finite world or lying within it. For in the reality of the infinite whole that truly (unceasingly) is, there is neither a confined God *opposed* to the world, nor the *finite* world, substantial and independent in its existence.[9] In other words, God is definitely not *a* being which, like an external force, would merely push the creature from without to come into being out of nothing or non-being. Such a God acting *from beyond* upon something else, as if placed outside himself (even when associated with void or disguised under the name of *nihil*), is inconceivable at all. This is simply because God *confined* does not exist.

Creatio Ex Deo

Thus, dualism as a valid conception is not an issue to Eriugena, because to him God is *truly infinite*. This means that outside the infinite whole of God's being there is absolutely nothing—nothing in the Parmenidian sense of the word (i.e., in the sense that nothing *is not* at all). Hence, by no means can the creation be understood in the way of *transition from non-being into being*. Coming forth into being out of nothing or out of nowhere should mean to a believer in the One God that *ex nihilo* may only signify *ex Deo*. Nothing whatsoever, when consistently thought of, can really be known as coming into being out of anything else (be it even relegated to *nihil* or void) apart

---

true being and, as the subject-matter of Book 5 of the *Periphyseon*, crowns the entire of his philosophical-theological system.

9. A panentheistic model of God's being, according to which all things are conceived to be *in* God, would be likewise inappropriate to the true knowledge of God. In fact, a panentheistic conception proves to be largely based on a *formal logic* assumption with its characteristic appeal to notions as *forms*, mainly treated from the perspective of their content volume. In particular, panentheism finds it theologically important to assert that "*God is greater than the universe held in Him*" while actually ignoring some essential deficiencies within this approach. One of them is that the "universe" included in God's being is assumed to be and *remain* "part" of a bigger "whole," and therefore is conceived to be nothing more than just *a realm of finite being*. Thus God, who is supposed to be "greater," remains in fact *opposed* to the finite universe created, and therefore *confined*, though, so to speak, from within himself. The deficiencies of this theology are quite obvious, and they will haunt theological thought until it keeps insisting on substantiality of the *finitude* of the universe created. As long as theological reflection tries to retain *status quo* of the sensual perception perspective as the only appropriate one for approaching the universe of creation, it will hardly succeed in developing a coherent theology.

from the true, infinite, Being that is God himself.[10] This is what Eriugena is convinced of and seeks to prove by the entire system of his discourse.[11]

In the reality of God's creation there is nothing alien to him, unless the *mind corrupted* makes believe otherwise. The very account of Genesis makes it explicit at Gen 1 that God is fully satisfied with what he makes, because there is no discrepancy between his will and act in creation or, as Eriugena puts it, between his will and being. Each "day" of creation is acknowledged by the Scripture to be *good*; the entire creation thus proves to be the realm of Goodness and can only be known as the realm of God manifest, where his will comes true.[12] As far as humans find it possible, however, to disagree with this fundamental truth conveyed by the Scripture, they doom themselves to live wrong life of not theirs (i.e., inappropriate to their true nature

10. In spite of being almost a commonplace among the theologians of the biblical tradition to take for granted the doctrine of *creatio ex nihilo*, there is surprisingly no evidence or clue in the Bible itself for the legitimacy of such a doctrine. The only reference to the Scripture, that is believed to provide ground for the doctrine in question, is usually associated with the second Maccabean book (i.e., the text written in the environment of Hellenized Judaism of Alexandria). To be exact, only a few lines, namely 2 Macc 7:28, are selected from the text to point to the matter: "I beg you, my child, to look at the heaven and the earth and see everything that is in them, and recognise that God did not make them out of things that existed. And in the same way the human race came into being." The ambiguity of these words (that is considerably enhanced by their contrast with the preceding context at 2 Macc 7:27) is so apparent, however, that an attempt to interpret them in the sense of *creatio ex nihilo* would rather look like a deliberate misreading of the text. Taking into account the circumstances of the text's origin, it would be not unfair to assume that the lines quoted are meant to refute the doctrine of *creatio ex materia* (creation out of some pre-existent matter), quite commonly shared by the Greeks and understood as a kind of formation of the primeval chaos. Even purely grammatical reading of the lines in focus gives to understand that God is meant here to make the world *not out of things*. It would be therefore too biased to interpret these scriptural words in the sense of creation *ex nihilo*. As for other scriptural references normally made in favour of this doctrine—such as Genesis 1:1; Hebrews 11:3; and Revelation 4:11—they appear to be even more irrelevant.

11. By no means would it be fair to confuse Eriugena's conception of *creatio ex deo* with the Greek philosophy's approach largely based on the truth that *ex nihilo nihil fit*. The fact is that whereas the latter categorically denies a possibility of conceiving anything whatsoever apart from a pre-existent matter's involvement, the doctrine of creation *ex deo* is likewise categorical in denying the existence of anything pre-given to God's infinite being or consubstantial with it. Thus, similarly denying *nihil* as the source of existence, both doctrines yet fundamentally differ in their understanding of the Divine nature.

12. By the way, St. Paul's reminder about the necessity of human beings' transformation by the renewing of their minds also contains a clear indication of the purpose of this transformation. In particular, all humans are called by the Apostle to be transformed by the renewing of their minds so that they "may discern what is the will of God—what is good and acceptable and perfect" (Rom 12:2).

coming forth from the only Source of all life), and thus actually rebel against God himself. In the reality of the infinite whole there can be no division indeed into *"this"* and *"the other"* world existing, as it were, alongside one another. The dichotomy between the real and the sensible world (as well as between God's being and the creature) is in fact nothing more than just a pernicious blunder made by the mind corrupted by its perverse motion. *The senses overriding the mind* is where sin and unrighteous life are rooted, making human beings fall out of the paradise of God's creation, as Eriugena believes it to happen in line with Gen 3. He is therefore convinced that the perverse motion of the mind subject to the dictates of the senses is where a genuine effort is to be made. The corrupt mind is what to be amended and brought back to the ways of its proper *rational motion.* This is consequently where and how the perspective of the true reality is to be restored so as to let all human beings return to the world to which they originally belong.

Dialectic, Reality, and the Book

Thus *dialectic*, as Eriugena's genuine "know how" and the very core of his philosophically innovative approach to Christian theology, comes into focus of the project which he gives the title of the *Periphyseon.* It is by means of dialectic, as he gives us to understand it by the entire system of his thought, that the restoration and return mentioned above come to be brought about. Responsible for a new way of thinking that overcomes dualism in the mind's relation with reality, dialectic provides a holistic vision of being as an effective remedy for healing the mind of its addiction to metaphysical divisions of all things into opposites.

In the course of this treatment under dialectic's supervision, the mind learns to refrain from mistaking these deliberately made dichotomies for true, and thus to restore the relation with the reality as it properly is according to its substantial order.

This substantial reality that properly is according to a certain fundamental order is but *creation*—that is, the reality that proceeds from the universal Principle of all, and proceeding from it never abandons this source of being. This is consequently the reality that by no means can be identified with that of sensible things as they are given to the mind through the sensual perception. The reality of creation is definitely something other than the world of appearance, which does not mean however that it lies elsewhere beyond the sensible world. It is the reality which includes the sensible one as well, though only when this sensible part is seen *anew* so as to be known not according to its corporeal appearance but as an organic member of the infinite and indivisible whole. This is therefore the reality hidden behind the veil of sensible images which needs to be searched for; and it is exactly what Eriugena does by resorting to a careful reading of the Book of Genesis. In this sense, not unfairly can his massive system of theological thinking philosophically disciplined be understood as an exercise of deep insight into the meaning of the first three chapters of Genesis. The reality he is looking for Eriugena clearly defines as that of "the sole Principle, Origin, and universal Source of all, Which Itself proceeds from nothing while from It proceed all things, . . . and Which, Itself ἄναρχος (that is, without beginning), is the Beginning and the End, the one Good, the one God" (741c).

This is the search that the author of the *Periphyseon* not unreasonably compares to a "perilous journey." And this "journey" is so hard and long that it can only be covered by *five books* in the dense text of his *opus magnum*, among which the most intriguing and at the same time important is the *fourth* one. It is actually in Book 4 that the whole strategy of Eriugena's exploration cardinally changes. Previously it seemed to smoothly follow a linear-like division of Nature into species, which must have been quite intelligible to those Carolingians who were familiar, among other conventional doctrines, with Augustine's conception of a threefold structure of the universe of creation.[13] Now, in Book 4, the strategy applied becomes obviously dialectical, bringing to the fore contraries and contradictions, and making its adherents not only reconsider their understanding of God's being and creation (including the place and role of human beings in it), but also look anew at the very structure of the entire treatise and its profound meaning. Moreover, it is in this book that "the conflict and clash of different interpretations" is said to take place, by which—as we shall see it below (with regard to the whole of the *Periphyseon*'s conception as well)—the author ultimately means nothing other but the "clash" of the conflicting paradigms of thinking in their attitude to the true Being that is neither preceded nor followed by non-being. "The difficulty of this part of our theme, the conflict and clash of different interpretations," says Eriugena about Book 4, "I find so formidable that in comparison to it the first three books seem like a smooth sea upon which, because of the calmness of the waves, readers could sail without fear of shipwreck, steering a safe course" (743d). "Now, however," he continues in a vividly poetic manner,

> we enter upon a voyage where the course has to be picked from
> the mass of tortuous digressions, where we have to climb the
> steeps of obscure doctrines, encounter the region of the Syrtes,

13. An outline of this conception and the way Eriugena treats it see in the chapter below.

> that is to say, the dangers of the currents of unfamiliar teaching, even in immediate danger of shipwreck from the obscurity of the subtlest intellects, which like concealed rocks may suddenly split our vessel; and the length of this course is such that we must extend it even into a fifth book (743d–744a).

Thus, in the author's words, "we shall pick through all these dangers the true and safe course, and reach the harbor which we seek" (744a).

Needless to say that to Eriugena this "true and safe course" is directly associated with *dialectic*, which alone, "steering a safe course" between the opposites, allows those learning from "the subtlest intellects" to overcome on their way to truth all "conflicts" and "clashes" of different teachings. Originally implanted in reality (749a), dialectic alone, when translated into *art* (or discipline of the mind) is understood, according to Eriugena, to be capable of following the *proper order* of the reality of creation, which he also calls "the natural sequence of events." This order (or sequence) is such, the Philosopher emphasizes, that genus is *first* "because all species are contained in it," and these individual species proceed from their genus (general cause) so as evolving within it to "achieve their unity in it" (748a), never actually departing from the universal itself, which at 750a is explicitly defined as "the One Universal Principle." "From this we may see," Eriugena points out, "that that art which concerns itself with the division of genera into species and the restoration of species into genera, which is called dialectic, did not arise from human contrivances, but was first implanted in nature . . . and was later discovered there by the sages who make use of it in their subtle investigation of reality" (749a).

All this gives us to understand that—as a proper way of thinking which starts from the universal and further proceeds towards the particular to make the universal manifest—dialectic brings human mind to perfect conformity to the substantial reality of creation. And thus it opens before all human beings a new prospect of life, which by "the unique teaching of God's kingdom" is meant to be nothing other in fact but living according to truth, that is, in harmony and union with him who truly is the infinite Being that unceasingly is. But this *true being* of human nature, when "it is brought back to the former condition of its substance in which it was made after the image of God" (445c), constitutes, strictly speaking, the subject-matter of another book—the *fifth* one, into which Eriugena intends, as clearly stated at 744a, to extend his most difficult and intriguing fourth book. What the author of the *Periphyseon* is not as explicit about, however, is that this subject-matter of the fifth book, smoothly proceeding from that of the fourth one, does also perfectly match the *fifth mode* of understanding of being and non-being, which is said to be observed by reason in human nature only and associated with living according to "the divine image in which it was properly substantiated" (445c).

And this perfect match with a mode of distinction between being and non-being actually raises a crucial question concerning the genuine structure of the *Periphyseon* itself: is Eriugena outspoken enough when he gives his readers an impression that the layout of the treatise is subject to a *fourfold* scheme of Nature's division articulated in the opening part of the work? Does not he play tricks on readers when, immediately after the *four* species of Nature, he offers *five* modes of understanding of being and non-being, and later, in Book 4, he makes an abundantly clear statement about his intention to write *five* books? Should not it mean that at the very heart of its discourse each of the *Periphyseon*'s books is focused in fact on one of the five *modes* of our understanding of being and non-being, but not on a species of Nature divided, as many believe while taking for granted Eriugena's own claims, including those, as we shall see it below, made in the opening lines of Book 4? Does not it after all mean that the author, being a staunch dialectician, deliberately creates a contradiction between the visible and invisible layout of the book as a whole, i.e., between its literal (fragmentary) and spiritual (integral) sense? Should it be the case that the author is determined to distinguish between the finite and infinite dimension of the book so as to let the misleading impression of particulars and the substantial meaning of the whole be clearly discerned, we may easily recognise in his intention a strong appeal to *truth* as the real objective of a profoundly philosophical text, the ultimate concern of which is fairly concurrent with that of the sacred one. Indeed, the truth itself, as considered above, is not merely an external authority that can be imposed upon those who claim their belief in it. Truth cannot be simply declared or given from without; it can only be really adopted when acquired from within, through reason and deep understanding, as Eriugena himself insists. For this, truth needs to be properly investigated by reason and therefore coherently *thought of*. Understood as a dialectical contradiction, the distinction between the visible and hidden layer of writings (i.e., between the particular of the sensible image expressed and the universal of thought defined) would undoubtedly be the best way, when properly followed, of approaching the profound meaning of these writings, concealed by the letter lying on the surface of their immediate appearance.

Such a sharp distinction between the contraries implanted in the very form of the treatise to be properly tackled in a dialectically coherent way looks like a very Eriugenian motif indeed. Little wonder, therefore, that at 744a, when the strategy of exploration is meant to be changing, Eriugena himself gives us a clue to complete reconsideration of the whole structure of his *opus magnum*. From the statement he makes there, it is quite clear that Book 5 was planned at the earlier stages of his project, even well before Book 4 came to light. It would be not improper to assume, then, that Book 5 has always been to Eriugena not merely an accidental extension of the previous one providing, as it were, a sort of supplementary material to its argument, but quite a necessary and independent element of a greater plan, appropriate to another scheme, completely different from the one overtly claimed by the author—namely, to *five modes* of our understanding of being and non-being.

The following detailed analysis of the text from Book 4 will enable us to considerably enhance this assumption. For it will become clear from this analysis that the argument developing in Book 4 is profoundly based on what is articulately formulated by Eriugena in the *fourth* mode of distinction between being and non-being. Furthermore, a striking affinity of this mode's formulations with the epistemological postulates of the Parmenidian ontology allows us also to better understand why Book 4 has a reputation of being the exceptionally important part of the entire project. It is particularly here, in Book 4, that it finally becomes utterly clear that the ultimate concern of Eriugena's is, similarly to that of Parmenides, to establish the truth of the totality of Being that infinitely is. Beginning at the very outset of Book 1 from *the fundamental division* of all things into those that are and are not, Eriugena actually seeks to overcome the ontological dichotomy in the totality of the infinite Being, which he finds appropriate to call *Natura* or *Φύσις* (441a). And it is in Book 4 where at last we come to clearly understand that Eriugena's true intention never consisted in the investigation of the division of Nature into separate species, hierarchically ordered and associated with God (both creating and uncreating), the world of created things, and the so-called primordial causes mediating between God and his creation. What Eriugena is really looking for throughout the whole of the *Periphyseon* is Nature's unity, the unity of the whole Being—that is, God's Unity or, to be precise, *the way we may know it*. For it is this type of knowledge which does allow us to be really at one with him who truly is the One.

In this sense, therefore, it would be not unfair to suggest that the entirety of Eriugena's *Periphyseon* should be thoroughly understood as an *anti-division* project.[14] This is the project which proves to be brought about

14. Since Thomas Gale's 1681 Oxford edition of the *Periphyseon* entitled by him (perhaps for some methodological reason suitable for his time) *De divisione naturae*, there has been quite a sustained tendency among readers of Eriugena's work to uncritically look at the *division* of Nature as its central theme. To the extent this view prevails, however, Eriugena remains an obscure thinker who is largely misunderstood.

on the ways of overcoming those forms of mind where the division of being into contraries is actually rooted. To Eriugena as a Christian thinker, it
is utterly unacceptable that these forms of the fundamental division, when
imposed upon the reality, give rise to different perspectives of its distorted
perception, and along with it to a prospect of human life in a spurious world
of things divided. The fundamental division into being and non-being is in
fact what separates all humans from the reality of him who truly is infinite,
and this is the major obstacle to be resolutely overcome on the way to the
One. The following consideration of Eriugena's text will help us to come
closer to a perspicuous vision of the deep meaning of his grand system,
which may not improperly be defined, as mentioned above, as the one of
theological thinking philosophically disciplined.

CHAPTER 4

The Text Unlocked

Review of Books 1–3

BOOK 4 OF THE *Periphyseon* begins at 741c–743c with a brief review of the three preceding books which appear to follow the sequence of the division of Nature into four species as they are presented in the opening part of *opus magnum* at 441b–442a.

Starting from a characteristic of Book 1 as the one where the nature that is not created but creates is considered, Eriugena defines its aim as that of proving the *superessentiality* of the Cause of all things. In particular, he says: "The aim and principal theme of our Philosophy of Nature was *firstly* to prove that uncreated and creative Cause of all things which exist and all things which do not exist, the sole Principle, Origin, and universal Source of all, which itself proceeds from nothing while from it proceed all things, the Trinity which in three Substances is co-essential, and which, itself ἄναρχος (that is, without beginning), is the Beginning and the End, the one Good, the one God ὁμοούσιος and ὑπερούσιος (that is, co-essential and superessential), is in fact ὑπερουσιώδης (or superessential) Nature" (741c).

Passing over to the second book where the second species of Nature that is created and creates is examined, Eriugena describes its theme as the analysis of the primordial causes of things that subsist in their principles. "For this nature on the one hand," he explains, "is created by that single universal Cause and supreme Goodness, whose property it is by Its unspeakable Power to lead all things forth from non-existence into existence; and on the other hand does not cease to create the things which come after It, by means of their participation in It" (743b).

And, finally, concluding his survey with the third book, Eriugena says about it as an inquiry into the third division of Nature that treats of "the ultimate effects of the primordial causes," or the nature which is created and does not create. "These hold the lowest rank of nature," specifies the author, "for the devolution of the universe ceases with them, having no further place whither to descend, for it is now established in the realm of corporeal objects" (743c).

Setting a New Aim

This brief review of the preceding books of the *Periphyseon* allows Eriugena, as he believes, to pass smoothly to putting forward a new aim which would determine the subject-matter of the following book. Having considered in detail in Book 3 Five Days (or Prophetic Meditations, as he also calls them) of the creation presented by the biblical account at Gen 1, Eriugena suggests that the next part of his *opus magnum* should start "with the works of the Sixth Prophetic Meditation of the creation of the universe" in order then "to consider the Return of all things into that Nature which neither creates nor is created" (743c). Thereby Eriugena intends to safely arrive at the fourth species of Nature, which is supposed to be the final destination of the "perilous journey" of his investigation of the Nature's fourfold division already postulated (although without any sort of explanation or logical underpinning) in the opening lines of Book 1. This final species of division is in fact the most problematic part of the entire work, since the obscurity of the reason for such a division is even more dramatically enhanced by a remarkably paradoxical statement that the fourth species of this division "is classed among the impossibles, for it is of its essence that it cannot be"(442a). So that now, after having reached along with the author of the *Periphyseon* the fourth stage of his massive work, one might expect to find at last a clear answer to the question what is really meant by that far mysterious fourth division of Nature which from the very beginning of the inquiry undertaken has caused a great deal of perplexity and seemed to be a stumbling block on the way to the truth sought.

Thus, following the way shown in the *Periphyseon*, one might hope to gain an understanding how it happens that, while bringing all things forth from himself, God *never departs* from himself but constantly stays within himself, as if *returning* to himself from his creation. As a result, a student of this highest truth might not only tune his mind to the universal pattern of the true reality that takes its origin from the sole Source of all (that is the "single universal cause"), but also bring in fact all his nature into harmony with the reality where the Beginning and the End are one, and thereby he might actually come to enjoy his union with God who is truly One.

This ultimate lofty aim of encouraging the human soul to enter upon the path of ascending towards the truth of God's Oneness seems therefore to be what Eriugena really implies to achieve by the extensive work of analysis of the fourfold division of Nature. And it is in Book 4, which is essentially focused on the perceptive interpretation of Scripture with regard to the Final Day of creation, that this ultimate objective of the entire project (only implicitly present in it before) is made at last explicitly revealed. " . . . in the sweat of her brow," says Eriugena about the human soul, "is she to get her bread (that is, the Word)—so she is commanded—and to till the field of Holy Scripture, prolific as it is of thorns and thistles (that is, a thin crop of interpretations of what is divine)," so that through the study of Holy Scriptures "she may return and reach again that which in the Fall of the First Man she had lost, the contemplation of Truth; and reaching she may love it, and loving it she may abide in it, and abiding in it she may there find her rest" (744b).

The Key to the Sacred Text

Use of dialectic, as Eriugena sees it, allows him to arrive at what constitutes the real target of the entire project undertaken by him—namely, a comprehension of the true meaning of the Message handed down to us through the Holy Scripture.

In particular, the matter that concerns the author of the *Periphyseon* above all is how to read the sacred text so as to understand the message conveyed. According to him, "there are many ways, indeed an infinite number, of interpreting the Scripture, just as in one and the same feather of a peacock and even in one and the same point of a tiny portion of the same feather, we see a marvelously beautiful variety of innumerable colors" (749c). It is important therefore to find the *right way* of approaching the meaning of the sacred text hidden behind the colorful veil of its form and literal sense. To Eriugena, who is well aware of the role of dialectic in bringing about the transformation of the whole of human nature (through which the latter returns to the reality of the Divine creation), this *right way* or fundamental principle, that human reason is to firmly adhere to as a clear strategy in pursuit of the meaning concealed, is precisely what he calls "the relation which exists between the Sacred Texts and reality" (749c). In the light of the above analysis, it is not hard to understand that the *relation with reality* meant here must be nothing other than *conformity to the substantial order* as it is established in reality from the very beginning of God's creation. About this *substantial order* as the one of *precedence of the universal to the particular* Eriugena says in the following words: "For there is a most general nature in which all things participate, which is created by the One Universal Principle. And from this nature as from an ample spring certain streams, so to speak, issue through the hidden pores of the corporeal creature, and pursue their different courses through the subterranean channels until they break out above ground in the different forms of the individual objects of nature" (750a).

With regard to the Scripture, all this might consequently mean only one thing: it is the search for the substantial order of reality as it is reflected in the texture of sacred writings that, like a holy key, unlocks the most secret recesses of their true meaning. In this way, man comes to initiation into the mystery of *return* to the true reality: by bringing his mind and nature into correspondence with the universal order of the substantial reality he starts his journey back to the world where he indeed is due to be. Hence, when equipped with the art of dialectic allowing the mind to properly follow the substantial order of God's creation as it is expressed by the sacred text, one really has an opportunity to go beyond the smooth surface of the literal sense of Scripture and to penetrate deep into the dimension of its genuine meaning, that is, the realm of the Divine Word. Approaching and accepting thus the Truth of the Word of God, every human being takes a chance to actually become what he or she truly is.

Man's Duality

According to Eriugena's reading of Scripture, man appears to be *dual* in his nature. "It is true," the Philosopher points out, "that the species of animal which is established in man is superior by virtue of reason and intelligence to the nature of animals which are in the same genus . . . " (750b). So that, on the one side, man is believed to be brought forth "within the universal genus of animals" (751a) as it should be in accordance with the substantial order of God's creation, whereas on the other side he seems to be something special among the animals and is even said, as the Scripture reads, to be made in the image and likeness of God (Gen 1:26-27). Thus the Prophet, in Eriugena's view, "records this greatest and most precious species of animal twice in his account of the events of the Sixth Day: first, under his genus, which is animal, he is commanded to be brought forth from the earth; and then somewhat later, when a brief classification of the animals has been given, mention is made of his creation as image and likeness of God" (750b-c).

Man's Uniqueness

However, a certain problem seems to arise here, for it is a surprising thing indeed that not the whole genus of animals but *man alone* appears to be made in the image of God. Thus, as Eriugena insists, the Scripture gives us to understand that "man was first brought forth from the earth with the cattle, reptiles and beasts of the field; and yet he alone is formed in the image of God, and so removed far beyond all comparison with the rest of the animal kingdom" (750d). Moreover, according to the Scripture again, man is preferred to all the animals, which he is believed to be brought forth out of the earth together with, as a living soul, and ordained to be master over them (750d). So that, after all these it might seem quite problematic indeed to understand how it could have happened that, unlike the other animals, man alone proved to be the image of God who created him like the rest of the creature.

The solution comes, as the Philosopher suggests, when it is sought in the following way. As the substantial order of creation requires, the whole animal (that is, "the living soul") is constituted "through connection with the body" (751a), or in other words, through the soul's manifestation in the form of body. Likewise man, being a species of the same genus, is established in accordance with the universal order of creation, within which the living soul comes to manifest herself in the form of the body. Yet, there is an essential difference between man and the rest of the animals. In particular, within the animal kingdom the link between soul and body, while exhibited in *sensation*, still remains unconscious (i.e., not subject to reason) and therefore unrevealed. The *proper order* of soul and body relationship is virtually irrelevant to sensation as such, whose function in effect consists in subjecting soul to the impulses coming from the body, which obviously breaks the substantial order of things in reality. Meanwhile, in man—about whom it is fairly said that he is "superior by virtue of reason and intelligence to the nature of animals" (750b)—the relation between soul and body becomes *intelligible* (i.e., subject to reason that is by nature relevant to the universal as such) and therefore gains an opportunity of being properly revealed. Thus, as Eriugena himself formulates it, "the animal is the juncture of soul and body in sensation . . . But this threefold motion becomes intelligible in man only, the only rational animal. For he has in subjection to his reason certain motions which may be symbolised by the word 'cattle', or 'four-footed things'" (751c).

Hence, in so far as the intelligible—which alone perfectly corresponds to the proper connection of soul and body—is actualised in human nature, man really comes (unlike the animals in whom this connection does not find its proper explication) to be the image of God.

Rational Motion

As follows from this conclusion, it appears to be beyond question that it is the *intelligible* as the most essential in man that allows him to be what he truly is—that is, the image of God. The only thing, however, that seems to need some more attention here to avoid any unwanted deviation from the very center of Eriugena's conception as a whole is to make it utterly clear *how* the Philosopher understands the intelligible to be actually brought about in man so as to let him overcome one-sided animality of his being.

While referred for this purpose to the context at 751c once again, careful reading immediately draws our attention to such a phrase as "subjection to reason" which appears indeed to be the key one in the fragment for understanding how the intelligible comes to manifest itself in human nature. As a matter of fact, this "subjection to reason" cannot imply (and the passage to follow unequivocally proves it) anything else apart from *the leading role of reason* with regard to senses, which comes to reveal itself, for instance, in cognition, as far as it is true and accurate. As Eriugena himself testifies to this "mechanism" of operation of the intelligible in man, "by his skilled zeal to understand the sensibles he moves his five-fold sense in disciplined order towards cognition of them" (751c) to acquire "true and accurate knowledge of all the sensibles, dispelling all falsehood" (751d). All this means that in order to let man know sensible things as they truly are and thus to bring him into the true reality, all human senses *are to be disciplined by reason* so as not to rule over reason but to be ruled by it, that is to say, to be moved by reason or, using the author's figure of speech, to be as obedient to its authority as "cattle" is to human will (751d). Being *prior* to the sense by nature, reason is also, as required by its leadership, *superior* by status. Therefore, when man's nature is brought into right order universal to the whole of creation so that his five-fold sense, while disciplined and led by reason, obediently follows its leader, only then man enters in effect the substantial reality of God's creation where, in accordance with its proper order, the universal precedes the singular (as it is the case with reasons and sensible things).

This properly ordered motion of human nature—in which soul precedes the body, and reason the sense, so as to let man really be the image of God in whom the universal embraces all the singular—is what Eriugena calls the "rational soul" (751d) or, as it emerges a little later in the text, the "rational motion" (752b).

Irrational Motion

As a matter of consequence, it logically follows that when the senses—in contrast to the rational motion of soul—are not obedient to reason but continually resist its discipline, they constitute the ground within man for certain motions which, being substantially hostile to his true nature, deservedly receive the name of *irrational motions.* "But there are certain irrational motions arising from the lower nature," says Eriugena, "which are resistant to reason—such as rage and covetousness and all the inordinate appetites of the corporeal senses, that make wrong use of sensible creatures" (752a).

These motions therefore occur in man when his senses, instead of being obedient to reason, entirely rely on what lies *outside* man, beyond the rational control. Being thus able to notice only discrete external things and taking them for true, these uncontrolled senses infect human nature with their wrong impressions of the sensible world and thereby unavoidably cause a bitter conflict between what is inside man and what is outside him. "And since these motions which infect human nature belong properly to the brute creation," continues the author, "they are not improperly called beasts, especially as they are in continual revolt against the discipline of reason, and can rarely, if ever, be tamed thereby, but are ever seeking to attack savagely and devour the rational motions" (752a-b).

Thus we are given to understand that, as far as man does not rationally control his senses but lets them run *ahead of reason* towards sensible things (turning them into merely corporeal objects perceived from outside only), this man actually dooms himself to untrue being in the midst of the sensibles, turning his nature into one of the corporeal things among other.

Subrational Motion

Meanwhile, apart from the two aforesaid types of motion of the soul, there is one more, as the Philosopher believes, to be counted in human nature. It is particularly the one that provides a living (or physiological) connection between soul and body, which brings them together into a single whole of a living being. This is the motion which performs what the author calls the "auctive and nutritive" functions of "the living soul." "Moreover in the rational animal," he says, "there are certain other motions, though not manifesting themselves, by which the body joined to it is administered. These motions are situated in the auctive and nutritive part of the soul. And since they perform their functions by their natural facility and as it were hiddenly—for they in no way agitate or disturb the disposition of the soul but, provided that the integrity of nature is preserved intact, penetrate by a silent progress the harmony of the body—they are therefore not improperly given the name of reptiles" (752b).

Being thus deeply hidden within the soul-body integrity of human nature, this living function may be fairly defined as *subrational* motion. Though, like the irrational one, this motion of soul stays *beyond* the rational control, it however does not revolt against human reason (as the irrational sense does), but simply remains out of reason's reach.

Manifestation of the Proper Order of Creation in Man

"Now in all animals except man," concludes Eriugena, "two only of these aforesaid three types of motion are found: that which resides in the sense and lacks the control of its own reasoning, and is therefore called bestial; and that which is attributed to the nutritive life force, and resembles the reptile" (752b–c). Consequently, one might clearly see from this that, though the "living soul" is substantially constituted by soul and body relationship, this foundation of the living creature remains revealed properly and in its full extent (so as to be the image of the Creator) in none except man. In particular, neither the *irrational motion* of soul (when she seeks to entirely rely on the bodily sense in her pursuit of knowledge of the outside world and thus allows the body to prevail over her) nor *subrational motion* (where it remains unknown which of the two precedes the other) can really show the soul administer the body. Only in man, as far as the rational motion prevails in him so as to let the soul precede the body by virtue of bringing the sense to reason's control and leadership, the proper order of the whole creation, according to which all the particular is caused to being by the universal, comes to be manifest. In this sense, it is rightly therefore said that "man is in all animals and all animals in him, and that yet he transcends them all" (752c).

Man's Choice

However, although human nature is destined to be by its very essence the image of God who causes the whole creation to being, yet in real life it is up to man to choose whether to bring his nature into right order by virtue of reason's discipline imposed upon the sense or to let senses override reason that would ultimately lead to complete disorder and destruction of his nature. Since God is the One and therefore subject to nothing outside him, so man, who is supposed to be God's image, should likewise determine his being *from within* (i.e., from the very heart of his pure nature) to be truly what he is and thus find himself in conformity to God's Nature as a whole. This precisely means that man should *freely* make his own decision (so that no one can do it for him) concerning his true being. Unless he is utterly free from any compulsion *from without*, he cannot become truly man. Hence, it is always an alternative for man whether really to be what he truly is by his nature or to remain among the animals and, while being administered by irrational and subrational motions of his soul, to simply live like a beast or a reptile. "For when consideration is given," as Eriugena points out, "to his body and his nutritive life force, to his senses and to his memory of sensibles, and to all his irrational appetites, such as rage and covetousness, he is altogether an animal; for all these he shares in common with all the other animals. But in his higher nature, which consists in reason and mind and the interior sense, with all its rational motions, which are called virtues, and with the memory of the eternal and divine things, he is altogether other than animal" (752c-d).

So that, unless man has made his choice and remains dual in himself, "it may rightly be predicated of him: 'Man is an animal'; and: 'Man is not an animal'" (752c).

The Outer and the Inner Man

In support of his view of man's duality, Eriugena refers at 753a to St. Paul's distinction between the "outer man" and the "inner man" expressly given at 2 Cor 4:16. This approach to human nature suggested by such an indisputable authority of Christian thought provides the Philosopher with the terms which seem to be quite appropriate for an explicit description of man, when he is understood to be "in a manner of speaking a two-fold creature" (753c): "And that part of him by which he is animal is appropriately termed the outer man, while that by which he transcends all other animals as well as the animal part of himself may be called the inner man" (752b).

Indeed, when man is considered on the one hand from the side of the body so that his being appears to be entirely reduced to bodily operations, then the term "outer man" may properly match human nature seen like this. For according to such a view, the soul (that is supposed to be understood as *the interior* of man) proves in effect to be widely exposed to the *outer* world and fully dependent on what is delivered to her by the bodily sense *from outside*. At the same time, however, when man is understood on the other hand to be administered *from within* by the rational motion, so that even his sense (while disciplined, as said above, by mind and reason) is formed inside man and receives the proper name of the *interior* one (752d), then the term "inner man" may adequately fit this view of human being.

The Spiritual and the Unspiritual Man

Nevertheless, despite its obvious merits and, above all, its emphasis on the inner part of human nature as superior to the outer one, the distinction between the "inner" and the "outer" man might yet bear in itself an implication of division of man into two contrasting sides of his being that would subsequently inaugurate man's duality as something substantially true. Meanwhile, the distinction between the "outer" and the "inner" in man should by no means signify an actual split within his nature into two different, as if separate, beings that could somehow mutually co-exist. Therefore, what this distinction does imply is that—although under certain circumstances man might appear as an outer being (surrounded by the world of external things appropriate to it)—such an outer state of his must be radically overcome as imperfect and fundamentally untrue. "For he who lives perfectly," the Philosopher admits, "not only altogether despises his body and the life force which administers it and all the corporeal senses together with the objects which they perceive, and all the irrational motions which he perceives in himself, together with the memory of all transient things, but also, in so far as he is able, does away with them and destroys them, lest they should in any way prevail within him, and (he) strives that he may become dead to them and they to him" (753b).

All this consequently means that the distinction between the "inner" and the "outer" man is not a rigid contrast, but a dynamic relationship. As a natural result of this relationship, the true superiority of the inner over the outer should consist not in establishing a higher position of one of them in contrast to a lower position of the other, when they both, as if satisfied with their discrimination, co-exist in mere confrontation. In effect, the real supremacy of the inner reveals itself in overcoming any contrast of mutually restricted opposites. It is such an overcoming which allows the inner actually to be what it truly is—that is, not merely an ever concealed side of being countered by the "outer" as its opposite, but a general principle which gives rise to the "outer" as its own specific manifestation. The truly "inner" therefore is to be understood not as that which is always simply different from the "outer," but as that which exhibits itself in the "outer," so that there can be neither discrepancy nor, all the more, opposition between the two.

Having said this, one may not unreasonably conclude that since the "outer" as such is to be truly understood not as a bare opposite of the "inner" but as an explication of it, likewise the "outer man" should be rightly viewed not as merely countered by the "inner man" but as the one in whom the "inner man" makes himself disclosed. In this sense, it would be fair to acknowledge that the distinction between the "outer" and the "inner" man, as far as it remains firmly confined to the contrast between the two opposite sides of human nature, proves to be quite imperfect with regard to comprehension of man as a whole and true being. For as a truly whole being, in whom the inner does not simply counter the outer but unfolds itself in the outward form adequate to it so as to prevail in human nature through and through, man virtually comes to be *Spirit*. "For in those," as Eriugena maintains, "who live according to the Spirit, in the words of the same Apostle, 'the outer man wastes, but the inner man is renewed from day to day'" (753b).

So that, unlike the inner-outer distinction, though explicitly true but implicitly fraught with a possibility of division of man into opposite parts of his nature, human being may more properly be interpreted—in line with St. Paul's language offered at 1 Cor 2:14–15—by virtue of comparison between the "spiritual man" and the "unspiritual man" (753a).

The Split of Reality

Hence, as far as man overcomes the duality of his nature so that the inner, while "renewed 'from day to day,'" comes to prevail in it, he really becomes a spiritual being in whom, as in the Divine reality, there is no division and who therefore finds himself fitting in with this true reality so as to be able to participate in it. On the other hand, if man does not overcome the duality of his nature so that the outer takes it over, while the inner remains in him only in potential as a hidden counterpart of the outer side of his, then such a man finds himself within the animal nature, that is, in the world of "transient things" perceived by the corporeal senses (753b), which is outside the substantial reality of "the things of God."

With regard to man's choice concerning the right order of his nature, according to which he might prefer to be controlled either by the irrational or the rational motion of the soul, man consequently finds himself facing two different prospects of being: either in the spurious (illusory) reality of transient things (i.e., sensible objects produced by the corporeal sense), or in the true reality of eternal things (subsisting in God by coming into being within him and never departing from him). Among these two modes of being, "one is animal . . . which admits nothing spiritual within itself," whereas the other is spiritual, "since it has communion with the eternal, spiritual, and divine substances, and is free of all animality" (753a). For as Eriugena puts it in Paul's words, man "in his animal nature . . . does not perceive the things of God," although "in his spiritual nature judges all things, but is himself judged by none" (753a).

Thus the words above give one to understand that in consequence of his choice man not only simply opens up before his mind two different perspectives of reality, but also actually finds himself in *two different dimensions of it*. So that, as a *spiritual* being, he gets into God's creation proper (where the universal precedes the particular) and, to the extent that his mind enjoys the conformity to the right order of creation, is able to judge all things. By contrast to this, remaining just an *irrational* creature, man stays in the world which proves to be outside the creation of God, for nothing of the Divine is said to be admitted within it.

All this convinces those who read the *Periphyseon* carefully that the question of man's duality and choice is not an idle matter at all. Indeed, because of this duality and the subsequent choice that man unavoidably faces, his nature appears to be cleft asunder. In particular, as follows from Rom 7:25, "that nature through which man is in communion with the animals is called the flesh; and that by which he participates in the celestial essence is called mind or spirit or intellect" (753c). Consequently, regarding the way man resolves the problem of the duality of his nature, he may actually destine himself to two alternative modes of being, that is, two different lives he might live—namely, that of an animal among the animals or that of a spiritual being among the "celestial essences," who is fairly said to be made "in the image and likeness of God" that is beyond all animal nature (753c). This means, as Eriugena concludes making use of the Apostle's words again, that in the result of his own choice man may virtually find himself in utterly different dimensions of reality subject to absolutely different laws and, subsequently, appropriate to different prospects of life: "By my mind I serve the Law of God, but by flesh the law of sin" (753c). Thus man himself chooses in fact whether to accept or to reject the destiny to come, for as said, "that part of him by which he partakes of the celestial essence he renews 'from day to day', that is, he ascends from virtue to virtue by the movement and cooperation and leadership and perfecting power of the grace of God" (753c).

It is in this way therefore that man proves in fact to cause the split of reality into that of the spurious (or illusory) one, which—being spread among transient things of the sensibles—only seems to be; and that of the substantial (or true) one, which—being originally established among eternal things of God—comes to be revealed to man. In this sense, it is right to say that the split of reality arises from man, and it remains there unless man completely brings his nature into right order so as to actually achieve the pristine state of union with the substantial reality of God's creation. This state of union comes to be lost in consequence of the disastrous delusion of man's mind becoming guilty (when imperfectly used) of bringing his nature into a devastating disorder by means of taking the outcomes (effects) of its motions for their beginnings (causes). The reunification of human being with the true reality visibly happens (or rather begins to happen) when the *transformation of the corporeal sense* into the *interior* one (i.e., the transformation of what is shared with animals into what is fully controlled, disciplined and led, by reason) comes to be apparently manifest in man. For only when man's reason does not counter itself to the senses so as to stand in its pride apart from all the senses taking them for something inferior and unworthy, such a reason may take up the role of the Good Shepherd (John 10:2–4) to call all the senses by name (i.e., giving their data a definite notion) and thus to lead them out of its own secret folds going ahead of them. Only then human reason (whose nature thereby comes to perfectly accord with the rational motion of the soul) may be properly called, as the Philosopher suggests, spirit or mind or intellect (753c). As such, man really becomes as whole as God Himself is, which enables him to embrace the entire reality beyond any division imposed upon it by the imperfect mind overridden by the exterior sense. Thus, by virtue of healing his mind (whose rightly ordered motion acquires later in the text the name of *recta ratio*), man really enters the world as it originally is since coming into being from the One God, and thus recognises in it the Kingdom of God that he has been obliged to find as the place appropriate to the high status of *imago Dei*.

The Unity of Reality.

It follows from what has been said that man's choice concerning the right order of his nature (and, subsequently, the modes of his being) does not imply that one part of it may be merely rejected in favour of the other, as it might seem to be the case with the distinction between the "inner" and the "outer" man. Indeed, just as no living being can be divided into parts and yet remain alive, so it is with the human nature as the living soul that it cannot be, as it were, cut up either into separate "outer" and "inner" sides, or "lower" and "higher" extremes, or "animal" and "spiritual" natures so that neither of the two contraries would admit anything of the other (see 753a). In this sense, it is fair to say therefore that in human nature there are actually no parts that could be understood to exist on their own.

Thus, being not countered by the body but incorporating it as the manifestation of its own wholeness, the spiritual nature constitutes the totality of human being, and for this reason cannot be rightly considered at all as merely a part of it. And it is in accordance with this spiritual unity that "the whole man" is fairly said at 755d to be "both an animal and a spiritual creature" in the sense that the "inner man" is inseparable from the "outer man," in whom the "inner" one is made explicit. If it were nevertheless somehow imagined that the spiritual nature could be only one of the constitutive elements of human being so as to break its living wholeness, it would be then, according to Eriugena's conviction, just an absurd opinion that no "true philosopher should maintain" (754a). For as he argues, if it were only the case that human nature consisted of co-existing animal and spiritual parts adjusted to one another as if from without, it would have to be maintained (though neither reason nor Divine authority permits it) "that in the one man there are two souls" (754a). In line with such a dichotomy, it would also have to be held that one of the two souls "administers the body, giving it life and nourishment and increase, and perceives the sensibles by means of the corporeal senses and stores the phantasies of them in its memory, and performs all the other functions which it is well known are performed by the souls of the other animals; while the other which subsists in the reason and the mind, 'is made in the image and likeness of God.' But this seems altogether absurd" (754a). However, in truth "man consists," the Philosopher concludes, "of one and the same rational soul conjoined to the body in a mysterious manner," and it is only "by a certain wonderful and intelligible division that man himself is divided into two parts . . . " (754b). As a matter of fact, his soul

> is whole in itself and its wholeness pervades the whole of its nature. For it is wholly life, wholly mind, wholly reason, wholly sense, wholly memory, and it is as a whole that it gives life, nourishment, consistency and increase to the body. As a whole it perceives the sensible species through the whole of its senses; as a whole it operates beyond the bounds of the bodily senses and treats, separates, combines and forms judgments upon the nature and reason of the sensibles; as a whole it extends beyond and above every creature, including even itself in so far as it is itself reckoned among the numbers of the creatures, and, purged from all vices and all phantasies, revolves about its Creator in an eternal and intelligible motion. (754c)

This gives us to understand that the split within reality arises from the split within man's own nature. Hence, in so far as the duality of his being is healed, man becomes whole in himself (as he truly is by his nature originally coming into being from the universal Principle of all), and along with the wholeness of man the division of reality gets overcome too. Becoming a single whole, man sees the same reality with new eyes which allow him to look beyond its old bounds, for this reality now appears to him in the true light of its being in the original state of the substantial wholeness of God's creation. Therefore, being one whole, as Eriugena says, the human nature "operates beyond the bounds of the bodily senses" (754c), and thus—by extending itself "beyond and above every creature" (i.e., every individual sensible object, the multitude of which forms the world of particular things)—his nature comes to revolve "about its Creator in an eternal and intelligible motion" (754c), which alone in its universal grasp is appropriate to the whole of the true reality.

In this regard, it is vitally important to understand that the restoration of man's wholeness, which makes him fit in with the wholeness of the true reality, happens only when man evokes within himself the *universal motions* of his nature, that becomes possible solely when the soul is occupied with "the Divine essence" or, at least, with "the natures and causes of creation" (754d). For solely when, exceeding "the bounds of the bodily senses," the human soul extends its capacity as far as to grasp such *universal* subjects as God's Nature and general causes of things, and thus acquires respectively the proper names of *mind* (also called by Eriugena spirit or intellect) and *discursive reason* (754d), only then man is made truly *one* (755d), both within himself and with the whole universe of God's creation. And this is rightly so; because it is in this way of being brought into conformity with the true reality subject to the Law of God that the human nature is converted into Spirit. So that, only when understood to be Spirit who follows the proper order of God's creation (where, according to the Law mentioned, the singular takes its beginning from the universal, but not *vice versa*), man really comes to participate "in the Divine and celestial essence" (755c). Thus, becoming one with the substantial reality as it truly is, man really achieves the state of his true being, through which he properly subsists in God's creation.

In contrast with this, in so far as man does not evoke within himself the universal motions of his soul so as to enjoy the perfect use of mind and discursive reason (755b) and thus to become whole (while restoring the original right order of his nature), he actually fails to cleave to the true reality and therefore cannot truly be. For as follows from 754d–755b, being content after the manner of the irrational animals with "the use of physical sense" and "the hidden operation within the body" (i.e., "the capability to administer his body", which is also called "vital motion"), man finds himself to be confined to "the bounds of the bodily senses," within which his soul "perceives the sensibles by means of the corporeal senses and stores the phantasies of them in its memory" (754a). Engaged thereby not with the things of the substantial reality that are *universal* by nature but with the *sensible objects*, which are not the things themselves as they truly are but, as said at 754c–d, just *perceptions* of "the sensible species" (i.e., of *individual* things, received by the soul from without through the exterior senses), man inevitably comes to face only the sensible world, which is rather the realm of man-made *phantasies* than reality as such. Having no suspicion neverthe-less of being captive to his own phantasies of sensible objects drawn by the memory from the sense (755c), man is led astray by the *irrational* motion of the soul into an illusory world. As a result of this, he finds himself among the external things as they appear in their discrete state and therefore only seem to exist on their own. Mistaking his sensible impressions of the sur-rounding world for the proper reality, man actually entrusts himself (and his fate) to the world of appearance, and thus deprives himself of the true being, both of being a true human and subsistence in the true reality. For this reason, it is rightly said of man that "it is by the freedom of his will only" (for man is free indeed to choose between the *rational* and the *irrational* motion of his soul) "that he is animal" (755d).

As a matter of fact, man is free to yield to animality in himself and thus to dishonor the dignity of his pristine nature, which is said to be "the dignity of the Divine image" (756b). The real trouble about this ill choice resulting in man's disgrace is, however, that by making it man does not simply find an alternative mode of being, less perfect then the substantial one, yet suitable enough to his animal-like needs and pleasures. Indeed, becoming animal in defiance of his genuine nature and thus corrupting its proper order, man violates the universal Law of God and, as a matter of consequence, dooms himself to *non-being*. For in the substantial reality of God's creation there are no such things at all that could subsist while being less true or less perfect than they essentially are, because nothing that *does not accord with its own proper nature* can truly be (see 756b). "Therefore man becomes animal," Eriugena admits, "and is so described, when he abandons those operations, which accord with reason and intellect and are concerned with the knowledge of the Creator and of creation, for those irrational activities which among the brute beasts are concerned with the appetites of the body—and falls through his wilful appetite, so as to gorge his interest with the deadly allure of the temporal and corruptible things which tend towards non-being" (756a).

After all this, it is not hard to understand that in so far as man makes a choice between the *rational* and the *irrational* motion of the soul, he actu-ally chooses not between one or another mode of being, but between *being* proper and *non-being*. For corrupting his true nature by bringing it into subjection to the senses so as to make it compatible with the finite things of the sensible world, man virtually lets the transient take him captive and gradually draw the entire of his nature (even against his will or intention) towards non-being as the only end of everything temporal and corruptible. Hence, as far as man is really concerned about his proper subsistence in the true reality so that he could reach in effect "the state to which he is destined by his immutable substance" (756b), man has in fact no other choice to make except to bring himself into perfect accord with his proper nature or, in other words, for being perfect as the Father in heaven is said to be perfect (Matt 5: 48). For only when his actual existence perfectly accords with his essential nature (which, being rational in its true status, is infinite and universal), does man truly come to properly subsist in the Divine reality, because he really becomes what he is meant to be from the very beginning of creation—that is, the image of him who says of himself: "I am Who I am" (Exod 3:14). Otherwise, if man understands the temporal existence after the manner of the irrational animals to be his fate, then he loses indeed the entire meaning of his life and cannot dare even thinking of himself to ever become the image of God who seems to him to be too far away and even alien to his imperfect being.

Mode 4 and the Unity of Being

Thus the inner logic of the text as it develops in Book 4, when focused on investigating the ontological implications of the contrast between the *rational* and *irrational* motions of human nature, brings us close to the formulations of mode 4 of the "division of those things of which it is said that they are and those things of which it is said that they are not" (443a). In particular, giving a fair distinction between the intellect and senses in their approach to being (which may not improperly be associated with the distinction between the ways of Truth and Delusion in Parmenides's ontology), this *mode* reads as follows, beginning with a clear reference to its affinity with what had been proposed by "the philosophers": "The fourth mode is that which, not improbably according to the philosophers, declares that only those things which are contemplated by the intellect alone truly are, while those things which in generation, through the expansions or contractions of matter, and the intervals of places and motions of times are changed, brought together, or dissolved, are said not to be truly, as is the case with all bodies which can come into being and pass away" (445b–c).

In the light of what is examined in detail in chapter 2 with regard to Parmenides's ontology and epistemology as well as what Eriugena concentrates on in Book 4 of the *Periphyseon*, it is not hard to understand what he means by saying in mode 4 about the ontological status of the things available to human mind through the sensual perception. In mode 1, appropriate, as we may clearly see it, to the division of reality into the transcendent and immanent realms (developing in Book 1 in the course of discussing the basics of the *apophatic* theology), such things available to the mind through the senses are apparently classed among those that are said *to be*. Introducing the theme of the *modes* of our understanding of being and non-being, Eriugena in particular maintains: "Of these modes the first seems to be that by means of which reason convinces us that all things which fall within the perception of bodily sense or within the grasp of intelligence are truly and reasonably said to be, but that those which because of the excellence of their nature elude not only all sense but also all intellect and reason rightly seem not to be—which are correctly understood only of God and matter and of the reasons and essences of all the things that are created by Him" (443a-b). However, in contrast to this purely metaphysical dichotomy between being and non-being, as a result of which God proves to be unfairly opposed to existence as such, the dialectical view of reality suggests, as the entirety of our analysis shows, that God's being as it truly is cannot be confined at all, neither from within nor from without. According to this, the true (infinite) being may only be properly known when it is coherently thought of as fully distinguished (by means of the dialectical contradiction) from the opposite, and therefore as neither preceded nor followed by non-being nor remaining con-substantial with it. So that, as soon as Eriugena makes it perfectly clear in mode 4 that the true being is utterly irreducible to the spatio-temporal realm of existence and is available to *the intellect alone*, he actually means to confirm by this his allegiance to the dialectical standpoint, explicitly stated at the beginning of Book 4 (749a).

According to the dialectical approach to being, the true infinity, as seen before, can by no means be found compatible with the finite dimension of reality, that is, with the temporality of all "bodies" spatially confined and anchored in the sensible world—the world unsubstantial by nature and packed with fleeting impressions that things leave upon senses while, as said, coming into being and passing away. By affirming the perspective of "genera" over the perspective of "species," as dialectic of "the sages" applied to "their subtle investigation of reality" requires (749a), Eriugena seeks in fact to exalt the point of view of the mind over that of senses, bringing the former thereby to its perfect conformity to the whole of being as it truly (infinitely) is in its unconfined totality. Thus, he believes, the fundamental ontological dichotomy is overcome and the way to the substantial reality, which is that of God's creation, is cleared. In this way, on account of the *imago Dei*, all human beings come to be at one with God, knowing him and therefore worshipping him in Spirit and Truth. But this radical transformation of human life in union with God, brought about through the perspicuous contemplation of the true reality of creation and actual participation in it (by perfection or making the inner nature adequately manifest), constitutes, as already mentioned, the focal point of mode 5 of understanding of the true being (445 c–d), and along with it the subject-matter of the following, *fifth*, book of the *Periphyseon*.

All this convinces us that the prime concern of the entirety of the vast project undertaken by Eriugena is indeed about "those who in the first man were lost and had fallen into a kind of non-subsistence," and whom "God the Father calls through faith in His Son to be as those who are already reborn in Christ" (445c-d). Not unreasonably therefore, in continuity with the profound consideration of the *rational motion* of human nature (developing in Book 4), does Eriugena add to the formulations of mode 5 an emphasis on the crucial role of the proper manifestation of the innermost recesses of that nature: "But this too" (i.e., God's call) "may also be understood of those whom God daily calls forth from the secret folds of nature in which they are considered not to be, to become visibly manifest in form and matter and in the other conditions in which hidden things are able to become manifest" (445d).

In the light of these insights into the meaning of mode 4, it would be fair to conclude that it is in the *fourth* book's inquiry into the relationship between the mind and the senses that we are given to understand how the true (unconfined) being comes to be knowable and therefore attainable. It is in fact through the *right order* of the mind and senses and their interaction that the proper manifestation of human nature and, accordingly, its actual participation in the substantial reality of the whole come about. As a rigorous discipline of the mind restoring human nature to the pristine dignity of its wholeness, *dialectic* seeks to establish the right order in question and thus—through the mind's conformity to the proper order of reality—to bring human beings back to the bosom of creation, where, as appropriate to *imago Dei*, they are properly due to be. This is what the following analysis of Eriugena's text in the next chapter allows us to understand better.

CHAPTER 5

The Doctrine of Contradiction

The Integral Approach

As FOLLOWS FROM THE above inquiry into the order of human being, man's existence in accordance with his proper nature may be rightly (dialectically) understood to come about by virtue of *negation of all animality* within himself, manifest par excellence in such purely corporeal features of his nature, taken on their own and separately from its inner dimension, as the external body and bodily senses. Not unfairly, therefore, should man in his proper existence be defined as *not an animal*. Indeed, it is in contrast to sensation essential to animals that *reason* only or, to be precise, the *rational motion* of the human soul (where senses are not just neglected or discarded but, as discussed above, *disciplined* and *led* by reason) adheres to the universal order of creation, making it manifest in man and thus enabling him to actually participate in the substantial reality. In this sense, it would be right to say, following Eriugena, that rationally embracing the whole genus of "the living soul" (i.e., adequately representing in himself the basic order of the soul-body relationship) man is at the same time among the animals and transcends them all (752c). For this reason, he is truly found to be simultaneously *an animal* and *not an animal*. "Therefore, the whole soul," the author points out, "is on the one hand produced from the earth in the genus of the animals, and on the other hand is made in the image of God. For this and nothing else is what must follow from the foregoing arguments . . . And no true and orthodox philosopher should doubt it, lest he appears impiously to tear in two this most simple and indivisible nature" (755a).

Thus, in the form of the paradoxical statement concerning man's animality and non-animality, contradiction comes into focus in Eriugena's discourse. " . . . how one and the same man can, as this discussion seeks to demonstrate," asks the Philosopher, "be, and yet not be an animal; possess, and yet not possess, animality; be, and yet not be, flesh; be, and yet not be, spirit. How can such contradictory and mutually opposed predicates be understood of one absolutely simple nature?" (755a). According to Eriugena, this contradiction should not however discourage those who are perplexed by its apparent difficulty: "From what has already been said it should be as clear as day to anyone who looks into the matter more carefully that everything which seems . . . to be contrary to the simplicity of human nature is in fact not only not contrary to but is entirely suitable" (755a-b).

Indeed, when applied to human being, the negative predicate "not an animal" should not be understood as a *bare negation* of animality as such. No negative predicate should be qualified as a mere *negation for the sake of negation*. If it were otherwise and the positive predicate could just be denied by the contrary one, then the whole statement concerning man's simple (i.e., undivided) nature, according to which he is *simultaneously an animal and not an animal*, would prove to be meaningless. Hence, when man is said to be *both* an animal *and* not an animal, it is quite reasonable to assume that the negation constituting the crucial part of this statement is meant to play a constructive role[1] rather than that of a bare negation—namely, the role of *affirmation*. And this specifically understood affirmation (i.e., *affirmation through the negation*), being different from the ordinary one that is usually believed to dispense with negation, is in fact a *true* affirmation. In its truth, affirmation as such is solely possible as the *overcoming of negation*, but not as asserting something contrary to anything opposite and therefore exposed to the following denial. It means that the true affirmation does occur from the *negation of negation* only, and thus may only be properly understood as the *overcoming of negation*. For being in fact the negation of the *finite* state of human being (which, in turn, itself is the denial of man's true nature), the negation of animality in man is supposed to result in *overcoming* the finitude of the fleshly one-sidedness of his being or, in other words, in *affirmation* of his true nature which is infinite in itself, as due to *imago Dei*. "For everything that is created in man according to nature," as the Philosopher argues, "must of necessity remain eternally intact and uncorrupted. For it is not in accordance with the Divine justice that anything should perish of that which He has made, especially as it is not nature herself who has sinned, but the perverse will which moves irrationally against rational nature" (760c).

All this consequently means that the affirmative and negative predicates of man's being—that is, "an animal" and "not an animal"—which seem "to be contrary to the simplicity of human nature," are in fact *not contrary* at

---

1. On the role of negation and contradiction in the Eriugenian approach to truth see, for example, Marler, "Scriptural Truth," 157–58.

all. When taken together in their integrity as the two inseparable aspects of a truly simple (undivided) and therefore really subsisting human nature, in which the inner and the outer cannot be severed, these predicates are to be rightly understood as *mutually complementary* or, as Eriugena himself puts it, "entirely suitable" (755b). For only in their *integrity* (suitability) do the opposed predicates—while representing inseparability of the inward and outward sides of a real being—prove in fact to be *ontologically applicable*. As such, they enable the human mind (and thereby human being as a whole) to exceed the limits of a formally logical appeal to purely abstract categories and thus to approach the substantial reality as it truly is. Otherwise, if the predicates in question were taken not in their integrity but separately (so as to be considered not in relation to the whole of human being but in their temporal sequence to one another), then both definitions—as being mutually countered and confined—would turn out to be no more than ontologically inappropriate abstract predicates, standing at best for some static *states* of being which, because of their separateness, are not there in reality. Hence, understood as *the negation of negation*, the negative predicate "not an animal" proves actually to be nothing else but the way to conceive *the mode of affirmation*, by which the restoration of human nature to its proper status is to be meant.

Thus, the paradoxical statement of man's being quoted from 755a at the beginning of the current chapter allows us to understand the following:

First, a higher status of nature (in the sense of its greater perfection or accordance with itself) is implied to prevail in man so as to raise him above the horizon of the sensible world, where in his present imperfect state of improper use of his own rational nature he exists among the external (i.e., finite or, in other words, temporal and corruptible) objects only.

Secondly, from the same statement it also follows that this affirmation of the surpassing nature happens in man not simply by means of *rejecting* the animality that is deeply rooted in him as the fundamental relationship between soul and body, but by *transforming* it into a radically new quality of its being by bringing the soul-body relation into *right order*, which comes to be manifestly realized in man precisely in the way of *subjecting the sense to reason*.

It means that it is in the result of this thoroughgoing *transformation of animality* within human being that the true nature of man (as it is expressed by the inseparable predicates discussed above) resolutely supersedes in him the negated one, which in its imperfection is akin to that of the brute animals. And thus, in the way of affirmation of the true nature in man, *the proper order* of the entire creation becomes adequately manifest in reality, so that even God himself comes to be fully revealed in it. It is therefore in this way that, metaphorically speaking, nothing but God's face is understood to be seen in man who is thus allowed actually to be what he truly is by his nature, namely the *imago Dei*. For *all men*—in so far as they are genuinely believed to come into being from the Sole Source of all (that is to say, from above)—are truly said in the holy words of St. John to become (on receiving the Truth revealed) "children of God, who were born, not of blood or of the will of the flesh or of the will of man, but of God" (John 1:12–13). That is why in agreement with this high truth the author of the *Periphyseon* enthusiastically admits: "For everything which her Creator primordially created in her" (i.e., human nature) "remains whole and intact, though remaining hidden until now, 'awaiting the revelation of the sons of God'" (761b).

It becomes therefore clear what Eriugena really means when, in response to the pivotal question raised at 755a with relation to the alleged duality of man's nature, he suggests in quite an extraordinary manner that the "contradictory and mutually opposed predicates" of being and not being animal (as well as flesh and spirit, as mentioned in the context) are to be rightly understood to apply to *one and the same subject* (human being) as "not only not contrary" to its simplicity, but also as "entirely suitable" (755b) to it. These are consequently the predicates that embrace the real wholeness of human nature in its true being which is said to be "everywhere a whole in itself" (761b). Indeed, the true being of man can in no way be understood to spread *beyond his nature's self-identity* into the realm of an illusory being that would emerge from separation of the outer from the inner (as well as from their substantial disorder, when the particular would seem to give rise to the whole), which therefore is nothing more than *non-being*. This finally means that man's proper nature can neither be conceived in its truth nor actually affirmed in reality *without the negation*, which in fact is but the negation of the one-sided finitude of his being, leading to the restoration of its proper wholeness. Such an integral approach to human being through a dialectically understood negation would further require, as we shall see it below, that the contradictory statements should be considered as being *simultaneously true*. If these statements however were considered separately in a dilemma-like *"either/or"* manner, in accordance with which it is sought to be decided whether man is *only* "an animal" or *only* "not an animal" (so as to choose only one of the opposing statements for true), then neither of the statements in focus would prove to be relevant to truth.

However, if in contrast to this dialectical (holistic) approach, these statements were dealt with *separately* and *independently* from each other so as to be considered, for example, in a dilemma-like *"either-or"* manner (according to which it would have to be decided whether man is *only* "an animal" or *only* "not an animal," and, as a matter of consequence, between the two opposed statements *only one* would have to be chosen for true), then anyone who is said to look "into the matter more carefully" (755a) would admit without hesitation that *neither* of the statements in focus could actually be true. For, as reciprocally countered, either of them would appear in affect to be rigidly confined to its finite meaning, which is of necessity encumbered with its own negation; so that, as a result, each of the two contradictory statements in its isolation from the other would inevitably prove to be equally *untrue*.

Thinking the Whole

By a dialectical treatment of the contraries with respect to their integrity, as seen above, Eriugena actually approaches the very fundamentals of a *radically new logic*. Dealing with the wholeness as such, both ontological and epistemological at the same time, this logic proves to perfectly match the substantial reality as it truly is while proceeding from and staying within the universal Principle of all. This is the reality which is embraced by the contraries and is therefore approached when coherently thought of by means of *contradiction*, aimed at overcoming all dichotomies between the opposites, including the ultimate ones of *being* and *non-being*. Thus the logic, appropriate to this reality and called *dialectic*, becomes an effective instrument which enables the mind both to restore the wholeness of human nature (by bringing the senses and reason into right order) and reach the reality of the whole. This consequently means that *inasmuch as man becomes whole in himself* (through the reason's control over the sense), he also becomes at the same time *one with the whole of the substantial reality of God's creation*, where the universal contains the particular, and the cause gives rise to the effects, but not *vice versa*.

In this way, by getting the wholeness of his nature restored through the mind dialectically disciplined, man is understood to come to the reality of creation to encounter God who is truly the One, while unfolding himself in creation and being thus *All in all*. It is in this sense, therefore, that man is fairly said to be both the image *and likeness* of God (Gen 1:26). "For just as God," Eriugena holds, "is both beyond all things and in all things—for He Who only truly is, is the essence of all things, and while He is whole in all things He does not cease to be whole beyond all things, whole in the world, whole around the world . . .—in the same way human nature in its own world (in its subsistence) in its own universe and in its visible and invisible parts is whole in itself . . . " (759a–b). "For even the lowest and least valuable part, the body," the Philosopher continues, "is according to its own principles whole in the whole man, for the body, in so far as it is truly body, subsists in its own reasons which were made in the beginning of creation; and since human nature is so in itself, it goes beyond its whole" (759b). It is for this reason, therefore, that the whole of man's nature is said *to cleave to its Creator* (759b). " . . . therefore we not improperly say," Eriugena concludes, "that human nature cleaves to its Creator. For possibility is often taken for realisation, and that which is bound to happen some day is regarded as happening now and already achieved" (760a). And this is precisely what appears to him to be unequivocally conveyed by the sacred words of the Gospel at John 12:26: "Where I am there is My servant also" (759c).

All this convinces a careful reader of the *Periphyseon* that the logic Eriugena is pursuing is all about the transformation of the entire human being (brought about through the cardinal change of the way the mind operates) and bringing it into the substantial reality of creation as it truly is in union with God. And what really makes this logic radically new is simply *contradiction*. That is why an extremely important question about the nature of contradiction inevitably arises in the context at 756b–757b, where the author appears to make a good effort to define it by focusing on its contrast to that of *difference*. A careful comparison between the two undertaken by him results in what may be reasonably qualified as a coherent *doctrine of contradiction*, in which—for the purpose of its better apprehension—two distinctive stages, as they successively occur in the course of its gradual unfolding, may be featured as follows: 1) *difference and contradiction*; 2) *uniformity of the subject*.

Difference and Contradiction

As it appears from Eriugena's discourse at 756b-d, no singular things (such as individual species of the animal genus) can *actually oppose* one another in so far as they remain simply separate externals. Likewise, no rational beings can oppose irrational animals, even though the predicates "rational" and "irrational" are fairly said to be "completely opposed to one another" (756c). Indeed, if the nature of individual (singular) things is considered more carefully, it becomes clear, according to the Philosopher, that these things, as some separate objects, can only be perceived as being in *external* relations to one another. For this reason, they prove in fact to be neither "mutually contradictory" nor "completely opposed," but merely *different*. It is to be understood with regard to this, therefore, that the negative prefix, explicitly present in such pairs of contrary terms as visible and *in*-visible, corporeal and *in*-corporeal, rational and *ir*-rational, stands actually for a *distinction* between some things designated by them and, consequently, "refers in many cases to a difference, not a contradiction" (756c). "For visibility and invisibility," Eriugena explains, "are two properties which are separate from one another but not mutually repugnant" (756c). Hence, however "completely opposed" the contraries might appear to be, in fact they are not *contradictory* at all if they refer to *different things* while standing for some particular (though contrasting) properties in them, as it is for example the case with the following pair of contrary statements: "Man is a rational animal" and "Horse is an irrational animal" (see 757a). This means furthermore that among such statements, in so far as they concern the *difference* between two separate things (that is held by the contrasting predicates regarding their essential properties), *either assertion is virtually true*, and neither contradicts the other.

From this, it is reasonable to assume that contradiction can arise solely when the contrary statements *contradict* each other. This may, clearly, happen if and only if "a pair of contradictories" is predicated of *one and the same* subject. According to common belief, however, contradiction is usually understood (or rather misunderstood) in such a way that one of the contrary statements is supposed to be true and the other false (756d). "For contradictory statements of one and the same subject," according to this belief, "cannot both at the same time be true or both at the same time be false, whether they be of a universal or of a particular application" (756d). And this is precisely what the *traditional* understanding requires of contradiction, but not that of Eriugena. According to his view, as follows from the context at 757b-c, a real contradiction does arise only when both contradictories are either *simultaneously* true or *simultaneously* false[2]. For otherwise,

2. This thesis might seem to common sense as unusual as the central postulate of *non-Euclidian* geometry of Lobachevsky is, in agreement with which two parallel lines—in defiance of popular belief—must *intersect*. Yet, it appears to be true in so far as a *real space* of the world that is spread over great distances, but not an abstract replica of it applicable to straight lines only, is concerned. Similarly, in the case of the doctrine of contradiction, it proves again to be the fact that abstract ideas—as it often happens when abstraction dominates in human reason—are just irrelevant to the true reality which they are supposed to correspond to. Therefore, however unusual it might seem that the true and the false do not contradict each other and that, accordingly, contradiction is not constituted by mutually excluding statements (of which one is true and the other false), one should ever remember the only thing—namely, the need for being in touch with reality as it truly is in and for itself. A classical exposition of the uncommon view, according to which a genuine contradiction does arise between the two contradictory statements if and only if they both appear at the same time to be true (or false), may be found for certain in philosophy of Immanuel Kant, namely in that part of his system which is called *Transcendental Dialectic*, where in particular contradictions, such as "The world has a beginning" and "The world has no beginning" or "The soul is mortal" and "The soul is immortal," are considered. True, it has to be also

if one of the opposed statements is recognised to be true and the other false, they do not constitute a contradiction; because in fact they prove to be just *separate* from one another, and for this reason do not come to contradiction at all. In so far as one of the statements is merely true and the other is respectively false there is only a disparity between the two and no room for a contradiction at all. Misunderstood however, in contrast to Eriugena's view, as a distinction between *the true* and *the false*, contradiction fails to conform to its own nature; for the true and the false do not contradict, but only *exclude* one another. It is as simple as that.

Contradiction therefore, as we can draw from this, should not be reduced to a mere *antinomy*, which in fact is not concerned about getting the contraries reconciled. In other words, contradiction should not be oversimplified and, like antinomy, only warn the mind against falling into delusion of formulating contradictory statements, and subsequently compel it to choose between the contradictories standing, as assumed, for truth or falsehood. Indeed, if *only one* of the contradictories were recognised for being true, it would necessarily mean that one of the contraries predicated of the subject is simply *irrelevant* to it and should refer to something else, namely, to *another* subject. According to Eriugena, however, contradiction should refer, as seen above, to *one and the same subject*, of which the contrary predicates should be understood in their unity, that is, in the way of being

admitted that, in spite of having rightly understood this chief peculiarity intrinsic to the nature of contradiction in general, the German philosopher nevertheless reckoned contradiction among the impossibles in terms of its complete irrelevance to anything real. To his mind, nothing true could ever be grasped by the opposed statements in so far as both of them proved to be equally valid. Hence, as Kant argues, if in his discourse man arrives at some contradiction, it must apparently testify to his reason's weakness and helplessness rather than to its merits and effectiveness. And since, furthermore, it cannot be firmly decided which of the contraries is really true (i.e., whether the world is finite or infinite, and the soul is mortal or immortal, and so on), contradiction as such comes then to be recognised as nothing else but a definite sign of delusion that human mind should carefully avoid on its way to truth. Thus, in his *Critique of Pure Reason*, while discussing in detail the antinomies of pure reason (which human mind finds itself to be trapped in as soon as self-assuredly tries to leave the solid ground of sensual experience and thus to transcend the utmost of its own capacity to look beyond the limits of the finite phenomena), Kant qualifies contradiction as an insurmountable obstacle on the way of cognition that does not allow human mind to go any further in its search for truth. Therefore, while severely criticizing the shortcomings of the Kantian approach to contradiction (mainly, the interpretation of it as a criterion of delusion), Hegel however highly appreciated Kant's contribution due to his recognition of equal validity of *thesis* and *antithesis*. And it was this equal validity of the contraries which allowed Hegel to suggest that contradiction is to be properly understood as a criterion of truth. Contradiction, according to him, lets human mind know that it is on the right way to Godly Truth as far as, by relying upon the integrity of the opposites, it resolutely breaks through the finitude of the phenomenal world towards the reality as it truly is.

appropriate to the *infinite* nature of the substantially true things. It is a matter of great importance therefore to realise what it really means to Eriugena to understand how contradictories can refer to *one and the same subject* and thus, taken in their integrity, uncover the infinity of the substantial reality.

Uniformity of Subject

In the result of the above analysis, one has to admit that *difference* as such is always found to be relevant to the *external dimension* of existence, for this difference (or distinction) is apparently rooted in separateness of external things, and it only occurs in language when some contrary predicates are applied respectively to different subjects. By contrast, therefore, it necessarily follows that if these contrary predicates are referred to *one and the same subject*, then *contradiction* arises, which with regard to human thought signifies its turn towards the *inner dimension* of reality. In this sense, it is consequently right to say after Eriugena that "whereas difference distinguishes one species from another," contradiction "is always held to be within one and the same species or part" (756c). So that—as he draws a conclusion—"if speaking of man one were to say of that species of nature which according to its substance is called man, 'man is a rational animal' and 'man is an irrational animal,' this would be the statement of a pair of contradictories" (756d).

Thus Eriugena's reasoning safely arrives at the question of the *nature of contradiction* itself that lies, as mentioned above, at the very heart of his entire enterprise regarding the development of a new type of logic properly called *dialectic*. And the first problematic thing to be tackled concerning this focal point is that of the status of the constitutive elements of contradiction which give rise to the contradiction itself. In this respect, it is to be particularly decided whether both *thesis* and *antithesis*, as the elements of contradiction, are to be counted for being equally valid so as to be truly held—as Eriugena insists on it—*within* one and the same subject defined (and therefore embraced) by their unity.

As a faithful dialectician who is totally committed to knowing the truth of the unity of reality that takes its origin from the universal Principle of all, the author of the *Periphyseon* leaves his readers in no doubt concerning the resolution sought, when with regard to the statement of man's being at the same time *an animal* and *not an animal* he unequivocally says that it is *equally true* that man *is an animal* and *is not an animal* (757b). Indeed, in accordance with what has already been said about the true nature of contradiction, one could easily agree that *falsehood* as such arises in effect only when each of the opposed statements is regarded *separately* from the other, as if having value while taken on its own as something *finite* (i.e., *in contrast to the opposite statement*). Furthermore it cannot be otherwise, for nothing finite—as being confined to its contrary—can be really true (or relevant to the reality of the whole). In consequence of this, it is not hard for those who look into the mater carefully enough to understand that man, as he truly is in his present state, cannot be *only* an irrational animal (i.e., merely a brute beast whose being is confined to body and sense) or *only* a rational animal (i.e., a pure mind which has nothing to do with animality itself as the union of soul and body). This means that, in so far as the contrary statements are only understood to be *mutually countered* so that one of them is accepted for true and the other is denied as false, both statements then inevitably prove to be *equally untrue* (or fraught in themselves with their own denial).

And Eriugena is really determined to deliver this challenging message to those who are concerned about knowing the Truth that is said to make them free (John 8: 32), i.e., fit for living in the substantial reality confined to nothing[3]. As a single whole of "a pair of contradictories," a proper contradiction enables the human mind to enter the infinite depth of truth correspondent to the infinity of the whole. For the true resolution of contradiction is seen by him on the way of *restoration of the wholeness*, but not on that of making contradictories mutually countered. This, in Eriugena's conviction, is the right way to properly safeguard truth from any delusion or wrongdoing.

All this allows us to understand that the genuine purpose of Eriugena's work is not as much to abolish the norms of the old (*non-contradictory*) logic as to bring the human mind, and along with it the entire human being, closer to the true reality, where no finite (*one-sided*) things subsist. To the Philosopher, contradiction is not a sign of delusion that reason should avoid on its way to reality, but a proper means of thinking of *the wholeness*, which alone—while spread between the extremes of *being* and *non-being*—is totally appropriate to the true being itself. Understood like this, contradiction becomes for the human mind nothing other than an effective instrument of uncovering *the infinite nature of things* as they genuinely are beyond their one-sided appearance, while belonging to proper (*unconfined*) being and actually participating in it. It is subsequently in this way of bringing the human mind into perfect conformity to the infinite nature of things that contradiction opens up before the "mind's eye" (as Eriugena calls it) the

3. The idea of freedom and existence interconnectedness is essential to any profound ontology. No wonder, therefore, that it echoes even as far as in Jean-Paul Sartre, in whose *Being and Nothing* freedom is defined as a focal point of his anthropological ontology, according to which man is destined to freedom in the sense that "he is either free or he is not" (Sartre, *Бытие и ничто*, 15, 156).

perspective of proper being, and thus allows the whole of human being to approach indeed the true reality of God's creation as it substantially is, ever remaining infinite in itself. For as Eriugena suggests following the Dionysian logic of the *Symbolic Theology* (757c-d), likewise to human nature in its true status "two mutually adverse predicates can be made of God, and can be true and in no way false, . . . as for instance when it is said that 'God is truth' and that 'God is not truth'" (757c). Being thus both *infinite* by their nature God and man meet in their communion, when properly conceived by means of contradiction, according to which "either statement is true" (757d). It is for this reason therefore that those who really come to enjoy this unity in their knowledge of the true being are not improperly said to acquire the name of *the sons of God* (761b).

From this it is fair to conclude that—in order to be appropriate to the reality of the infinite whole—the contradictories may only be predicated of the *uniform subject* in the proper sense of the word. This subject is the one which is no longer considered as something particular opposed to some objects external to it. This subject is *the whole* that perfectly fits the *totality of being* and, as the universal indeed, itself holds particular objects. Therefore, as infinite in-and-for itself that is confined to nothing, this truly uniform subject does exceed any limits in order to embrace the entirety of God's being. And thus the uniform subject really becomes *the true being* that is not only *in itself* but also *for itself*, and is therefore *at one with God* while sharing "the unity of substance with Him" (761a). For as the Principle of all, God likewise is understood to be nothing other than the *Universal Subject* who, while bringing everything forth into being and comprising it, never moves beyond himself but only "from Himself in Himself towards Himself" (453a). In this sense, as Eriugena puts it, the Divine essence "is correctly said to be created in those things which are made by itself and through itself and in itself and for itself" (454c).

This further means that in the true reality as it substantially is there is ultimately nothing save him who is properly thought to be the Beginning and the End of all or "the one Who alone by Himself truly is" (518a). For God is fairly said to be *the One* who "sees in Himself all things that are while He looks upon nothing that is outside Himself, because outside Himself there is nothing" (452c). In other words, in so far as God is truly believed to be *the One*, it has to be admitted that he cannot be just *one among many* (as appropriate to the particular only), but is *infinite* indeed. God is the *universal* Being that is absolutely incompatible with anything finite, and thus indispensably is *one with the whole of creation*, but not opposed to it as to something one-sided and isolated in its independent existence. For coming out of God (i.e., being *of one essence* with him or, using the conventional term, ὁμοούσιον⁴), this creation never actually departs from him with whom it is of the same essence, but ever remains *within* God himself, whose being is fairly defined as "the invisible Unity which is what He Himself is" (520a). All *individual* things therefore substantially are (i.e., participate in the true Being) in so far only as they manifest their *infinite* nature that is *in* and *for* itself. Otherwise, no entity could be really co-essential with the very nature of the Uniform Subject where it takes its origin from to participate in the universe coming out of him. For according to Eriugena, "everything which is said to exist exists not in itself but by participation in the Nature which truly exists" (454a). And only when perceived from the perspective of the *external world* (and not from that of *creation*), these individual things are seen *from outside* and therefore seem to be particular (separate), as appropriate to *the finite* that appears to be torn off the Principle of all beings. As such, they can only be found, as it were, *outside* the universal Being and unable to take part in him who is truly the One—that is, the only and uniform Subject who is countered by nothing separate or opposite.

---

4. About the sacramental formula Ομοουσιον τῳ Πατρι (*co-essential to the Father*) first introduced to Christian dogmatics by Athanasius the Great and adopted by the Church at the Council of Nicaea (325 AD) see, for example, Kartashev, *Вселенские соборы*, 13.

CHAPTER 6

The Doctrine of Knowledge

Two Perspectives on One Reality

AFTER WHAT WAS CONSIDERED in the previous chapter, we may have no difficulty in realising what Eriugena means to suggest when he asserts that God "has created in man all creatures visible and invisible, for the whole spread of creation is understood to inhere in man" (763d). He certainly does not intend to say by this that "bestiality, quadrupedality, volatility and all the differences of the divers animals and of the other things, together with all species and properties and accidents and all the other innumerable attributes" are made in man to be actually present in him (765b). Otherwise, if all the attributes of animality, while "so far removed, were indeed found in man, he would rightly be considered not a man but the foulest of monsters" (765b). Hence, what Eriugena really means to suggest by his assertion is that since all of "this sensible world is fashioned in man" so as to be in its entirety held by his mind (764a), "the whole spread of creation" cannot actually exist apart from being perceived by man as a whole—both by his reason and body, where even "the pupil of the eye, although the least of all the members in physical size, yet exerts the greatest power" (764b). From this it follows therefore that man's grip on the world created extends as far as his rational nature (or, to be precise, *rational motion*) is engaged. Accordingly, "everything which is known by the intellect or the reason or imagined by the sense can somehow be created and produced in the knower and perceiver" (765c). It is consequently in the sense of relation of the entire creation to the human mind that the following words of Eriugena should be understood: "No part of it" (i.e., creation) "is found, either corporeal or incorporeal, which does not subsist by being created in man, which does not perceive through him, which does not live through him, which is not incorporated in him" (764a). Thus, as a focal point of the whole created nature, man is understood to have a chance to know that no finite being exists on its own nor takes its origin from the Principle of all beings that gives rise to nothing finite. It means that anything finite may only be known as an accident appropriate to the subjectivity of human perception. Therefore, to be properly known in its truth (i.e., as a real member of the universe of creation but not as one of the transient things), any particular being must be grasped as it is *beyond its finitude* (or appearance), while coming from the universal Principle of all and remaining in ever-lasting unity with it. In this way man comes to the starting point of his knowledge leading him to the substantial reality of creation: this starting point is a clear vision (available to the "mind's eye") that nothing finite "which is not from God can by any means be understood, because it does not exist in any way" (765a). As Eriugena further suggests, it must be as clear as light that only those things truly exist (and can therefore be properly known) which are from God as the universal Principle, and thereby belong to being or subsist as essences (764d–765a). On the contrary, those things which only relate to essence or substance "are not to be reckoned in the number of the universe of things—in fact are altogether without being . . ." (764d). As a result, knowing things as they truly are, man actually transcends the power of the corporeal senses that insidiously make him imprisoned among finite things. Thus he broadens before his universal (properly ordered) mind the horizon of creation up to the utmost of knowledge of the Very Creator. "Reason then permits us to say," the author of the Periphyseon draws a conclusion, "that God willed to place man in the genus of the animals for this purpose: that He wished to create every creature in him, . . . because He wished to make him in His image and likeness, so that, just as the Primal Archetype transcends all by the excellence of His essence, so His image should transcend all created things in dignity and grace" (764b).

From this it follows that—depending on whether man's attitude to the surrounding world is subject to the sense or to the mind, so that either *finite* objects or *infinite* nature respectively come into focus—one and the same reality of creation may be considered by man from the perspective of two dimensions. "For every creature," says Eriugena in this regard, "is considered under one aspect as it exists in the Word of God in which all things are made, and under another as it exists in itself"[1] (770c). Hence, when considered

---

1. The Latin version of the quotation given reads: "*Aliter enim omnis creatura in verbo dei in quo omnia facta sunt consideratur, aliter in seipsa.*" When in this context *in seipsa* is rendered as "in itself," it should be rather understood in the sense of the

from the perspective of "the Wisdom of God," all things are known according to their substance (or true being), for, as is said, *substantia omnium omnia est* (770c). This is the perspective of reality where the right order of things is established and sustained, so that according to this order the *inner* essence precedes the *outer* existence, and the *universal* cause gives rise to its *singular* effects, but not *vice versa*.[2] By contrast, if "the intellectual and rational creature" assumes—as it further appears from the context at 770c—that it possesses "intelligence of itself" in so far as "it is in itself" (i.e., on its own and, hence, regardless of any relation to God as the source of every being), then the knowledge produced by this creature approaches the same reality from another perspective, according to which all things are seen as externals that seem to subsist on their own. This knowledge, therefore, appears to correspond to something else in addition to (or even instead of) the true being—that is to say, to the so-called "second substance" (770c), different from the "first" one (770c–d) and, at best, co-existing alongside it.

By this we are given to understand that in so far as these "substances" or *two aspects* of one reality are understood in an abstract way to be mutually countered in like manner to the diametrical opposites, then the uniform reality, indivisible by nature, would *seem* to fall apart into different realms, first in the human mind and subsequently in his practical conduct. In consequence of this delusion resulting from the improper use of the mind (by which both the theoretical and practical attitude of all humans to the world is determined), human nature as well appears to be *divided within itself*. "Under one aspect," Eriugena says, "the human substance is perceived as created among the intelligible causes, under the other as generated among their effects; under the former free from all mutability, under the latter subject to change; under the former simple, involved in no accidents, it eludes all created intelligence; under the latter it receives a kind of composition of quantities and qualities and whatever else can be understood in relation to it, whereby it becomes apprehensible to the mind" (771a).

Be it the case however that such a split of reality and human nature were accepted for true so that one substance might be considered under two aspects (771a), the nearest result of this division of the reality of the whole

---

Kantian *Ding an sich*—namely, as a thing that is *on its own* or *by itself* (i.e., without being perceived or conceived) but not in the sense of perfect accordance with its own inner nature. Hence, the "aspects" meant here are those of being *with God* and *without God* ("in itself"), i.e., on its own, as it would appear to the sense. By being *in itself* is therefore meant that, in spite of any changes that occur in the course of perception, an object perceived seems to a perceiver *to exist on its own*, remaining independent of man and safe from his interference

2. In connection with this, see also 770c, especially with regard to what is indicated of the so-called "first" substance.

into the opposite (and therefore mutually confined) counterparts would then be *finite* knowledge. Being solely appropriate to the world that appears to consist of finite things, this kind of knowledge seeks to comprehend *what* individual things are (see 770d) as purely external objects. The major defect of this type of knowledge is however that its intentions are doomed to failure for the simple reason that no finite thing may be known as to *what* it is in itself (770c). Indeed, anything *external* (as it is undoubtedly the case with all finite things) is *concealed* and, as being external, cannot ever disclose *what* it is in itself. Moreover, as *spurious* being confined to *non-being*, nothing finite can truly exist and, because of this, be ever liable to proper understanding. For as is clearly stated at 765a, that which does not exist (i.e., is not seen as coming into being from God and remaining in unity with his infinite nature) can by no means be understood.

Consequently, it has to be admitted that if one and the same universal reality of creation, uniform by nature, is considered from the different perspectives (as appropriate to the aspects indicated above), it appears not only to cleave asunder but also to remain *unknown* in both of its parts. As mutually countered and devoid of their unity, these two parts would appear to be nothing more than just finite realms of spurious being. "So it is," concludes the Philosopher, "that what is one and the same thing can be thought of as twofold because there are two ways of looking at it, yet everywhere it preserves its incomprehensibility, in the effects as in the causes, and whether it is endowed with accidents or abides in its naked simplicity: under neither set of circumstances is it subject to created sense or intellect nor is it understood by itself as to what it is" (771a-b).

Phantasies and Concepts

From the above analysis, it can be further deduced that in so far as the universal reality is understood to be fissioned within itself when considered under the contrary aspects, such a division of reality indispensably entails *two different types of knowledge*. Although these types of knowledge are initiated by the split of reality in two, they do not simply correspond to the mutually opposed realms of being but result from the contrast between the *holistic* and *differentiative* approaches of the mind. This means that the types of knowledge in question are respectively understood to be either *adequate* or *inadequate* to the universal reality as the two essentially different *perspectives* of it, of which only one is able to adhere to the fundamental order of procession of causes into their effects (785d). As a result, depending on whether the reality is considered as *a whole* or as *divided within itself* (so that the inner and the outer, the immanent and the transcendent, and the like seem to set apart as the confronting counterparts), *two different successions of concepts*, as appropriate to the rational and irrational motions of the mind respectively, do come into focus in Eriugena's ongoing discourse. As we may see from Eriugena's statement to follow, these two successions of concepts (while progressing, as is clear from the context below, in the opposite directions) determine two opposite *orders* of the knowledge content and, accordingly, the contrary *types* of it—namely, those of the knowledge *from without* and *from within*:

> . . . the species of sensible things and the quantities and qualities which I reach by my corporeal sense," the author explains, "are in certain way created in me; for when I imprint the phantasies of them in my memory, and when I deal with them within myself by division and comparison and, as it were, collect them into a kind of unity, I notice a certain knowledge of the things which are external to me being built up within me; and in the same way when I seek earnestly within me after certain concepts resembling the intelligible species, concepts of intelligibles which I contemplate with the mind alone, as for example the concept of the liberal arts, I feel them born and becoming within me (765c–d).

From the quotation given above, it may follow that the two types of knowledge, as they are highlighted in it, should be distinguished with a great deal of certainty as the *produced* and the *prior* (concerning the latter see also 779c). Indeed, when on the one side knowledge appears to follow the corporeal (exterior) senses and is provided by their perceptions of externals (which despite being "built up" in man, remain external both to a knowing subject and to one another as merely discrete objects), such knowledge inevitably becomes *fashioned after the exterior sense* or, in other words, *formed from without*. At the same time, on the other side, in so far as knowledge does not refer to the corporeal senses as to a reliable source of information concerning "the species of sensible things" nor does it take its beginning from these senses (and to this extent evolves independently of them[3]), this knowledge proves *to rise from within* or, as the Philosopher puts it, to be *born* from the human mind (765d). Accordingly, the former kind of knowledge entirely relies upon the senses; and though the bulk of it is said to result from such mental operations as division, comparison and

---

3. This *independent* status of knowledge is definitely the case, according to Eriugena, with the *liberal arts*, which not unreasonably should be thought of (in the framework of his discourse, at least) as the *cognitive faculties* of the *independent* (liberated) mind.

collection (765c), this sort of knowledge may yet be only understood as no more than the *sensible* one that proceeds from the sensible phantasies, and in this respect it apparently comes to be a *produced* (or made) one. On the contrary, when conceived *to precede* the exterior (corporeal) senses (see 766b–c) so as in accordance with the *rational motion* of the mind to discipline and rule them for the purpose of gaining a perfect conformity to the truly infinite nature of things, this kind of knowledge turns out in effect to be the *intelligible* or the *prior*[4] one (see 776a–b; 779b–c). It is the latter therefore that comes forth from the innermost depth of the mind to be thus perfectly appropriate to the inwardly infinite nature of things as they truly are. And it is by this type of proper knowledge that both the human mind and being are brought to conformity to the fundamentally right order of the universe of creation, where the inner precedes the outer, and the universal causes the singular, but not *vice versa*.

As for the difference between the *successions of concepts* as they pertain to the types of knowledge distinguished above, it ought to be explained likewise by "the relation between this knowledge and the things themselves which are its object" (765d). This particularly means that the difference sought fully depends on the *order* in which knowledge and its object occur to the mind. If knowledge places its object among the things as they are immediately given to the sense and, for this reason, is commonly believed to derive from the things themselves (or their images imprinted in memory), then knowledge like this provides the mind with a concept which proves in fact to be nothing more than just a *replica* of the things seen from outside or a *phantasy*. For as rightly said at 765d, the corporeal species of a certain animal, grass or tree cannot be of the same nature with the knowledge of them produced by the incorporeal nature. To confirm this crucial point of his doctrine of knowledge, Eriugena refers to the word of authority found in Augustine, from whose monumental treatise *On the Trinity* (Book 9, chapter 11, as the author scrupulously indicates, underlining thus the importance of the point made) he quotes as follows: "'When we learn of bodies through the sense of the body, a certain replica of the bodies is created in our mind: this is a phantasy in our memory. For it is certainly not the bodies themselves that are in our mind when we reflect on them, but replicas of them'" (766a).

On the other hand, if knowledge does not associate its object with individual things but finds it among the universal concepts of the mind,

---

4. To the extent that a certain affinity between the basic principles of Eriugena's and Kant's systems may be acknowledged, it would be beneficial for a better understanding of both thinkers to note that the *prior* and *produced* forms of knowledge, as they come to the fore in the course of Eriugena's speculation, could be fairly qualified in the Kantian terms as *a priori* and *aposteriori* knowledge respectively.

then this knowledge results in understanding of what the *concept proper* is. Similarly to replicas, the concept of this knowledge is likewise said to differ from the things themselves, though not as their obscure images but as being *more exalted* than them (766a). This difference, therefore, is of another kind—namely, not that of a phantasy which is torn off the things and merely resembles them, but that of discrepancy between what is defined to be of a *better* nature (766b, 776a) and those things which are straightforwardly seen as the *sensibles* only. "For it is a doctrine according to reason," Eriugena admits, "that that which understands is better than that which is understood" (766b). Indeed, as he further argues, being the knowledge of all things the Divine Wisdom is "incomparably superior to the things of which it is the knowledge. And if so, I believe that the same relationship proceeds from the Divine providence throughout all creation, so that not only every nature which has a concept of that which follows it is better and superior, but also the concept itself, through the dignity of the nature in which resides, greatly excels the object of which it is the concept" (766b).

All this gives us to understand that what is thought to be of a *better* nature is actually meant to be *closer to Good* as such, which consists—as the course of the entire inquiry shows—in nothing other than the universal *Self-identity* as *the perfect accordance of the inner essence with its outer existence*. Thus the infinite itself (i.e., the whole of the Divine reality as the living Spirit who alone everywhere explicitly is what he implicitly is in himself) comes to be actually manifest through this self-identical Good and the Concept, as its adequate form, which in its ultimate status is *Logos*. For God is the One, and there is no discrepancy between him as the Creator (the Supreme and Universal Cause) and the outcome of his creation (the effect of the Cause), between what he wills and what he does—so that, what he wants or says to be, exactly that (and nothing else) comes to be. That is why the Philosopher later points out at 786b with regard to the Genesis account (Gen 1:4–31) that "in the text 'God saw the light that it was good' the Holy Spirit is intended, as also on the other days" (of creation) "wherever it is added 'And God saw that it was good.'"

Thus, unlike phantasies, concepts are to be understood not to derive from sensible things, as would be the case with purely abstract forms. Conversely, being as *exalted* over things themselves as the *universal* truly is in relation to the singular, concepts, according to Eriugena, *precede* all things, so that even "the concept of the intelligibles precedes the intelligibles themselves" (766b). And if in continuity with this, as he further suggests, it could be, for instance, argued with regard to the *liberal arts* that their concept "was not formed from the arts, but the arts from the concept," the argument would be running then along the right lines (766c). It is subsequently in this way that, forming all things but being not formed by them (766c), the concept as such—understood as "a kind of multiple source of inexhaustible depth" (770a)—constitutes indeed the very basis of the *prior* knowledge that comes forth, as said before, from the innermost nature of the mind and is found to be in conformity to the inwardly infinite nature of things.

From this it follows therefore that the concept as such may be understood to be *different* from things only in so far as they are taken *on their own* as sensible objects, which merely seem to subsist by themselves. However, if the same things are properly considered as they truly are in their inwardly infinite nature that comes forth from the Supreme Cause of all, then the true concept, while defined as exalted over all things, turns out to be *universal* by nature. And thus, like the prior knowledge initiated by it, this properly understood concept proves to be appropriate to the infinite nature of things as they are perspicuously seen through it according to their reasons (769c) and, in this sense, implicitly contained by this concept.

As a result, all things *as they appear to man in the light of their true being*, which is solely attainable by virtue of knowledge or "the perspicuous vision of all things," should be fairly acknowledged to be *established in the human mind* (769b). This means that not only the animals (or "every living soul"), but also the things "which nature contains besides the animals, such as the elements of the world, the genera and species of grasses and trees, quantities and qualities, and all the innumerable multitude of differentiations" (769b) come to subsist, as Eriugena specifies, "in the notions of them contained in the soul of the wise" (769d). "For where they are comprehended," the author adds, "there they are; and they are nothing other than the understanding of themselves" (769d). And this is reasonably so; for in accordance with Gen 2:19, all living creatures are supposed to receive from man the names proper to their nature (as due to "the very concept of the living soul"), which the Philosopher understands to be the way man enters the substantial reality of creation that the Holy Scripture itself clearly points to (768d–769a).

All this, from Eriugena's point of view, may be summed up as follows: "True knowledge of all these is implanted in human nature, although it is concealed from her that she has it until she is restored to her pristine and integral condition, in which with all clarity she will understand the magnitude and the beauty of the image that is fashioned within her, and will no longer be in ignorance of anything which is established within; for she will be encompassed by the Divine Light and turned towards God in Whom she will enjoy the perspicuous vision of all things" (769b–c). Hence, unlike the image as a replica of things that is imprinted in the mind of man after they have been perceived by his corporeal senses, the Concept is to be understood as the true Image which is fashioned in human nature after the Supreme Being himself so as not to come from without (inasmuch as nothing can subsist outside the true being) but to be inborn from within. And being thus innate in the human mind, this Concept opens before man the perspective of the true reality of God's creation to let him be properly in it or, as is said, restore his nature to the dignity of her "pristine and integral condition."

With regard to what has been revealed of the concept as such and the true knowledge as a clear vision of the nature of things, it may be counted for certain that the "inner concept which is contained in the human mind constitutes the substance of those things of which it is the concept . . ." (770a). "What is so remarkable then," the Philosopher refers to those puzzled by this, "if the concept of nature, created in the human mind and possessed by it, is understood to be the substance of the very things of which it is the concept, just as in the Divine Mind the concept of the whole created universe is the incommunicable substance of that whole?" (769a). According to Eriugena, there is nothing extraordinary in this understanding of the concept to be puzzled by. For just as we may call "the concept of all intelligibles and sensibles in the whole of things" to be "the substance of those intelligibles and sensibles," so we may also say "that the concept of the differences and properties and natural accidents are the differences and the properties and accidents themselves" (769a-b). Likewise, as the author further underlines, even "the concept by which man knows himself may be considered his very substance" (770a).

By no means should the true concept be understood therefore as merely an *abstract* form. The concept cannot be reduced to a purely cerebral phenomenon contrasted both with the rest of the human nature and reality itself. Otherwise, human nature would be relegated to nothing more than the corporeal side of it (i.e., to such of its physiological functions as sensation brought about by bodily senses), and reality would simply appear then to consist of a number of sensible objects only. In fact, as a *concrete* form which perfectly fits reality as such while embracing the whole of it without residue, the proper concept determines the human being *as a whole* so as to effectively control all parts of his nature, including both the mind and the sense and the body itself. And only as such, the concept—"through contact with the 'variable object . . .'" (769d) mediated by the sense, fully disciplined and guided by this concept—constitutes indeed the totality of things in all particular details of their differences, properties and accidents as they are perspicuously seen from the perspective of the integral mind. That is why, in line with this, Eriugena later adds with confidence: ". . . for the soundest reason teaches us in no uncertain way that one man, alone, is greater than the whole visible world, not by the bulk of his parts but by the dignity of the harmony of his rational nature" (784c).

From this it follows that to the extent that the phantasy is controlled by the mind subject to the inner concept, it turns into what Eriugena calls the *interior sense* (see 787c). This is the sense that rises from the midst of man's rational nature and thereby essentially differs from the *exterior* one.

Crucial to the distinct types of knowledge discussed above, this difference between the exterior and the interior sense allows us not only to distinguish the opposite types of senses but also to indicate the *diametrically opposed perspectives of the mind*. These are the perspectives that Eriugena describes at 783c–784c by means of an allegorical interpretation of the celestial luminaries as they appear in the Genesis account (Gen 1:14–19), presenting them as sense-related metaphors.

In particular, with relation to "the larger luminary" Eriugena is quite certain that, in his view, it appears to symbolize the sense which announces to the mind "without danger of error the species of the sensibles," so that "with the greatest ease and without labor the mind is able to form unclouded judgments upon these species in all clarity" (783c). This means that, by analogy with the sun, this kind of sense might be unequivocally associated with a centrifugal motion of the rational nature that, led by the central luminary of the mind, goes along its rays. So that, when illuminated by the intelligible light, this sense penetrates into the darkness of the unknown so as to actually see things as they truly are; "for it does not deceive the mind, but with all the brightness of the sun uncovers every sensible species and lays them bare before the reason" (783d).

As for "the lesser luminary" (i.e., the moon that lights not by itself but with reflected rays), it reminds the Philosopher that mode of sensation which receives impulses from without and, because of this, often deceives the mind, "as though wandering uncertainly through some nocturnal dusk" (784a). This comparison allows him to clearly demonstrate that, instead of focusing on things as they truly are, the mind is deceived and misled by the exterior senses, due to which it deals in fact with some obscure phenomena of sensual origin that only seem to stand for the things themselves. As it further follows from the context at 784a, among these deceptions of the mind such examples may be counted as "the oar which appears to be broken when it is dipped in water," or "the reversed face in the mirror," or "towers which appear to those sailing to move," "and a thousand other illusions of this sort, which are found naturally in all the senses of the body" (784a). This therefore entails that as long as submitted to the sense undisciplined and thus fully dependent on its hectic impressions of outer things, the mind "cannot easily form true judgments upon objects which it receives through sense" (784a). "And the rational soul, when forming its judgments," the author concludes, "must employ the greatest skill and utmost industry to distinguish these from true appearances. For these have no existence in nature, but are formed in the senses and frequently deceive the mind and put it into the error of taking false things for true" (784a).

And finally, as for the opinions of the mind that are formed by it under the impact of the exterior sense, they are not the mind's own ideas, but the ones which in all their particular details entirely derive from sensual perceptions. And though elaborated and possessed by the mind so as to seem to have some relevance to the inner senses, this sort of innumerable opinions prove yet to be basically sensible (but not intelligible) by their content, as due to those of the *external* origin. In the light of such an understanding, therefore, the sense-related experience appears to Eriugena "under the metaphor of the stars of different brilliancies" (784c). For according to him, when numbers of sensible forms are poured into the mind through the senses, it "attempts by means of certain logical processes to make statements which will to some extent resemble the truth, and to be certain about things which are themselves uncertain. And it disputes about the minutest reasons of visible nature in various ways: sometimes offering opinions which, like bright stars, show a degree of clarity and proximity to the truth . . ." (784b).

Two Types of Knowledge

The results of the preceding inquiry could be summarized as follows:

Knowledge

Produced	Prior
subject to the sense and fashioned after it;	independent of the sense while preceding and leading it;
proceeds from without—from the exterior sense: its concept is the image—replica or phantasy—of sensible things (formed by abstraction of the diverse attributes[5]);	proceeds from within, i.e., rises from the midst of the mind: its concept is the image of God (based on the universal principle of self-identity to be appropriate to the infinite nature of being[6]);
accommodates human mind (and, through it, man himself) to the sensible world.	introduces human mind (and, through it, the whole of human being) into the reality of creation.

5. As it appears from 769c, among these may be counted, for example, qualities, quantities, forms, magnitudes, smallnesses, equalities, conditions, acts, dispositions, places, times, etc.

6. Since, in Eriugena's conviction, the true concept (that is appropriate to the infinite being) constitutes all things according to their substance of which it is the concept, it indispensably follows from this that "the concept by which man knows himself may

Thus, it is seen from the above that the proper concept—as it appears in relation to the *prior* knowledge which enables the mind to contemplate all things as they truly are—constitutes the basis of the *true knowledge* that is all about the infinite nature of the universe of God's creation. Being actually *inborn* or "implanted in human nature" (769b), this true knowledge nevertheless remains hidden from man until he is restored to his "pristine and integral condition" (769b).[7] In this condition "with all clarity" man would be able to understand "the magnitude and the beauty of the image that is fashioned within" him, so as not to be any longer "in ignorance of anything which is established within," but to enjoy in the Divine Light "the perspicuous vision of all things" (769c). Hence, only restored to the pristine and integral state of his being in the original and ultimate reality of God's creation (which is ever the absolute one), man does find himself to be "encompassed by the Divine Light" or, in other words, to be able to see in the perspective of this Light, so as truly to know all things as they substantially are. Thereby, through the true knowledge of things according to their substance or infinite nature (i.e., when causes and their effects are comprehended to be one), man actually enters the true reality of creation, where the absolute essence and its existence are inseparably one. In this sense, therefore, to gain true knowledge by virtue of comprehension of the proper nature of concept[8] means in fact nothing other than to reach the true reality itself and

---

be considered his very substance" (770a). And this is rightly so; because just as the concept as such inaugurates all things in their true status, likewise the mind and its proper concept—as the very essence of human nature—undoubtedly determine man's true being. In this way, the inner essence of his proper nature comes to perfectly accord with its outer existence, as the principle of self-identity universal to the entire substantial reality requires it of necessity. With regard to this, it would be quite fair to remind of "an extremely true and very well tested definition of man" (768b) that the author of the *Periphyseon* gives: "We may then define man as follows: Man is a certain intellectual concept formed eternally in the Divine Mind" (768b). This definition of man "as he is intellectually comprehended to be" (768b), which Eriugena himself calls *substantial*, apparently contrasts with any other unsubstantial ones that do not define the human being itself but only describe its accidents or, in other words, "what relates to the substance from the attributes acquired by the substance from outside itself through generation" (768c); as it, for example, does when Eriugena suggests that "man is a rational mortal animal capable of sense and discipline" (768c).

7. This is the point at which Eriugena's understanding of the innate knowledge would considerably differ from the empiricists' approach to it. Thus *John Locke*, for instance, assumed that if any ideas were innate, they would be available to *everyone* and *everywhere*. By contrast, in accordance with Eriugena's vision the innate concepts (and the knowledge based on them) become available to man's mind not until the entirety of his nature is restored to its true integral state (i.e., to the unity of essence and existence).

8. This cognitive task will become the prime concern of the philosophical comprehension in the system of Hegel to ensure the further progress in philosophical studies to come.

to be actually in it, when the whole of human nature (including the body itself) is brought to what it is genuinely meant to be by its very concept. "For there is innate in him" (i.e., in *man*) "intellect and reason, as well as the innate principle of possession of the celestial and angelic body," Eriugena explains, "which after the Resurrection shall appear more clearly than light . . .; for it will be common to all human nature to rise again in eternal and incorruptible spiritual bodies" (764a). It is subsequently for this purpose that man is supposed *to bring his essence* (the inner nature of his true being) *into accordance with his actual existence*, which unequivocally implies that he *must live according to the mind* that is deeply hidden in him and really constitutes the profound essence of his nature. For this, man's intellect is strictly forbidden "to cherish visible forms" in order that he could be, in the words of St. Paul, "not fashioned after this world" (780d). And to achieve this goal, the mind is to be carefully *cleansed* of any impressions it receives from the *corporeal senses*. For as Eriugena argues, is it not obvious to any true philosopher

> that this sensible world was created for the sake of man, that he might rule it as a king rules his kingdom and as a husband his household, and that he might use it to the glory of his Creator, subordinated to no part of it, in no way dependent on it, but raised above it ruling it alone? For if man had not sinned" (i.e., submitted himself to the power of senses) "he would not be ruled among the parts of the universe, but would himself rule the whole of it as his subject; and he would not employ for that purpose these corporeal senses of the mortal body, but would govern eternally and faultlessly the whole and the parts of it in accordance with the laws of God, without any physical act in space or time, but solely by the rational apprehension of its natural and innate causes and by the easy use of right will. (782b–c)

As a result of the complete purification of the mind that is effectively carried out by its submission to *the substantial order* of the universe of creation (which the true Law of God consists in), a rigorous *discipline* of this submission comes to be imposed upon the mind's *skills* (or faculties) referred to the particular targets, which in fact are nothing other than its potential *manifestations*. And in consequence of this, the *exterior* sense proves to be replaced by the *interior* one—that is the sense which is *ruled from within* when illuminated by the mind's light or, to be precise, controlled and led by it, as due to the *rational motion* of human nature. Through this *transformation of the sense*, mind *truly comes to manifest itself*. Through the ability of *inner sight* acquired thereby, it comes to see all things *from within*, and thus enters the substantial reality, where all things subsist *according to their proper nature.* "Just as the Creative Wisdom, which is the Word of God," Eriugena expounds, "beholds all things which are made in It before they are made, and that very beholding of all things which are beheld before they are made is their true and eternal and immutable essence, so the created wisdom, which is human nature, knows all things which are made in it before they are made, and that very knowledge of the things which are known before they are made is their true and indestructible essence" (778d–779a). And further he concludes:

> We can then sum up everything that we have been trying to teach briefly as follows: Just as the understanding of all things which the Father made in His only begotten Word is their essence and is the substance of all those attributes which are understood to be attached by nature to that essence; so the knowledge of all things which the Word of the Father has created in the human soul is their essence and the substance of all those attributes which are discerned to be attached by nature to the essence: and just as the Divine intellect is prior to all things and is all things, so the intellectual knowledge of the soul is prior to all the things which she knows and is all the things which she fore-knows. (779b–c)

Since "the knowledge in the Creative Wisdom is itself rightly held to be the primary and causal essence of the whole of creation," whereas "the knowledge in the created nature" is considered by contrast as "the secondary essence" that "subsists as the effect of the higher knowledge," (779a) all things due to this are believed to "subsist as causes in the Divine understanding, but as effects in human knowledge" (779c). It does not however mean, according to Eriugena, that "the essence of all things in the Word is something other than the essence of all things in man, but one and the same essence is contemplated by the mind under two different aspects, as subsisting in the eternal Causes, and as understood in its effects . . ." (779c). It is consequently apparent from this that—being *one* in the true reality or *reconciled* in "one and the same essence"—causes and effects should not be *separated* in the true knowledge. Otherwise, if they are considered by the human understanding separately (i.e., as *only* the causes and as *only* the effects), neither of them can be known at all; for as said, nothing *finite* is permitted to be known (see 779c). Subsequently, to be *true* (i.e., appropriate to the reality as it truly is), human knowledge must resolutely approach the *inseparable*, and thus the *infinite* as such. And for this purpose, the perspective of knowledge (which is that of "the created wisdom") must *perfectly concur with the substantial order* of the Creative Wisdom or, in other words, be as *prior* to all things as "the higher knowledge" is. For as Eriugena maintains, an accurate examination of the universal nature clearly shows that "whatever circumstance attaches to the substances in the human intelligence," it "proceeds through the created wisdom from the knowledge of the Creative Wisdom" (779b).

All this should convince students of Eriugena's thought that the mind, as it truly is in accordance with its innermost essence, comes to be manifest in man when it is purified from the sensible phantasies, and the universal *self-identity* inherent in the reality of creation *is properly thought of*. This is, clearly, achievable not so much by means of ascetic practices of wrestling with the flesh but by virtue of a thorough application of the fundamental principle of self-identity to the task of *comprehension of causes and effects in their proper unity.*[9] Indeed, it is the mind's self-discipline provided by an effective use of *dialectic* that allows man, as discussed above, to really resist the sway of the corporeal senses correspondent to finite (sensible) things only. It is consequently by means of dialectic, becoming thus an art of living in the true reality, that a proper distinction between the *exterior* and the *interior* sense is brought about to give birth to the *inner sight*, which opens to man the reality in which all things are perspicuously seen as they subsist according to their reasons. Purified thereby, the mind itself becomes adequately manifest in its true wholeness, due to which the senses are not merely neglected and discarded but disciplined and led by the mind.

This *dialectic* therefore proves in fact to be nothing else but precisely that *discipline* of the mind which leads it to its *proper condition*. In this condition, while preceding all particular things, the mind actively forms them, using the concepts innate in it. For it is, no doubt, these concepts that really enable the human mind to clearly see all things *according to their proper self-identical nature*, in which the universal essence of all particular things and their actual existence are at one. Thus, as Eriugena further argues (see 766d–767b), the mind comes to be understood as being brought into accordance with its constructive *skill* and *discipline*, which are not accidents to it but the "substantial and constituent parts." For, in so far as the image and likeness of God (that is, human nature) is thought to be created not by

9. Surprisingly or not, in *Zen Buddhism* likewise (as probably in any other esoteric doctrine that similarly sets itself a task of bringing man to a perfect harmony with his true nature), *the unity of causes and their effects* is traditionally treated as nothing but the *gateway* into the Ultimate Reality. Thus, as Hacuin's *Song on Meditation* (that is crucial to the ordinance of preparation for the lectures in the Buddhist monasteries) particularly reads, "the gate of unity of causes and effects opens before them" (i.e., the seekers), "and they enter upon the straight way, on which nothing dual nor triple can be found" (Suzuki, *Основы Дзэн-Буддизма*, 269).

accident but by substance (767c), its *skill* and *the discipline* are not accidents to the mind, but "are naturally present to it" (767c). "For although," the Philosopher continues, "through the accident of its transgression of the Divine command whereby it became forgetful both of itself and its Creator, the mind is born unskilled and unwise, yet when it is reformed by the rules of doctrine it may discover again in itself its God and itself and its skill and the discipline and all those things which subsist in it according to its nature . . ." (767c). And thus the mind, its skill and the discipline will form "a kind of trinity in one essence" (767d).

"A Doctrine According to Reason"

In connection with the preceding analysis of the *Periphyseon's* text, it is not hard to understand that the *doctrine* mentioned above, in accordance with which the mind is meant to be reformed to uncover its proper nature, is nothing other than "a doctrine according to reason" (766b). This is the doctrine which consists in teaching about *the intimate proximity of the intelligible nature to the universally self-identical Good.* According to this doctrine, as previously seen, "that which understands is better than that which is understood" (766b), and hence is *nearer to Good.* As discussed before, this Good is to be properly understood as the Divine being in its *self-identity* or as the *self-knowing* Spirit. Being thus ever in and for himself, never departing from himself but remaining within himself throughout everything so as to know himself (or to see himself from within) as the universal Good, this Spirit of God has nothing inside nor outside himself to counter him, and thus to disrupt his being or to cause any deficiency in him. Likewise, the human mind in order to be true (i.e., appropriate to the true reality) is supposed to arrive at its own self-identity, which brings it close to the infinite being of the Spirit of God who truly knows himself as the universal Good.

From the "doctrine according to reason" it is clear therefore that the human being comes to conformity with the substantial reality of creation in so far as the human mind, brought into harmony with its own nature, attains *knowledge of itself.* As a form of overcoming the finitude of all individual things brought together into the unity of the universal concept, the mind's *self-knowledge* becomes a means of the restoration of man's wholeness and, consequently, of his *participation* in the substantial reality of the whole. It is indeed by knowing himself as a universal being, who thoroughly understands all things as they truly are, that man actually becomes identical to himself and, thereby, a *participant* in the universal reality. In this sense, it is right to say after Eriugena that, when restored to its

Good-like self-identity by virtue of self-knowledge, "the human mind, and its concept by which it knows itself, and the discipline by which it learns itself so as to know itself, subsist in one and the same essence" (770b). Understood thereby as the true being of human nature *identical to itself in all of its essential manifestations*, this "one and the same essence" should further be known as *Spirit* to whom, where appropriate, Eriugena refers throughout his discourse as a fair definition of human being. "For no one knows," the Philosopher holds, "what things are in man, save the Spirit of man which is in him" (770a). This consequently means that becoming infinite and universal through his self-knowledge, man actually encounters the self-knowing Spirit of God, who likewise is "one and the same essence" that embraces the entire being of creation.

Thus the notion of "one and the same essence," as it occurs in this context, seems to be central to Eriugena's discourse concerning the issue of encounter of the human and God's Spirit. Indeed, in the light of the *uniformity of essence*, the *Spirit* of man and the Spirit of *God* can hardly be understood as *two* remote entities merely co-existing as the different substances; rather they should be known, as the very notion requires, as "one and the same essence." For it is undeniably true that the *absolute* being is *indivisible* within itself and, being essentially *one*, cannot consist of *separate* (isolated) parts. In the absolute reality, the infinite God cannot be set apart from his creation so as to look upon it from afar as if something alien to him. With reference to this it is right to admit, following Eriugena, that "if every creature whether visible or invisible is in itself most perfectly created and since the Creator is perfect and more-than-perfect, it cannot be believed that He has created anything that is imperfect . . ." (775d).

All this consequently means that in the reality of "one and the same essence" any particular being can properly subsist, and therefore be truly known, as *the infinite* only. And although these issues (of uniformity and infinity) "seem to be extremely difficult since they pass beyond the limit of simple doctrine" (774b), nevertheless the Philosopher assures that whoever "looks intently into the nature of things will soon find that this is the way in which they are constituted" (775b).

Knowing the Infinite

If it is assumed that—in order to be self-identical (or to know himself)—man must know all things *as they truly are*, this certainly does not imply that these things ought to be known *in themselves* as a sort of individual beings immediately taken *by themselves*. For when regarded on their own (so as to appear to exist independently of the causes of their being), any things prove to be impenetrable and therefore utterly incomprehensible as to *what* they are. In contrast to this incomprehensibility in their *finitude*, all things nevertheless may be really known as they truly are when conceived of *in their relation to the infinite nature* (which is both the Ultimate Cause and the inner essence of their being), and thus understood as belonging to the *true being* that ever is and never ceases to be. It is consequently by knowing things not as to *what* they are but that they *are,* that man actually cleaves to the substantial reality of God's creation proper, where all things are necessarily self-identical while retaining their living link with the true infinite nature and strictly following the fundamental order of it. Being actually the knowledge of the infinite as such, *dialectic* therefore is of great help to man on this way to the reality as it truly is.

As is said at 771b, when a contradiction concerning man's knowledge of all things (and accordingly of himself) arises, it is hard to decide for sure whether man knows all things (and, as a result, himself) or not. An instrument that man has at his disposal to master such contradictions and ensure his progress to truth is *dialectic.* Thus in particular, if on the one hand the human mind appears to know itself, whereas on the other does not, then according to dialectic, as previously discussed, either part of such a collision the mind comes into ought to be treated as *equally true.* "Both assertions," Eriugena argues with regard to this, "have the full support of reason. For the human mind does know itself, and again does not know itself. For it knows that it is, but does not what it is" (771b). It would be fair to conclude from this that it is a dialectical treatment of the contradiction in question (leading to the unity of opposites) "which reveals most clearly the image of God to be in man" (771b). Indeed, in so far as the opposed statements are grasped in their unity (but not in an *"either-or"* manner), the human mind is enabled thereby to conceive of the wholeness as appropriate to the unconfined infinity. And this integrity of the opposites becomes for man the way of approaching the universal nature of his being, which is never confined to *non-being* and therefore perfectly accords with the infinite nature of him who ever *is* and never ceases to be. "For just as God is comprehensible in the sense that it can be deduced from His creation that He is,"[10] the Philosopher

10. This assertion of Eriugena's should by no means be interpreted in the manner of the scholastic arguments for the existence of God, such as a *design* argument and alike (especially those of the cosmological and teleological ones). What Eriugena means to suggest here has obviously nothing to do with an abstract way of reasoning in favour of so-called "arguments," which are supposed to postulate God's being. In particular, seeking to give human mind logical evidence of the reality of God as a superior being that causes all other things, this sort of reasoning—be it Anselm's speculation on ideally great quantities or Aristotelian contemplation of causal sequences (elaborated by

insists, "and incomprehensible because it cannot be comprehended by any intellect whether human or angelic nor even by Himself what he is, seeing that He is not a thing but is superessential; so to the human mind it is given to know one thing only, that it is—but as to what it is no sort of notion is permitted it" (771b–c).

It is clear from this that a contradiction concerning man's self-knowledge requires a *dialectical* way of its treatment. It particularly means that none of the contrary statements, in so far as each is taken *in contrast to the other*, could be chosen as true. When, however, dialectically considered as being simultaneously in their integrity, *both* counterparts of the contradiction should be accepted for being true at the same time. In this sense, therefore, it is *equally right* to say after Eriugena about human self-knowledge as follows:

Man does know himself;

Man does not know himself.

In this way, the Philosopher intends to suggest that, from the dialectical point of view, it is impossible to say of man that he *only* knows himself or *only* does not know himself. According to the integral approach to human

---

Aquinas into "five ways" of reflection on the Divine) or Paley's observation of the design apparent in the universe—appeals in fact to the experience of the senses. The finite ideas that this sort of reasoning employs for argumentation prove actually to be induced from sensual perceptions (always particular by nature) and therefore fit the sensible world only, but not the superior being of the infinite and eternal. As for Eriugena's argument that it can be deduced from the creation that God is, the *Periphyseon's* context convinces everyone who looks intently into the matter that it does not mean at all to affirm that *a* God exists "*elsewhere*" solely because "*here*" (within the mind's grasp) there is a creation that needs its cause or designer. When Eriugena says that God's being can be deduced from his creation, he rather implies to maintain that the proper *being* of God is to be necessarily thought of in its *inseparable unity* with the whole creation. For only when dialectically understood as opposed to nothing different, God may really be known as he truly *is*, while coming to himself in everything singular and thereby actually asserting himself as ever-lasting universal being that is confined to nothing finite or, more specifically, diffuses itself in no individual things but remains the unfathomable (i.e., or infinitely self-identical) source of their existence. All this consequently means that, according to Eriugena's way of argumentation (implicitly present in the words quoted, but explicitly evident in the context as a whole), the necessary being of God might only be properly known in so far as he were dialectically conceived of as *one* and *all* at the same time. Likewise, Nicholas of Cusa later sought to express the same idea by means of mathematical allusions when posited that God may be not unreasonably thought of as being the *centre* and the *circumference* at the same time. For further reading see, for example, Hegel's *Lectures on the Arguments for the Existence of God*, which apparently gives a classical pattern of refutation of any attempts of abstract reasoning to "prove" God's existence (see Hegel, Философия религии, Т. 2, 337–467).

being which alone is appropriate to the wholeness of the true being as such, man may only be properly known when dialectically understood to know *and* not to know himself at the same time. And this is truly so; because, as Eriugena specifies at 771b,

> The human mind does know *that it is,*
>
> but does not know *what* it is.

This consequently means that in order to know himself as he truly is in accordance with his proper nature, man must *conceive of his being* as the *infinite* one. This further entails that everything finite—when taken by itself in contrast to the infinite—should be regarded as irrelevant to man's proper being and therefore rejected as the *untrue* predicate of it. Hence, in order to really know that he *is*—that is to say, *truly* is (while never disrupted by *non-being*)—man must resolutely deny any finite knowledge of himself or, better to say, any knowledge of himself as a finite being. That is why, as appears from the second half of the contradiction presented at 771b, the human mind is unequivocally said not to know *what* it is, i.e., not to know itself as anything *finite,* that is limited by something other and therefore seen, as it were, from without as a particular "what." And it cannot be otherwise, because—in contrast to the Aristotelian approach[11]—nothing at all may be truly known as to *what* it is. For strictly speaking, *it is definitely impossible to know anything finite at all.* Even God himself, as confirmed at 771b, is understood not to know *what* he is. Indeed, nothing finite can be thought of otherwise than in the way of being *confined to its limit,* resulting from its encounter with *something other.* Being thus in its existence dependent on *the other,* no finite thing can ever be understood to subsist *in a true way,* so as in its outer existence to be *an adequate manifestation of the inner essence.* Nothing finite can actually pertain to *being*: remaining within its own limits, it is always fraught with *negation,* and therefore burdened with *non-being.*

Since Spinoza it is well known that *omnis determinatio est negatio.* Everything finite, according to this, inevitably turns into its opposite. Likewise truth, in so far as it is understood to be limited (or appropriate to the finite only), inevitably turns into *falsehood.* To remain itself, truth must be appropriate to the *infinite* alone. It means that only *the infinite itself* can be the genuine object of the true knowledge or, in terms of the above contradiction, the knowledge of "*that it is*" type.

---

11. Common belief normally appeals to the Aristotelian understanding of definition (*Metaphysics* 1031a), according to which it should take shape of a statement "what a thing is" (Aristotle, *Сочинения,* 194–95).

From this it follows that only that which *truly subsists*, but not merely appears to exist when perceived by senses, can be really known. And although it seems natural to popular sentiment to know not the infinite but finite things only, which are immediately given to the sensual perception (and for this reason seem to lie within the mind's grasp), in fact only that which is coherently conceived as being infinite in-and-for itself can actually be *known* and therefore *belong to the true reality* that is inseparably one with the universal and infinite Principle of all being. Despite common belief's fear of infinity as something incomprehensible, the infinite being cannot in fact remain *unknown*. The true reality cannot merely hide itself, as if it were something non-existent. On the contrary, it actually exists by *revealing* itself (i.e., unfolding its unfathomable depth), as due to the Uniform Subject.[12] The problem therefore is in the mind's conformity to the reality like this. In its proper state of *likeness* to the substantial reality of God's creation, the mind is supposed to be universal and infinite too. It is consequently this *proper nature* of the human mind that is to be uncovered. Through the mind's *discipline* of self-identity and *skill* of being perfectly congruous to the infinite reality, the whole of human nature, as due to *imago Dei*, comes to conformity to the true Being that ever *is* and never *ceases* to be.

Thus, it follows of necessity that the statement that man's being is *infinite* (i.e., the affirmation that it *is*) does not yet express the infinity itself, unless it comes to collision with the opposite statement, according to which man is just a finite being or, in other words, a particular "*what.*" Indeed, as a real target of contradiction, the infinity (or proper being) is not anything individual only: it cannot be merely declared to be *this* or *that*, nor indicated to take place *here* or *there*, for it is neither seen *from without* as a particular "what" nor placed next to anything *other*. Hence, the infinity cannot be properly conceived of and therefore truly affirmed without *the true negation* of all finitude, when everything individual is perfectly grasped with regard to "an extremely true and very well tested" *substantial definition* (768b–c). This is the definition through which nothing but *the true being* reveals itself by the complete denial of "what relates to the substance from the attributes acquired by the substance from outside itself through generation" (768c). According to this *substantial definition*, appropriate to the *substance* as "the true existence" (774a), man's proper being "cannot be called by this or that name, for it stands above all definitions and all groupings of parts, for it can only be predicated of it that it is, not what it is. For that alone is what a truly substantial definition does: it asserts only that it is, but does not say what it is" (768c).

12. On the Uniform Subject, see chapter 5.

This means that the infinite can only be known when all the knowledge of the finite (i.e., of every individual "what") is *negated*. The *true affirmation*, which alone is adequate to the infinite reality, may therefore result from the *true negation* only, that is by its nature nothing but *overcoming* all *finitude* (or *knowing* things as they truly are in their relation to the infinite). Speaking in terms of dialectic, this affirmation should be understood as *the negation of negation*.

This *negation of the finite knowledge* is what Eriugena calls ignorance,[13] which means that nothing can ever be truly known as to what it is. In this sense, "ignorance" becomes a crucial factor of the knowledge of the infinite. Not unreasonably therefore is the human mind held to be honored in its "ignorance," which to some extent is ever more praiseworthy than the abstract knowledge itself. Indeed, it is full awareness of the limits of the finite knowledge, and *not the knowledge of the finite things themselves*, that really opens the way to the true knowledge as such.[14] Without this sort of awareness and the subsequent overcoming of all restrictions of the spurious knowledge applicable to the improper being of finite things only, no true knowledge, appropriate by its content to the true reality, is attainable at all. "And, a fact which is stranger still and, to those who study God and man, more fair to contemplate," says Eriugena, "the human mind is more honoured in its ignorance than in its knowledge; for the ignorance in it of what

13. With regard to Eriugena's discourse, this sort of *not knowing* should by no means be interpreted in the grammatical sense of the expression and understood as being close to that of *tabula rasa*, to which such expressions as "full lack of knowledge," "sterility of the mind," "complete illiteracy" or anything else of the kind might be found to be appropriate. On the contrary, in accordance with its use by the Philosopher, the "ignorance" ought to be rather dialectically understood as a certain condition of knowledge that inevitably results from the awareness of some knowledge invalidity, and thus as a reliable means of overcoming quasi-knowledge that provides a sustained approach to the true one. It is consequently this dialectically coherent meaning of the term that Eriugena is deeply concerned with, which in turn betrays in him a speculatively subtle thinker who might deservedly stand close to such authorities in Philosophy as *Socrates* with his famous statement "I know that I know nothing," and *Nicholas of Cusa* with his paradoxical conception of "knowing ignorance" (see Nicholas of Cusa, *Сочинения*, 47–184).

14. According to *Nicholas of Cusa*, for example, the way of approaching the Truth implies *the unity of the opposites in the infinite*. In so far as the finite things are one-sidedly perceived to belong exclusively to the physical world, they are found to be opposite to the infinite; but when understood to subsist in God, these things and all distinctions between them come of necessity to be in unity: the opposites only occur when finite things are countered to the infinite, but are absent in the absolute. God therefore is, in the words of Nicholas, "*complicatio oppositorum et eorum coincidentia.*" "All this," G. Reale admits, "leads to overcoming the views of common sense, which are based on the principle of non-contradiction" (Reale and Antiseri, *Западная философия*, 256).

it is is more praiseworthy than the knowledge" of that kind (771c). "There-fore," he continues with regard to the infinite nature of the true knowledge, "the Divine likeness in the human mind is most clearly discerned when it is only known that it is, and not known what it is; and, if I may so put it, what it is is denied in it, and only that it is is affirmed. Nor is this unreasonable. For if it were known to be something, then at once it would be limited by some definition, and thereby would cease to be a complete expression of the image of its Creator, Who is absolutely unlimited and contained within no definition, because He is infinite, superessential beyond all that may be said or comprehended" (771c–d).

CHAPTER 7

Overcoming the Division

Partaking in the One Indivisible Reality

IN THIS WAY, OUR inquiry into Eriugena's doctrine of knowledge brings us to a clear understanding that the reformation of the mind, leading human being to the reality of the infinite whole, directly depends on the proper (infinite by nature) subject-matter of its knowledge. This means that once the mind of man draws "the whole of his attention to the contemplation of the Cause of all things, and then of the principles according to which and in which all things were made" (844b), it actually opens before this man *an utterly new perspective of being*. It is from this new perspective that, by contrast to his outward existence among the contingent sensible objects, man proves to be not an alien, exposed to hostile (exterior) forces any more, but a real *partaker* of the one indivisible universe coming forth from the only Cause of all.

This perspective of the one indivisible universe becomes available to man, according to Eriugena, after he is "purged from every disease of body and soul," (858c) which is their discord (or cardinal disorder of human nature) resulting, as well seen before, from "the perverse motion of the rational soul" (844d; see also 855d–856a). As a result, the human mind allows everyone to realise indeed that, proceeding to all particular beings, the universal Principle of the entire reality nonetheless neither decreases nor departs from itself but, paradoxically enough, remains *ever identical to itself*. As a matter of fact, it is because of its *universality* that the Principle of all gives rise to *everything particular* and thus—in like manner to the fruitful Tree of Paradise (the metaphor Eriugena is keen to use)—does nothing other in fact but unceasingly manifests *itself*, while retaining its genuine universality by being *substantially homogeneous* to the totality of all its manifestations. And in this way indeed, causing all things to come into being, the universal Principle of the whole reality *never departs from itself* to get eventually dispersed among the singular. Instead, unfolding itself into actual being, the Principle ever *returns* to itself and thus properly is *in* and *for* itself, never transcending (as the *universality* itself requires) the boundaries of its absolute totality. And this is truly so, because nothing alien (*non aliud*) to the very nature of the properly universal Principle of all things, visible and invisible, is ever brought to light in the course of its *self-disclosure*.

In this sense therefore, being an outcome of the Creator's self-disclosure, the creation as such proves to genuinely subsist in so far only as it *returns* to its Creator as being essentially *akin* to him by its pristine nature, pure from any distortions imposed upon it by the irrational motion of the corrupt mind. Indeed, having in itself *nothing alien* to the Source of its origin (for there is certainly nothing other apart from that which comes forth from the only Beginning of all beings), the creation cannot properly subsist otherwise than by remaining *substantially one* with the Primal Cause of its being, as if it were ever *returning* to the place where it originally belongs (see 858b–859a). It is perfectly obvious, then, that *nothing alien* to the Ultimate Principle itself should ever be recognised to subsist in creation: where the Beginning and the End are understood to be one, there the true (self-identical) Being-in-and-for-itself properly is. Besides, it is also apparent in line with this that, grasping the profound truth of *a return-like mode of being* of the Universal itself, the mind of man inevitably gets rid of sensible illusions about the world he lives in, so as to find himself actively engaged with nothing else but *bringing the whole of reality back to the way it truly is.* Thus man does become a real *partaker* of the one indivisible universe of creation—that is, the domain of God's self-revelation.

All this consequently means that the entire creation as it properly is beyond the phantasies of the finite (sense-dependent) knowledge may not be truly known, unless it is consistently conceived—appropriately to the return-like pattern of the true reality—as being *brought back* "to the condition in which it was first created" (855a). For only then all things, including the human nature restored to the integrity of its pristine state, appear to the mind (after the labors of its "purgation in practice and theory") to be perspicuously seen indeed according to their true nature (see 855a). And thus the mind comes to know the nature which ever remains in "the immutable stability of the primordial causes" (858b) and, for this reason, abides "at peace and in harmony in itself and with its Creator" (855c). "For God does not curse," the Philosopher pinpoints, "the things which He made, but blesses them . . ." (848c). That is why "freedom from error," as fairly said, is guaranteed without fail to "those who, bathed in the splendor of the Divine ray, take the path of right contemplation and seek themselves and their God; for in these the knowledge of the Creator precedes the knowledge of the creature" (844c). And it cannot be otherwise indeed, in so far as "the rational inquiry into truth" is concerned (858b); for such is the "order of the Divine Law" (843c) that the universal Principle of all does precede everything particular caused to being. And it is *the rational motion of the mind* which alone—when the corporeal senses do not any longer resist it (see 856a)—enjoys the perfect conformity to the proper order of the entire human nature and creation, and therefore is really able "to observe the most just and beautiful order of the Divine Law" (843c).

The Logical Dilemmas and Paradoxes

Thus we are given to understand that—coming back through the proper operations of the mind to the state of his pristine integrity with "the One Creator of the whole creature, visible and invisible" (843b)—man attains "the perfection of wisdom" which truly enables him to "reason together with God concerning the principles of visible things" (843b). With regard to this, therefore, it would be right to admit along with Eriugena that man does realise that all the beauty of the creature ("whether the inner beauty of the principles or the outward beauty of the sensible forms") is to be referred "to the glory of the Creator" (843c). And thus approached, this undeniable truth should certainly imply after all that in creation as a whole nothing at all properly subsists separately from the Creator *manifest*. This further means that, in so far as the true being as such is concerned, neither the creature nor the Creator can actually dispense with one another. If it is so, however, that the creature and its Creator are in fact *mutually dependent* in their being, it may further mean only one thing indeed—namely that, in consistency with this valid proposition, it would also be logically sound to acknowledge that *as the Creator* God is hardly conceivable to subsist *before* the creature has been brought to being. Likewise, from the logical standpoint it remains utterly unclear what *the Creator* needs to do *after* the act of creation has been completed. Moreover, on the one hand, it appears logically faultless to assume after all that he, whose essence and existence are said to be one (Exod 3:14), should definitely face his own "glory" in all the "beauty" of the creature (which undoubtedly is the explicit harmony of its essence and existence). On the other hand, when the totality of distinct things is concerned, this assumption yet seems too extraordinary to be accepted. Indeed, it would be indispensable to suggest then that the Creator, although *uncreated*, nevertheless *encounters in creation none other but himself*, as if he who is uncreated, could also be—as highlighted at 452a and 454d—somehow created while all things are coming out of him into being.

What are all these logical difficulties about—do they mean to challenge the human understanding of God's eternity or to indicate some apparent imperfections of the very conception of creation? Is it just inadequate to consider the absolute God as *the Creator* only or to confine his infinite being to the relations with the creature alone? Should the very approach of the human mind to the infinite nature of the Divine be improved or simply some additional postulates, like those of the continuing act of creation or sustaining the creature, be allowed for the conception of creation? After all, no matter how many other questions of the kind could be raised in this regard, it should be quite evident to everyone who carefully follows the inner logic of *the Periphyseon* that the only constructive way of tackling the dilemma in focus is supposed to agree with that plain insight that *it is impossible at all to think of God's being without falling into contradiction.* In no way does it mean, however, that the contradictions, by which the mind is haunted in its attempts to know the infinite, prevent man from making any progress towards knowing God's truth. On the contrary, the real implication of this insight consists in highlighting the basic axiom of *dialectic* that it is nothing other than the contradictions themselves, when properly treated, that truly become an effective instrument for overcoming any obstacles on the way to the infinite as such. For it is the vigour of negation latent in them that brings to the fore the fundamental inadequacy of any *finite* definitions to the Divine being, despite they flourish in abundance within the scope of *cataphatic* theology, specifically keen on ascribing some conventional attributes to God and, as a result, honoring them for the real properties of his true nature[1].

From this, it necessarily follows that the true knowledge of God (which the righteous are undoubtedly directed to by their faith) is to be all about resolutely *overcoming the contradictions*[2] into which the human mind inevitably falls as soon as it sets out to think of the infinity of the Divine in

---

1. A set of attributes usually ascribed to God's being in dogmatic theology includes such definitions altogether abstract in their extremity as *omnipotence, omniscience, omnipresence,* etc. On this one-sidedly abstract approach to God's nature see, for example, Thyssen, *Лекции,* 93–104.

2. That the *apophatic* way of thinking is entirely aimed at transcending the finitude as such and, as a consequence, at overcoming all contradictions of human thought, it had always been a firm conviction for those who readily paid a tribute to Greek Fathers as the forerunners of their own doctrines. Russian religious philosophers of the twentieth century, and notably Nikolai Berdyaev, may definitely be counted among them: "The ultimate union, where all contradictions and antinomies of human thought and integration are resolved, is achievable in *apophatic* way alone, that is, the way of apophatic knowledge of the absolute, which is also the way of being in communion with God in God's Kingdom" (Berdyaev, "Я и мир объектов," 258).

terms of creating and non-creating, as well as of being respectively created and uncreated.

To many present-day theologians however (especially those largely influenced by Kierkegaard's vehement rejection of human reason's ability "to answer the basic religious questions of life") such paradoxes seem so utterly insoluble that they find it fair to assert that "the truth of Christianity is grasped only by faith and not by reason."[3] By contrast, to such early Christian thinkers as Eriugena—with whom, as Hegel says, "the genuine philosophy begins"[4] —it is apparent that the true faith in the One God, allowing everyone to "rightly believe and understand" (860c), should only encourage, and not humiliate, human reason, without which the nature made in the *image and likeness* of God would simply be inconceivable.[5]

From this point of view, it would be fair to expect of a faithful Christian *not to give up*, when on the way to the truth of God's revelation he finds himself confronted, as he thinks, by some flagrant paradoxes, which on closer examination prove nevertheless to be not as insoluble as they first appear; because in fact these paradoxes are not of the matter man seeks to know, but of *his own reasoning*.

Indeed, speaking of this in general, it is true to admit that all paradoxes of human knowledge may finally be understood only as stemming from nothing other than knowledge itself or, to put it more precisely, from *the way the matter of knowledge is approached*. Hence, if any paradoxes do occur, it is not matter that is to blame for it nor, all the more, is the problematic matter to be forbidden to knowledge. In fact, reason alone is guilty of its own failures; again, however, not because reason is merely instrumental and serves man's practical needs or is simply unfit for the task of knowing anything obscure at all (and ultimately the truth as such), but solely because the very *logic*, which reason adheres to in its cognitive activity, proves to be just *inappropriate* to the complex nature of the matter itself. This obviously means then that human reason should not try to escape the paradoxes it encounters on the way to knowledge, nor seek its consolation in faith troubled by no paradoxes. Neither of these would actually save man from being what he is supposed to be by his pristine (proper) nature. Rather man should do his best *to bring his reasoning into perfect conformity with the matter he seeks to know*. And if this concerns the knowledge of the infinite as such (without interest in which no true belief in God is possible at all), then *the very logic*

3. Grenz and Olson, *20th-Century Theology*, 64–65.

4. Hegel, *Лекции по истории философии*, Кн. 3, 195–96.

5. As discussed in chapter 1, Vladimir Soloviev highly appreciated Eriugena's way of treatment of faith and reason as one of the cornerstones of his system, apparently present in the *Periphyseon* at 511b.

of thinking that man uses to solve the cognitive task he sets himself is to be *radically changed* so as to thoroughly fit the nature of the infinity in ques-tion, that is evidently achievable when the infinite depth of thought is un-concealed and aptly applied. It is for this purpose hence that, surprisingly or not, nothing other but *paradoxes themselves* must be well employed. In fact, it is a dialectically coherent treatment of the *theses* and *anti-theses* in which the paradoxes consist that really becomes the proper way of their resolution. And it is subsequently in this way that the mind is allowed to break through the gravity of the finite (sense-dependent) knowledge of "what it is" type to the boundless horizon of the *true being* that *unceasingly is*. In the result of this, the finitude as such (ultimately expressed by mutually confined con-traries of any logical contradiction) is radically overcome to open up before the human mind the perspective of the reality of God's creation as it truly is in its indivisible unity with the Universal Principle of all being. Through this gateway of the dialectically resolved contradiction man is invited to enter the reality, not improperly compared in the Scripture to that of the garden with the Tree of Life in its midst, to enjoy the communion with him outside of whom there is nothing, because he ever is the all-embracing One, the Beginning and the End of all.

The Triune Nature Dialectically Conceived

By seeing perspicuously *the entire* creature, while contemplating it "with the reasonable sense controlled by the dictates of the mind" (843c), man is understood by Eriugena to bring this creature back to the way it truly is ac-cording to its proper (original) status of the intimate unity with the Univer-sal Principle of its provenance. And at 860b this is qualified as "the Return of the natures into their primordial causes and into that Nature which . . . is God Himself." Having thus realized by means of dialectical view of the absolute (self-identical) whole that, in accordance with the "order of the Divine Law," God's creation as such may only be treated as the *disclosure* of his own Nature, man does arrive at *a new understanding* of God as the Triune One (see 455c-d).[6] For once God is genuinely believed to be the

6. When spoken of in terms that are close to the established way of approaching it, "the great truth that the Cause of all things is of a threefold substance" (455c) may ap-pear articulated, as found in the *Periphyseon*, like this: "For, as we said, from the essence of the things that are it is understood to be; from the marvelous order of things that it is wise; from their motion it is found to be life. Therefore the Cause and creative Nature of all things is, and is wise, and lives. And from this those who search out the truth have handed down that in its essence is understood the Father, in its wisdom the Son, in its life the Holy Ghost" (455c). And though this conventional language describing the

Supreme Cause of all, he may solely be known in truth as the *universal* Principle which, because of its absolute universality, is *never transcended* and therefore inevitably is not only the Beginning but also the Middle and the End of all being, so that nothing at all can ever be understood to properly subsist outside of him.[7] Indeed, from what the Philosopher appears to be aware of from the very outset of his quest and clearly states in the beginning of the *Periphyseon*, it unambiguously follows that—to the faithful mind well-disciplined in dialectic—not only should God be properly known as "the principal Cause of all things which are made from Him and through Him" (451d). In fact, he should also be known as "the End of all things that are from Him, for it is He towards Whom all things strive. Therefore He is the Beginning, the Middle and the End: the Beginning, because from Him are all things that participate in essence; the Middle, because in Him and through Him they subsist and move; the End, because it is towards Him that they move in seeking rest from their movement and the stability of their perfection" (451d). In this sense, therefore, it is fair to say that God is perfectly known—according to "the path of right contemplation" that Eriugena is immensely concerned about—only when "unity and trinity" are simultaneously predicated of his absolute being (455d).

From this, it obviously follows that in no way should "the Return of the natures" mentioned above be understood as a sort of *spatio-temporal movement* of the creature back to a primary state of its pre-existence, where it becomes as it were absorbed by the Creator again. Rather, it should be understood conversely as a *spiritual* process taking place within the human nature restored to its perfect integrity.[8] Indeed, when faithfully following

---

triune nature of God is fairly thought to be infallible, its use nevertheless should by no means be accepted for the only way of treating the matter behind it, especially if a clear understanding of the truth conveyed is concerned.

7. As A. Brilliantov holds while referring in particular to 527c, 528a, 688b, and 690a, "it is necessary to admit that the creature and its Creator are one, for in its creation the absolute reveals itself, so that beyond it there is nothing. The one and universal nature is therefore the Divine nature. The whole is one and, to be precise, is God, for God is the whole: God is the beginning of all, as it were, the middle and the end, or the purpose, and is Himself present in all" (Brilliantov, *Влияние восточного богословия*, 259).

8. From what A. Brilliantov for example says about the central point of Eriugena's views, it is quite clear that the return of all the creature to its "ideal state" consonant with its "original predestination" may only be properly understood as being brought about *in* and *through man's mind*: "Everything external (i.e., the external world) will return to the human nature, to man's spirit; it will return exactly in the mind of all human individuals, for even now in fact the world exists in human nature. As for the human nature itself, it will return to God and into God and will abide in Him" (ibid., 263). And again, speaking of Book 4 as a whole, he particularly admits that approaching "the doctrine of the process of return of all to God," it proves to be entirely focused

the *ontologically* proper order of creation, the *rational motion* of the mind leads man out of the corrupted world of sensible phantasies (where since the Fall he has been captive to the sin of subjection of his pristine nature to the power of the exterior sense), and thus *opens up before him the perspective of the entire of the true reality*, as if bringing it back to the ways it has been originally set up within "that Nature which is God Himself" (860b). But if it is true that in giving rise to the creature God does not yet transcend himself as the absolute being, and accordingly encounters in the integral whole of creation nothing other apart from his own Nature disclosed, then not improperly—as the author of the *Periphyseon* insists beginning with the opening lines of his massive work (441b)—should God be also thought of as the One who *does not create*.

Thus, after "the Return of all things into that Nature which neither creates nor is created" has been considered in the way discussed above, the *fourth species* of Nature, the most obscure in the overall account of its division (441b), eventually comes to the fore in Eriugena's conception of reality of the whole. At 860b it is brought into focus of the Philosopher's inquiry into the meaning of what seemed at the beginning to be "classed among the impossibles" (442a) and to cause a great deal of perplexity among those who found it "of its essence that it cannot be" (442a). A careful reader of the *Periphyseon* is thereby led finally to understand what the author of this voluminous work truly implies by introducing such an extraordinary and highly problematic species of Nature, and what consequences for the whole doctrine of the fourfold division of Nature it really entails. And this time again, as it always was before when a coherent thinking came across any flagrant contradictions on its path, nothing other but *dialectic* is to be appealed to for assistance to the human mind. Since the *fourth* species of Nature apparently opposes the *first* one, which according to the fourfold scheme of division stands for God (442a) understood as the Nature "which creates and is not created" (441b), it is logical to assume that by introducing this opposition the Philosopher actually means to articulate our thoughts of God in the form of contradiction to get an opportunity of overcoming any finitude in our knowledge of God.

It is obvious to Eriugena that the true infinity of God's being, exceeding the limits of a *non-contradictory* approach, is properly conceivable *by virtue of contradiction only*. When it is treated in a dialectically coherent way, contradiction becomes a means of knowing the infinite as the *negation of finitude* or, to be precise, as its overcoming, possible solely along

---

on considering the *human nature*, for it is *in* human nature and *through* human nature that the process of return is brought about (see ibid., 308).

with the concomitant affirmation of somewhat positive of a superior or absolute nature. For such is the way of knowing him who is really *the One* while never abandoning himself and containing *everything particular* in himself; because he truly is the Absolute—that is, the Beginning, the Middle, and the End—and beyond him there is utterly nothing. And no faith is subsequently true, unless the knowledge of God, as the way of encounter with him who is the foundation and the ultimate meaning of all being, is really pursued by man.

The Cardinal Contradiction

No wonder therefore that—from the very outset of his quest for a profound understanding of the truth of Revelation—the author of the *Periphyseon* appears to be determined to identify, as seen from 441b–442a, a *cardinal contradiction* in our knowledge of God. When dialectically treated, this contradiction alone may allow the mind of man to break down the bonds of the finite (sense-dependent) knowledge that holds him back from knowing the true God who, being absolutely universal by his Nature, is *confined to nothing.*[9] Nothing of the kind seems to have been ever done before Eriugena—neither, say, by Augustine, whose legacy apparently was an indisputable authority for the Carolingian scholars; nor in the Dionysian apophatic theology which, despite (or perhaps thanks to) its obscurity, intrigued them so much. Indeed, even the latter, though greatly appreciated by the Philosopher for exercising the principle of negation in its treatment of the Divine matters, did not actually search among the contraries' collisions for the only *cardinal contradiction*, a constructive use of which could definitely revolutionize the mind's attitude to the very concept of God and, as a consequence, considerably advance the entire knowledge of his being. Likewise, Augustine's theology did not seem to be concerned about finding such a contradiction, resolution of which could become a means of improving human knowledge of God. Instead, it is in lack of antinomies that his theology saw a guarantee of its own consistency and validity, and for this reason

---

9. This truth is supposed to be commonplace for faith. Nevertheless, it is frequently blurred by those who believe that God and creation have always been *opposing* one another. To them Vladimir Soloviev reminds about this plain, yet basic, tenet of Christian faith: "If the Divine essence were not all-embracing and did not include everything in itself, it would follow then that something could exist outside God; be it the case, however, God would be limited to this being external to Him and would not be absolute, i.e., would not be God" (Soloviev, "Чтения," 85).

sought to eliminate from the knowledge of God's Nature any possibility of falling into contradiction.[10]

Thus, as seen from Augustine's discussion of the substantial order of creation (*On the City of God*, bk. 5, ch. 9),[11] he finds a hierarchy-like *three-fold division of causes* to be appropriate for giving a non-contradictory account of the Divine reality as a whole. According to this threefold division, all the causes are thought to successively proceed from the most general Ultimate Cause to the particular ones so that no room seems to be left there for anything contrary that could ever impede their smooth procession: 1) "Thus, the cause of things which produces, but itself is not produced, is God." 2) "Another one both produces and is produced, as it is for example the case with all the spirits created, especially those of the intelligent ones." 3) "Then, the corporeal causes are the ones which, being rather produced than producing, should not be counted among those that give origin to the effects; for they are only able of doing what the will of spirits does with them."[12] As a result, the whole of the Divine reality seems to be coherently described in this way because, as the author of the doctrine believes, "there are no other causes giving rise to anything that happens, apart from those depending on the will, . . . i.e., on that nature which is the spirit of life"—that is, the spirit "who gives life to all things, and is the creator of any body. And this spirit of every creature is God himself, the spirit in no way created."[13] So that those, who are convinced by this straightforward approach to the matter, might agree with Augustine that the knowledge of God is only attainable in a *non-contradictory way*, when the entire course of reflection upon his Nature adheres to the monistic principle of supremacy of a single Supreme Cause over all the effects it causes.

Eriugena however apparently thinks otherwise. Once he enters upon "the path of reasoning" (441a), which is supposed by its nature to be free from any sensible phantasies, his approach to knowing God's being inevitably comes into conflict with that of Augustine's. Moreover, it is likely the

---

10. As it is well known, this trend of intellectual quest has eventually culminated in Kant's critique of metaphysics and his attempt to tidy up in philosophical meditation by allowing it never to operate against the *law of contradiction*, according to which A can be B and not B' at one and the same time (Kant, *Критика чистого разума*, 131). In fact, in the *Critique of Pure Reason* Kant particularly holds that "contradiction altogether undermines and eliminates knowledge" (ibid., 130). The knowledge of truth is therefore identical, according to him, to banishing delusion and falsehood originating from *contradictions* (see ibid.).

11. See Augustine, *О граде Божием*, 253–55.

12. Ibid., 255.

13. Ibid., 254.

latter to which the author of the *Periphyseon* tends to object.[14] Indeed, the Ultimate Cause of all may only be properly conceived of not so much in a linear way, so to speak, as a single *starting-point* of a sequence of actions, but rather in an integral way as the all-embracing *Universal Principle*, beyond which there is nothing in reality at all. For only then, as those taking their origin from the Cause that is supposed to be essentially unfathomable and inexhaustible, all things may be truly understood as contained by it. Its *singularity* therefore, as far as considered in a coherent manner, should no doubt be conceived of inseparably from its *universality*.

Meanwhile those who, following Augustine, seek to avoid (as they think) any dualism in their understanding of the Ultimate Cause by taking no opposites into consideration, actually arrive, despite their intentions, at just the opposite result—namely, the *duality* of the Cause in question or, to put it more precisely, its *confinement by the opposite*, on account of which it cannot be self-dependent any more. In fact, after being produced by the Cause, the particular effects, as they appear according to Augustine's scheme, eventually turn out to be inert. And even though this Cause happens to be referred to as "the spirit of life," and the effects themselves are called "the corporeal causes," all these cannot really help thinking to escape the invisible pitfall it stubbornly makes its way to. Indeed, "the corporeal causes"

14. As a matter of fact, the works of Augustine were deeply respected by the Carolingians, and in the first instance none other but Charlemagne himself was apparently responsible for this respect. It is well known in particular that he greatly enjoyed reading Augustine, and actually was so well-read in his writings that could even quote by heart extensive passages from them (see Levamdovsky, *Карл Великий*, 114). Especially enjoyable reading of his, as A. Levandovsky points out, undoubtedly was *On the City of God*, to which the emperor frequently referred as a source of inspiration for the most challenging of his social projects: ". . . the treatise *On the City of God* by the Bishop of Hippo was not only his favorite book, but also a direct living guide and the great plan he envisaged to fulfil in reality" (ibid., 124). The enormous task of building the *City of God* was Charles's "haunting idea" which he sought indeed to realize in practice (see ibid.). As a result, the central message of this particular treatise by Augustine had become a real agenda for the Carolingian scholars (see ibid., 125–28), which consequently means that all of them (with no exception of Eriugena, of course) must have been well acquainted not only with its general contents, but with the particular doctrines coming from it as well. Little wonder, therefore, that even at first glance there is a striking affinity in the opening lines of the *Periphyseon* between Eriugena's doctrine of the fourfold division of Nature and that of the threefold division of the Cause found in Augustine, at least as far as the first three subdivisions in it are taken in comparison to those three in the other one. Anyway, hardly could such an affinity be just a coincidence. As mentioned, it is plausible enough to assume that, like many of his contemporaries, Eriugena could be well aware of Augustine's threefold approach to interpreting the order of creation. But in contrast to those who agreed with that doctrine, he found it necessary to respond to its logical defects and, consequently, to wrong theological (as well as anthropological) conclusions to follow from them.

are understood to be completely obedient to "the spirit of life," while doing only "what the will of spirits does with them." As a result, having proceeded into a number of other causes, the Supreme one proves nevertheless to be after all *opposed* by its own produce, entirely passive and having therefore nothing in common with the very nature of "causes." By no means, hence, can such an outcome of the one-sided treatment of the matter be found compatible with knowing the universal nature of the Principle of all being.

By contrast to this, a proper approach to the nature of the Ultimate Cause should not mean avoiding the dualism of *singularity* and *universality*, but should rather dialectically tackle their unity, which alone may clear the way to the advanced knowledge of the Divine. In fact, solely that cause may be counted for being truly *single* which has nothing other *alongside itself*, and thus is properly known at the same time as the true *universality* which counters nothing other *beyond itself*. From this perspective, it is therefore not hard to see that it is nothing but the universality as such[15] that may be properly understood as a real starting-point[16] of anything that has ever happened in God's creation.

15. This "general name," which obviously stands "for all things, for those that are and those that are not" (441a), seems to be precisely what from the very outset of the *Periphyseon* Eriugena means by a general term *Natura* (441a). "For nothing at all," he explains, "can come into our thought that would not fall under this term" (441a).

16. In contrast to quite a common practice of associating the singularity of the Primal Cause of being with a *mathematical point*, the universality might be envisioned in like manner to an immense *globe* comprising the entire being. And if in the case of singularity a sort of outward motion of expansion starting from a certain center seems to be natural for the whole stuff of the Universe, in the case of universality something opposite, or inwardly directed, should be counted for a generative movement within the Universe. As a result, unlike the latter the first model of genesis would appear then easier to be grasped and therefore more acceptable to common sense so as to remind in many respects the modern cosmology theory of Big Bang, so popular nowadays that even believers often find it possible to acknowledge some similarity of it to their vision of creation. According to this cosmological theory (and subsequently the model of the Universe it provides), it is particularly assumed that the entire visible Universe "must have emerged from a mathematical point—a singularity—at a definite time in the past" (Gribbin, *Almost Everyone's Guide*, 206). When that infinitely dense point (a "cosmic egg" or "primeval atom") spontaneously exploded, it created all the matter in space in the form of stars and galaxies, which have been rushing apart in all directions ever since and thus making the Universe continuously expand. "The birth of the Universe," cosmologists suggest, "was like a cosmic hurricane, but with the winds all blowing in one direction—outwards" (ibid., 214). If so, however, and if Edwin Hubble was right while hypothesizing, after the effect of "red shift" had been discovered, that "the Universe is expanding and the galaxies are expanding along with it" (ibid., 128), it yet remains unclear for the scientists whether the Universe will continue expanding for ever until it gets dispersed in space (so that the very space and time vanish), or it will slow down and eventually stop in order then to collapse back in on itself and suffer a similar final of annihilation (or perhaps of rebirth in another "big bang"). Despite an obscurity

It is quite unequivocal then with regard to this that there is actually no other way to conceive of the universality than by reducing all possible contradictories concerning the knowledge of the Ultimate Cause just to one *cardinal contradiction*. For that is the contradiction which would allow the mind, when dialectically resolved, to bring all the extremes to the *absolute unity* of the Universal. Moreover, it is in this way of the true knowledge of the Divine that all humans may get released from their bondage to *sin* (or wrongdoing), inevitably resulting from the entire dependence of both their mentality and mode of being on the *knowledge of the finite*—that is, the knowledge appropriate to the world of sensible phantasies only, where the opposite extremes appear to be set apart and nothing substantial is assumed to exist. This way of conceiving the proper nature of the Ultimate Cause,

---

concerning the actual fate of the Universe, both theorists and observers nevertheless agree (or, better to say, used to agree until recent discoveries) that, under the influence of gravity dominating across the Universe, its expansion has at any rate to be *slowing down*. However, in the light of the new discoveries recently made by Saul Perlmutter and his team it has become clear that this belief cannot remain infallible any longer. As the results of their extensive project originally focused on measuring the rate of the universal slowing down showed, the expansion of the Universe is not slowing down; it is in fact *speeding up*, and the galaxies appear to be pushed further away into deepest space, as if being affected by a mysterious force much more formidable than that of gravity. All the scientists have been greatly confused by such an unexpected result which seems to be the greatest discovery of the century shattering the fundamental conceptions of Science: should it be true that the Universe is pushing itself apart faster and faster (though many still find it hard to believe), the known laws of Physics formerly assumed for those of Nature are to be radically reconsidered. Could it not just signify that through this epoch-making discovery Nature presents a new face to us, and that accordingly neither the very foundations of knowledge nor the models based on them simply suit the reality as it truly is? If the Universe is really speeding up in its motion, could it not be just because the entire cosmos is moving not from a point-like center to an utmost periphery but in the opposite direction—towards the genuine center and the source of unimaginable energy to eventually face him who is invisible now? Is the problem not all about a radical change of our point of view and the logic we adhere to so as to become really able—after they have fundamentally changed—to conceive the unity of singularity and universality, as appropriate to the true nature of the Universe origin. The answer to all these is obviously quite simple: once the mind abandons the way of delusion that it used to grope obediently following the dictates of the sense, and after it becomes able to contemplate the proper order of things in reality, a new scenario of the origin of the Universe, alternative to that of the "big bang," will come into vision. According to this new approach, the origin of the Universe will be understood as being caused not by the energy of destruction but by the energy of creation, hidden not in the infinity of density but in the infinity of universality, that is, the infinity of all-embracing Love and Goodness. Hence, depending on the way the Ultimate Principle of all is coherently conceived of, the mind can offer two different models of the Universe, the nearest consequence of which however is that all humans thereby are actually offered two different kinds of life they may live—either life full of meaning or the one devoid of it. It is up to humans therefore to choose where to start and which way to follow.

therefore, proves actually to lie at the very heart of Christian faith. Indeed, this manner of thinking, which no consistent faith can really dispense with to be not confined to darkness of ignorance, virtually becomes an effective means of restoration of the corrupt mind to its true status. From its wandering in the obscurity of sensible illusions, the mind thereby is brought back to the ways it properly operates as *recta ratio*, while keeping the whole human nature (inseparable from its innermost essence) in unity with the Principle of all being. As a matter of consequence, it is primarily this restoration of the mind which does enable all men and women *to perspicuously see* the substantial reality as it truly is, so as to let them thereby, while finding themselves belonging to it, *actually join* this reality known to the faithful as God's *creation* or the one coming into being from *the only Cause of all*. For solely that is the reality taking its origin from God which is ordered in such a way that the universal in it precedes the singular, and the whole the particular, but not otherwise.

Novelty of the Fourfold Division

From this, it follows therefore that—as long as looking for the Kingdom of God, or the true being, as required by their faith—only those truly are who, beholding the God-centered reality with the eye of their minds, seek to participate in it in effect by bringing their being into perfect conformity with the proper order of creation. To gain a right view of reality as it substantially is and thus to restore the mind to its original capacity of "right contemplation" (or proper speculation), God's being is to be conceived of as a *single whole*, that is, according to its universal nature. This is, clearly, attainable in a dialectically coherent way only, when thinking in contradictions allows the mind to embrace the ultimate extremes of the true (infinite) being with a prospect of having their indivisible unity comprehended. Such is the way of getting the faithful (who genuinely believe in their belonging to eternity) to be saved from captivity in the sensible world of transient things (the construct of the corrupt mind). In other words, this is the way of getting them fit for subsistence in the reality of God's creation, not improperly called his Kingdom, where all beings truly are according to their substantial nature, but not a mere appearance. This is the reality given not to the senses only (whom the mind perverted serves as their obedient instrument), but to *recta ratio* alone, when it is fairly understood, as previously considered, to guide the "reasonable senses," which are unambiguously said to be the ones "controlled by the dictates of the mind."

That is why—as a Christian thinker who is fully committed to following the truth revealed to the faithful and is therefore deeply convinced of the necessity of advancing the knowledge of the Divine making their faith certain—Eriugena appears from the very beginning of his thoroughgoing inquiry to be determined to develop the doctrine of the substantial order of creation. And he really does so—even despite a great deal of perplexity and paradigmatical difficulties it causes (similar to those indicated at 442a)—by introducing the "fourth species" of division of the universal *genus*, which is understood to contain in itself, as he puts it, absolutely *all things*, "those that are and those that are not," and is fairly chosen by the Philosopher to be named, more adequately than by that of Cause,[17] by "a general term" of *Natura* (441a). In fact, as clearly seen from the context at 441b–442a, this *fourth* species of Nature and subsequently a coherent consideration of "the division of Nature by means of four differences" (441b), really proves to become a new development in the evolution of Christian thought—namely, a distinct attempt of approaching in a dialectically advanced way the proper knowledge of the universal-singular relationship ever articulately made before in the course of systematic speculations on God's being. And it is actually nowhere but in the *Periphyseon* itself that, as follows from 442a, this uncommon and quite intricate teaching, with a highly problematic fourth species of division of the absolute whole in its focus, is first ever introduced to be unequivocally qualified by the author himself as *his own opinion* (441b). That is the opinion which is naturally supposed to differ from any other ones relevant to the subject-matter and therefore to be liable to "sound criticism" (441b), as solely due to a distinctively new standpoint whose articulation needs to be well verified. "It is my opinion," says Eriugena, "that the division of Nature by means of four differences results in four species" (441b). By applying this innovative *method* to considering the Universal's "division by differentiations into species" (441b), he obviously means not only to present "a true account of this matter" (441b), but also to challenge those of his opponents who likely found fewer differences and fewer species to be suitable enough for interpreting the division of the

---

17. In addition to what has already been said about causes before, it would be vital as well to remind here that as an abstract notion of the beginning of all things "cause" appears to signify a factor very much *external* to the effects it precedes, as it is for example the case with the Aristotelian *Prime Mover* (an archetype of "uncaused cause"), that is understood to stand *outside* a never-ending chain of actions. Meanwhile, apart from its antecedence the cause as such (or the first one) should also be thought *to contain all things in itself*, as due to a real *source* of their being. In this sense, therefore, the term "cause" might happen to be not entirely suitable for conveying the idea of being *the principle of all.*

whole, as it certainly was the case with the Augustinian conception of the *threefold* order of creation.

Thus, largely paraphrasing Augustine's definitions of the first *three* forms of this substantial division, and apparently finding their succession incomplete for giving "a true account" of the matter, according to which the universal whole should be perfectly understood *to remain itself after being divided into species,*[18] Eriugena adds the *fourth* form which is meant by him to be *contrary* to the primary one, so as to guarantee that the universal does not disappear after being divided into the particular. As a result, he has got a pair of the *contraries* that are to be certainly understood not as mere opposites attributed to *different* things (as those of created and uncreated nature, according to the account of division), but as being mutually *contradictory*, when predicated of *one and the same* subject. And this subject, taken in its ultimate sense as the *one preceding any action*, should be indisputably detected as the *nature uncreated.* So that, since among all the forms of Nature, as they are examined according to the substantial order of creation, "the first creates and is not created," it is logically required, when a dialectical train of thought is followed, that this form inevitably "has as its contrary that . . . which neither creates nor is created" (442a). As the contraries referred to one and the same subject that precedes everything but itself is preceded by nothing, these two forms of Nature appear to be altogether appropriate, when taken in their unity, for a cognitive approach to the proper nature of the universal as such. Indeed, making itself manifest through the particular, the universal in fact never departs from itself (i.e., does not transfer to the particular nor breaks down to pieces) but, as it were, returns to itself, because outside it nothing particular may ever subsist. Thus the universal Principle of all beings comes to be truly known in its unbreakable integrity as the One beyond which there is nothing other (alien), and which therefore may only be properly treated as the Nature that creates and does not create at the same time.

In this way, hence, the author of the *Periphyseon* actually arrives at the fourfold division of Nature as a comprehensive model of the absolute wholeness, in accordance with which God comes to be known as the true One who is *confined to nothing alien.* Nature is divided, says Eriugena, "first into that which creates and is not created, secondly into that which is created and also creates, thirdly into that which is created and does not create, while the fourth neither creates nor is created" (441b). Indeed, the reference of this division to God and his creation, directly confirmed at

---

18. To put it in other words, the universal should be understood not to disappear from being at all while getting dispersed among its particular forms, but rather conversely to manifest itself through them and thereby to affirm itself as a real whole.

442b, is entirely evident. However, only as a fourfold division does it really bring all parts of the Divine being to their absolute unity, so as by all means to stand for the true Oneness of God, who as a single whole can neither be split up within himself nor opposed by anything alien. As for the first three forms of Nature as they are believed to proceed in the course of creation, everything seems to be clear and no questions at all, as said at 442b, need to be raised concerning them. In particular, it appears utterly undeniable that "the first is understood to be the Cause of all things that are and that are not, who is God; the second to be the primordial causes; and the third those things that become manifest through coming into being in times and places" (442b). If, however, a full account of the division of the universal whole did not proceed as far as the fourth species of Nature but suddenly stood still at its third stage, as in Augustine's doctrine, then God, the knowledge of whom is solely sought by means of such a division, would inevitably prove to be diametrically *opposed* by his creation in its purely external (spatio-temporal) dimension, and therefore *confined* to it as his counterpart, which is evidently wrong. For this reason, to avoid such a discouraging result, "the opposition of the third species to the first" (442a) should not be ignored in favour of a non-contradictory approach to the knowledge of the Divine, but by all means taken into consideration with a prospect of overcoming it, and along with it the chasm between God and his creation imposed upon the absolute being by the ill-disciplined mind that readily sets the absolute and the tangible apart, as if the universal whole could be at all confined or split in two.

The Universal and Particular from the Dialectical Perspective

A distinctive feature of Eriugena's innovation is just the one therefore which consists in tackling in a thoroughgoing manner the finitude and other imperfections of human knowledge of God as they are above all displayed in contradictories and any sort of opposites that the mind gets entrapped in as soon as it attempts to approach the infinity of the Divine. In fact, at the center of this distinction of the Eriugenian approach from any other attempts of advancing the fundamental knowledge of this kind there definitely lies *a radically new attitude to the opposites as such.* Thus, whereas the upholders of a non-contradictory treatment of the matter seek to take no opposites into consideration to escape any inconsistencies in knowledge, Eriugena does exactly the opposite. In systematically uncovering and subsequently overcoming all oppositions, which any interpretation of the infinite is largely encumbered with, he sees the way of perfection of our knowledge of the absolute. Regarding this, it is important to understand however that in order to break through these oppositions as they appear in the knowledge of the absolute Nature, after the mind, according to Eriugena, identifies the "pairs of opposites" (namely, of the third and the fourth species of division to the first and the second ones respectively), no dialectician should actually permit their reconciliation at the expense of any *additional postulates*. Such extra measures would undoubtedly prove to be entirely *extrinsic* to the doctrine itself and, for this reason, would diminish its validity, as is apparently the case with an assumption of subjection of anything particular in creation to "the will of spirits" that was additionally made by Augustine with respect to the order of causes to explain their cohesion, as he saw it.[19] Instead, should the dialecticians find, and Eriugena really does, some *inner means* effective for the purpose of getting all the opposites reconciled—that is, the means *intrinsic* to the very logic of the doctrine of division of the absolute whole.

According to this logic, as it follows from what Eriugena suggests, after being totally divided the universal nevertheless does not get dispersed among the particular at all but, on the contrary, *remains itself*. Moreover, it is through giving rise to everything particular that the universal actually becomes *itself* or, in other words, what it is supposed to be by its proper nature—that is to say, *all in all*. The universal as such (which not unfairly is called by the Philosopher *Natura*) does come to be truly known only when it is dialectically thought to release and encompass everything particular at the same time. In the light of this logic, therefore, it may be clearly seen that the *inner means* in question, that is decided in the course of the present scrutiny to be necessary for effective overcoming the oppositions (dividing the universal whole), is all about a constructive treatment of the *contradiction between the universal and the particular*. Since, furthermore, in its true sense this contradiction does refer to the way the only Cause of all is properly thought of (both in its singularity and universality taken together), it is also evident enough to realise then that this is the contradiction which alone may be reasonably qualified as the *cardinal* one—that is, the one lying at the very heart of the most fundamental knowledge, which undoubtedly is our knowledge of God. Indeed, once dialectically resolved, this contradiction allows the mind to overcome all the oppositions that tear the infinite whole into pieces, and thus to really advance in knowing God *unconfined*, who truly is the Ultimate Cause of all while being neither split

19. See Augustine, *О граде Божием*, 255.

within himself nor opposed from without by anything whatsoever, be it even brought forth from him.[20]

Overcoming a Dualistic View of Creation

That is why, as 442a reveals, Eriugena sounds pleased rather than upset or confused while holding that within the four species of Nature established according to his method "there are two pairs of opposites." Indeed, when examined in their successive order, it is really hard to miss that "the third is the opposite of the first, the fourth of the second," and Eriugena articulately admits it (442a). What is more, however, he lingers over the evident difficulty of understanding the fourth opposite, from which it may be fairly deduced that it is actually the second of these two pairs that seems to be of a greater importance and especially dear to the Philosopher, as if he sought to introduce the fourth form of division for no other purpose than having this problematic pair of opposites brought to light. And there would be nothing extraordinary at all about making such an assumption; for once its origin is perfectly understood, this opposition proves to elucidate the proper nature of the universality as such and thus to clear the way to the *cardinal contradiction* in question.

As a matter of fact, the role of the opposition of the second form of division to the fourth is absolutely crucial for the whole doctrine of Eriugena's. In particular, unlike the first of the two oppositions detected within the fourfold division of Nature, this one allows the mind to overcome in effect all the opposites that our understanding of the infinite is inevitably encumbered with, and in this way to successfully progress to the true knowledge of God as the only universal Cause of all. Thus, when the explicit opposition of the first species of Nature to the third (or of "the Cause of all things" to its ultimate effects, if to put it in more conventional Augustinian terms) is sought to be approached in a non-contradictory way with a prospect of overcoming the impassable gulf between God and creation which is obviously there between the opposites mutually countered within their opposition, some *intermediate* that produces, though itself is produced, is normally placed in

20. Generally speaking, by no means could Eriugena ever assert, and the course of reasoning really shows it throughout the *Periphyseon*, that "anything opposed to God or conceived alongside of Him exists" (458d). In fact, this is undeniable truth to him, for it unambiguously refers to the absolute universality of God's being, beyond which, as he gives us to understand, no room for anything whatsoever may be found: "By 'opposed' I mean either deprived of Him or contrary to Him or related to Him or absent from Him; while by 'conceived alongside of Him' I mean something that is understood to exist eternally with Him without being of the same essence with Him" (458d).

between to bring the opposite extremes close to one another. Nevertheless, regardless of a variety of names under which this intermediary agent might appear in different doctrines either as "the will of spirits" or "the primordial causes" or anything else, the nearest outcome of such an attempt of making the extremities of the Divine reality meet yet becomes utterly unacceptable for any further development of a coherent conception of creation. For despite their intention to avoid any contradictories in the course of reasoning concerning the Ultimate Cause of the whole being, those who readily resort to this auxiliary remedy to fill the gap between the Cause itself and its multiple effects in the realm of particular (finite) things eventually gain just the opposite result. Indeed, whereas prior to any discourse the Cause of all is straightforwardly declared to be *one*, it proves however to be duplicated and therefore deprived of its substantial uniqueness. It happens in the result of a non-dialectical treatment of the matter, when the finite (produced) effects are assumed to be concordant with the infinite (unproduced) Cause while being mediated by some *semi-causes*, which though caused are also meant to cause a vast range of particular effects so as to distribute, as it were, a primary impulse from the First Cause to every single thing. So that, with respect to this unexpected metamorphosis of the matter in focus, it is not hard to realise that as far as the only Cause of all is believed to be facilitated in its action by some auxiliary means, it actually *splits in two*, which regarding the doctrine of creation must be fundamentally wrong.

From this, it follows therefore that if all things were understood to be created both by a Prime Cause and the secondary ones, then the act of creation as such would happen to have *more than one beginning*,[21] that must be impossible by the very notion of creation. In truth, as Eriugena puts it, "only of the Divine Cause of all things is this rightly predicated" that "it is the supreme and unique Cause of all things which take their existence from it and exist in it" (452a). For, according to the true account of creation, God "alone is the principal Cause of all things which are made from Him and through Him, and therefore He is also the End of all things that are from Him, for it is He towards Whom all things strive" (451d). And it cannot be otherwise indeed; for as right reason suggests, "from the One all things which take their being; from two or more, nothing" (459b). In other words, "it is the one beginning of all things, and there one end, in no way at discord with itself" (459a). All this consequently means that once an improper division of the Ultimate Cause into any intermediary causes as a means of producing

---

21. From the very definition of the first and second species of Nature, as it is explicitly presented by the fourfold account of division at 441b, it is obvious that they both (i.e., "the Cause of all things" and "the primordial causes") are meant to do nothing else but *to create*, that is, to bring all things from non-existence to existence.

its multiple effects is taken for granted, such an apparently dualistic view of the act of creation would inevitably lead the faithful mind astray—namely, towards a flagrant *misconception* of God. In fact, in this way the faithful would be offered a deceptive perception of the Trinity, presented in the form of a Unity of three Substances,[22] as if one and indivisible being of God might consist of three layers of reality existing alongside one another.

A Coherent Treatment of the Opposites

To escape the fatal error of linking the opposites together (when their opposition is sought to be overcome) by placing a certain *intermediate* between them, the mind should instead appeal to the dialectical approach of *recta ratio*, which alone would allow it in effect to get the opposites reconciled

22. As Eriugena gives us to understand in Book 1 of the *Periphyseon* (455c–457c), it is hardly disputed by theologians how difficult it is to express "the mysteries of the Divine Unity and Trinity" (456a) by means of articulated speech otherwise than by using the names of Father, Son and Holy Spirit (see 455c). ". . . but in order that the religious inclinations of pious minds," he further argues, "may have something to think and something to say concerning that which is ineffable and incomprehensible. . ., these religious expressions by which the Faith is symbolized have been both devised and handed down by the holy theologians so that we may believe in our hearts and confess with our lips that the Divine Goodness is constituted in Three Substances of One Essence" (456a–b). "And even this truth," the author continues, "was discovered only in the light of spiritual understanding and rational investigation: for in contemplating, as far as the enlightenment of the Spirit of God would take them, the one and ineffable Cause of all things and the one simple and indivisible Principle they affirmed the Unity; and then by observing that this Unity did not consist in any singularity or barrenness they gained an understanding of the Three Substances of the Unity, namely the Unbegotten and the Begotten and the Proceeding" (456b). Meanwhile, "it comes to be known by those who investigate it in the right spirit" (454d) that "the Cause of all things is of a threefold substance" (455c), which includes rather three *conditions* of being unbegotten, begotten and proceeded, and thus actually reject that paradigm of reasoning according to which they are seen as three distinct substances respectively: "For as we said, from the essence of the things that are it is understood to be; from the marvelous order of things that it is wise; from their motion it is found to be life. Therefore the Cause and creative Nature of all things is, and is wise, and lives" (455c). All this consequently means that "the great truth" of the Divine Unity is that this Unity is properly conceivable in a *threefold* way only, when he, who truly is the absolute whole, is perfectly understood to be in himself through himself and for himself, and therefore is not unfairly defined as being "the Beginning, the Middle and the End" (451d). So that, the "mystical names" of the Holy Trinity (the Father, the Son and the Holy Spirit) should be accordingly qualified as those conditions detected above that refer, as Eriugena suggests, to one and the same Nature, but not to the tree distinct natures (455c, 456c–457c). And this is rightly so; for as the Philosopher fairly argues, with God "nothing is found to be co-eternal which differs from Him by nature" (459b), "because outside Him there is nothing" (452c).

and their opposition overcome. This is precisely a collision of these two diametrically opposite paradigms of thinking[23] that the author of the *Periphyseon* largely deals with from the very outset of his extensive inquiry into
the matter of division of what he calls *Natura* (441a). On the one hand, it is
utterly clear to Eriugena that no opposites or their opposition can be really
overcome by virtue of mediation, when some intermediary is believed to
bring the counterparts together. On the other hand, it is likewise obvious
to him as a firm believer in God's truth how vital it is that all the opposites,
which tear the indivisible nature of the infinite into pieces (and thus impede
the mind's approach to the true reality), ought to be completely overcome.
Therefore, for the solution of this problem the Philosopher chooses to focus
on a coherent treatment of *the opposites themselves* according to their rela-
tive nature. And this is the decision, a crucial significance of which he emphasizes in the first words of the voluminous work, where the profundity of
his attitude to the *fundamental division* as such appears to be formulated as
a basic principle of the entire project to be fulfilled. "As I frequently ponder,"
the author says, "and, so far as my talents allow, ever more carefully investigate the fact that the first and fundamental division of all things which
either can be grasped by the mind or lie beyond its grasp is into those that
are and those that are not, there comes to mind as a general term for them
all what in Greek is called Φύσις and in Latin *Natura*" (441a).

Thus the Philosopher gives us to understand that, even prior to the
inquiry itself, the opposites as such, the opposition of which fundamentally divides the totality of things (and in this way prevents the mind from
knowing all things as they truly are in their absolute integrity), may only
be properly regarded as those of *being* and *non-being*. Indeed, if anything
whatsoever appears to be the opposite of something else, then for the sake
of simplicity and clarity their relation may not inadequately be described
in formal terms as that of *A* and *not A*, in accordance with which one of
the counterparts indicated, *is* and the other *is not*. In other words, if any
A is understood to signify an affirmation of some properties with respect
to a certain entity, then *not A* proves of necessity to be the negation of the
same properties with respect to another entity, because of which the two
entities are recognised to be mutually opposed. Likewise, when God is
not unreasonably defined as the nature "which creates and is not created"
(441b), then the opposite of him, that common belief normally associates
with the creature (and in the fourfold account of division is explicitly identified with its third form), should be accordingly defined as the nature "which

---

23. Not improperly, in line with Eriugena's discourse, should the resolution of this
collision be sought in a dialectical overcoming of the tyranny of finitude entirely rooted
in the *irrational motion* of the sense-dependent mind.

is created and does not create" (441b). So that, it would be fair to admit in this regard that, as long as they are defined in these terms, both God and his creation appear to oppose one another as the two completely different entities. And those who from force of habit contrast the finite creature with the infinite Creator would probably find nothing wrong with such a sharp distinction. Meanwhile, quite a crucial detail, that might escape their attention but which cannot be ignored by a deeper insight into the matter, threatens to shatter a mosaic picture of the universe of creation which they tend to compose of some poorly matching fragments, similar to those of the opposites dividing the totality of the true (infinite) being into separate pieces. This crucial detail is the one that is to be found in a faulty association of opposites with opposite *entities*.

As a matter of fact, when clarified, this key detail sheds light upon that weak point of a non-dialectical paradigm of thinking which, like a stumbling-block, impedes the faithful mind's motion along the way of treating God's being as a single whole. This obstacle on the way to the profound knowledge of the real integrity is nothing other than the *principle of contradiction*, in accordance with which any opposite properties may be thought to refer not to one and the same entity but to different ones only. Unless this implicit weakness of the logic entirely resting upon the principle which rigorously requires of no entity to be simultaneously *A* and *not A* is revealed, the reasoning guided by such a logic remains however fully confident that nothing at all might ever be grasped as *being* and *not being* at the same time. Indeed, the opposite properties that this sort of reasoning deals with are by no means assumed by it to be just the mutually countered sides of *one and the same thing* (merely suitable, when taken together, for a speculative treatment of its wholeness). Instead, these properties are mistaken for the ontological features that can pertain to *different things* only. Thus, in so far as God and creation are perceived in line with the contrasting definitions of their nature as the diametrically opposite *entities*, they both inevitably prove to be *mutually confined*, as if they were nothing more than finite things only. But if it were the case that God's being could be confined and therefore confronted by something finite, then, paradoxically enough, neither God nor his creation improperly defined in like manner to the opposite entities would actually come to be compatible with the true being of the Divine, which obviously allows nothing particular to exist *outside the universal* to counter it.[24] For as clearly said, God alone may be truly understood to be

24. This quite basic truth of dialectic is utterly crucial for treating the absolute being, and no coherent theology can actually dispense with it. Thus speaking of Lev Karsavin's views of this matter, N. Lossky particularly admits: "Like many other Russian philosophers (i.e., Vladimir Soloviev; Fr Sergei Bulgakov; and Semion Frank),

the Principle of all (453b) "to Whom nothing is opposed, and with Whom nothing is found to be co-eternal which differs from Him by nature" (459b). As the universal Principle, therefore, God "is everywhere, without Whom nothing can be, and beyond Whom nothing extends. For He is the place and the circumference of all things" (453a). In this sense, it is not unfair to assert with respect to the universal nature of the Divine being that "everything which is said to exist exists not in itself but by participation in the Nature which truly exists" (454a).

Irrelevance of the Divisive Approach to the Divine Reality of Creation

Hence, as it can be drawn from what Eriugena suggests, a logical *aporia* concerning God and creation is that neither of them can actually subsist in so far as they are found to oppose one another and therefore, as something finite, to alternate as *being* and *non-being* in pendulum-like manner (depending on which of the two is counted to lie within or beyond the mind's grasp, and is accordingly affirmed or negated). To avoid this logical *aporia*, a non-contradictory reasoning (fearful of any antinomies that impede its smooth discourse) seeks to insert between the two extremes an *intermediary stage of creation*, as if it could be a mediating link between the Creator and the creature, where both might encounter before they split away from one another as far as the opposite extremes. Indeed, when conceived according to their truth, neither the universal can *decrease* at all while giving rise to anything particular (otherwise it would eventually get dispersed among the singular things), nor the singular can ever exist *outside* the universal so as to counter it from without. But if the universal and the singular are envisioned as the two distinct and remote poles of the universe of creation, it might seem reasonable to common belief to assume then that apart from these opposite extremes there must be something else in between that would mitigate their mutual alienation (inevitably fraught with their mutual negation) by allowing the singular *to participate*, as it were, in a more general element that would bring it somehow closer to the universal. As a result, in the overall account of the division of Nature there comes up its *second form* to fill the gap between the first and the third ones. This is the form that in Eriugena's account is defined as

---

Karsavin assumes that if something, be it even created, were ontologically external to God, it would put a limit to God. Therefore Karsavin persistently asserts that God is all-unity...," because, he further argues, "if God were not all-unity, then alongside Him there could exist another god and the third and the tenth and so forth" (N. Lossky, *История русской философии*, 384–86).

the nature that "is created and also creates" (441b), by which "the primordial causes of things" (529a) are explicitly suggested to be understood.

Despite being seemingly appropriate for the task of making up a coherent account of creation, however, this *auxiliary construct* (resulting of necessity from a non-dialectical mode of treatment of the "fundamental division of all things") does not yet allow the mind to jump over the gulf between the Creator and the creature, which opens wide in its discourse as soon as the opposition of the universal and the singular cleaves asunder into counterparts confronted. As a matter of fact, such a paradigm of thinking, within which any opposites are tackled as the diametrically opposed entities, cannot actually help to understand how *finitude as such*—that is, the finitude of the mutually confined opposites—may be overcome, and the way to the true knowledge of the infinite be opened. On the contrary, once the universal and the singular are thought to be set apart and mediated in their reciprocal relations by some additional means, *the finitude* resulting from this non-dialectical treatment of the opposites is inaugurated in effect as the principle of *division*, altogether relevant to the reality of finite things. And its power, utterly evident in the realm of the finite, seems so unrestrained that is also believed to extend that far as the domain of the Divine things. As a consequence, even the Ultimate Cause, the universal nature of which alone truly is the beginning of all, is found then exposed to the universal impact of *dichotomy*. As a result, the uniqueness and omnipotence of the Ultimate Cause come to be challenged by the so-called "primordial causes" that common belief is so much determined to place next to what is allegedly accepted by it for being the Principle of all. But how can this duplication of the Cause comply with the truth that there is no, and could never be, such a reality that might come to being from *more than one beginning*? Indeed, once having become subject to the on-going division (in the course of which alongside the Primary Cause there first emerge some *primordial* ones), the universal of the Principle—regardless of any attempts of common belief to postulate its *status quo*—would fully flow over without residue into the singular and, replaced by the infinite number of individual things, would inevitably prove to be reduced to *naught*. Nothing of the kind is however possible at all, when seen from the perspective of the reality as it truly is according to its substantial order; otherwise, it would have to be acknowledged that there could be such a reality that would continue to exist after the Principle of its being vanished or that, similarly to this, after having the entire creature brought forth to light, God would utterly cease to be.

From these reflections, encouraged by Eriugena's discourse, it is quite evident therefore that the account of creation provided by a non-dialectical mode of reasoning would prove in fact to be basically *incompatible* with the creation itself, in so far as the latter—as the very nature of it requires—is conceived to take its origin from the only Source of all beings and to exist inseparably from it, while never transcending the infinite boundaries of its universality. To some extent, a *threefold* model of creation, as Augustine and his Carolingian followers saw it, might probably fit the reality of sensible things, where the finitude reigns through and through; yet such a model would be altogether inadequate to the reality of the Divine things, the infinite nature of which is utterly inconceivable in a non-contradictory way. As a matter of fact, at the basis of a non-dialectical paradigm of thinking (as well as the construct of a single universe it provides) there definitely lies that *false premise* according to which, as already seen, the universal and the singular may be set apart and subsist independently, remaining as it were *external* to one another. But what might seem from this perspective to be true concerning the finite things (such as tangibles and externals), turns out indeed to be absolutely wrong when applied to the infinite ones, such as the Divine Nature and God-centred reality of creation. For by its proper nature, the universal is such that nothing whatsoever may ever be *outside* its absolute integrity; and it is because of the infinity of this absolute integrity that the universal as such is adequately thought to be at once *the beginning and the end* of all. As for the realm of the finite, however, the opposites there are countered as the entities, and therefore, as Eriugena holds, "are correctly thought to belong to the things which are subject to coming into being and passing away. For those things which are in discord with one another cannot be eternal. For if they were eternal they would not be in discord with one another, since eternity is always like what it is and ever eternally subsists in itself as a single and indivisible unity. For it is the one beginning of all things, and there one end, in no way at discord with itself" (459a).

Hence, in continuity with what the Philosopher explores here, it would be not unfair to suggest that the need for the substantial correction of the blunder concerning the way the opposites are treated as the entities standing in a diametrical opposition would imply in fact to make a good effort for replacing an old (*paradox-free*) paradigm of thinking by a new (*dialectical*) one. This would be the way to succeed in approaching the task of developing a radically new account of creation to make it thoroughly appropriate to the reality of God's creation as it truly is. And for this, first of all, the principle of *finitude and dichotomy* is to be counterbalanced by its opposite—that is, the principle of *infinity and integrity*, which is supposed to be all about the *preservation of the universal nature* of the Principle of all beings on account of comprising the opposites of the universal and the singular. In fact, this is precisely what Eriugena does when *in contrast* to the second form of Nature introduces the *fourth* one to the overall account of its division. Thus he actually crowns the mind's motion towards the truth of *the absolute wholeness* (that is disrupted by nothing and therefore never ceases to be) by offering a new definition of Nature, in accordance with which it comes to be known as the *true* Principle of all—that is, the Principle which is not only the Beginning, but also the Middle and the End of all. As a result, thought in this way, God comes to be known as he *truly* (*infinitely*) *is* without getting confronted by any *other being* or *non-being*— namely, as the Principle *truly universal* by nature. Giving rise to the totality of all things, God never abandons himself nor disappears among the things created, but comprises everything that has ever been brought to being, so that nothing whatsoever proves to be lost, that is, to subsist separately from him. And it is apparently in this sense that God should be rightly understood to encounter *nothing apart from himself* in the entire creation, the universal whole of which is intimately and indivisibly one. This is exactly what Eriugena means when refers to the Scripture in the following words: "For 'God shall be all in all'—as if the Scripture said plainly: God alone shall be manifest in all things" (450d). Thus the truly *universal* Nature comes up at last to be defined with respect to its absolute *self-identity* as the one which "neither creates nor is created" (441d).

The Meaning of God's "Rest"

At first glance, this new form of Nature may look appropriate to the state of God's "rest" that, according to Gen 2:2–3, comes when God, as it were, shrinks into himself after the act of creation has been completed. By virtue of introducing the fourth form of Nature's subdivision, Eriugena might therefore seem to merely follow the letter of Scripture concerning the *seventh* "day" of creation, without which the Genesis account (and likewise the division of Nature that is meant by the Philosopher to stand for the stages of creation) proves incomplete. In fact, however, the scrutiny of Eriugena's discourse undertaken so far does convince those carefully following it that the actual reason why the author of the *Periphyseon* does so is essentially different and may be better understood in relation to his attention to the *spiritual* meaning of the sacred writings in focus. This is the meaning that can have nothing to do with the transient world of *temporality*, where all things are said to be "subject to coming into being and passing away" (459a).[25]

25. Discussing Eriugena's attitude to mathematical numbers as "the models of reality," Dominic O'Meara admits that the author of the *Periphyseon* saw them as those giving "insight into the eternal paradigms after which the physical world is organized" (D. O'Meara, "Metaphysical Use," 145), and thus allowing us to approach metaphysics,

Indeed, it is hardly possible for those following Eriugena's logic (and thus brought to the *fourth* form of division) to disagree with his conclusion about the way the universal Principle of all comes to be known—namely, the way that *by allowing all things to be according to their substantial nature* (which is inseparable from the Principle of their being) God actually does nothing other apart from *making himself manifest* (454b). This is the way in which God can truly be known as him "Who is everywhere, without Whom nothing can be, and beyond Whom nothing extends" (453a). So that, it may be clearly seen from this point of view that when the letter of the Scripture says about God's "rest," it should actually imply the undeniable truth that, as the Primal Cause of all, God *does not disappear* among the things after they have been caused to being, but *remains himself*—the same God as he has ever been before. As a staunch upholder of the *spiritual* understanding of Scripture, Eriugena seeks to further deepen the proper knowledge of this fundamental truth by referring its validity to the infinite reality as a whole, where the beginning and the end of being are not severed by the duration of time. In this way, he safely arrives at a firm conviction that not only at the end of procession of all things into being, but also since the very beginning and at every successive stage of its ongoing action it happens true that the Ultimate Cause *neither decreases nor ceases to be*. And it could not be otherwise indeed; for the only Cause of all, beyond which there is certainly nothing, has been continuously retaining its *absolute universality and self-identity* while giving rise to the totality of things, and thus proves in effect to be *indivisibly one* (comprising utterly everything in itself), both in the Beginning and in the Middle and in the End of creation. In this sense, not unreasonably counted for the *spiritual* one (that must be thoroughly compatible with the living reality as it truly is in its entirety), God's "rest" is to be inevitably viewed not as *the end of that "motion"* which is directly associated with creation, but as the *stability* (or *self-identity*) of God's abso-lute being which accordingly goes hand in hand with the course of creation itself, coming about solely *within* his truly universal Nature. This is what allows Eriugena to fairly express as being perfectly true that all things that come forth from the Divine Essence "are made by itself and through itself and in itself and for itself" (454c).

Regarding this therefore, it would be sound to assume that—despite the literal (grammatical or finite) meaning of the Holy Scripture but in line

---

that is, the science of the Divine (see ibid., 142–43). As such, numbers on the whole, and particularly that of 6 explicitly standing for 6 "days" of creation or its entire process as "a symbol of perfection," "function rather as symbols, figures and types that permit the passage from the literal to the spiritual sense of the scriptural text. They act as signs of the presence of various deeper meanings in the revealed word" (ibid., 148).

with its spiritual (symbolic or infinite) truth hidden behind the surface of visible writings and amenable only to a dialectically coherent treatment of the contradictories (including those of Genesis 1 and Genesis 2 narratives)—God should be properly conceived not as him who *first* creates and *then* does not, but as him who *creates and does not create at the same time*. For God's "rest" the Scripture points to, when no creation appears to be brought about any longer, should not be actually interpreted according to the letter as a *state* of his being that chronologically *follows* a sort of "motion," by virtue of which all things are brought into being. Rather, this "rest" should properly be understood as the way God enjoys with no disruption the *stability of his Nature*, which ever remains identical to itself while giving rise to the totality of things. "Not without reason," the Philosopher argues with respect to this,

> for of all things that are at rest or in motion He is the Cause. For from Him they begin to run in order that they may be, since He is the Principle of them all; and through Him they are carried towards Him by their natural motion so that in Him they may rest immutably and eternally since He is the End and Rest of them all. For beyond Him there is nothing that they strive for since in Him they find the beginning and end of their motion." (453b)

"For of God it is most truly said," he does infer therefore, "that He is motion at rest and rest in motion (452c).

Hence, when defining God as the Nature that "neither creates nor is created," Eriugena gives us to understand that God apparently is not simply meant to come to rest *after* "all the work of creating" has been done, as the letter of the Scripture seems to suggest, saying: "By the seventh day God had finished the work He had been doing; so on the seventh day He rested from all His work. And God blessed the seventh day and made it holy, because on it He rested from all the work of creating that He had done" (Gen 2:2–3). As a matter of fact, one can easily understand with Eriugena's help that the true knowledge of the *universal nature* of the Principle of all requires both "motion" and "rest" (that is, creating and non-creating) to be coherently understood as *simultaneously* correlated with the way God is, so as to describe him as the infinite being, just as the Beginning and the End perfectly do, when simultaneously taken with reference to "the sole Principle, Origin, and universal Source of all" (741c). "For He is at rest unchangingly in Himself, never departing from the stability of His Nature" (452c), Eriugena explains. " . . . yet He sets Himself in motion through all things," he continues, "in order that those things which essentially subsist by Him may be. For by His motion all things are made" (452d).

In this sense, therefore, aptly is God's being defined in a dialectically coherent way as "motion at rest and rest in motion." For when known as the infinite being that truly (eternally) is, God cannot be conceived otherwise than by means of *the opposites in their unity*, like those of "motion" and "rest" equally taken for being *true* at the same time, that is, correlated with the substantial reality as it properly is. Indeed, as the "single universal Cause and supreme Goodness" (743b) that the Book of Genesis is explicit about, God finds himself *well pleased* with what has been caused by him to being each "day" of creation, because he recognizes it not as something opposite lying in front of him, but as being "*good,*" that is essentially akin to him who is universally and indivisibly One. That is why it would be right in fact to say, following Eriugena's *dialectic*, that, allowing *nothing alien* to himself to subsist, the infinite God never "moves beyond Himself, but from Himself in Himself towards Himself" (453a), "because outside Him there is nothing" (452c). "For it ought not to be believed," Eriugena further holds, "that there is any motion in Him except that of His Will, by which He wills all things to be made; just as His rest is understood not as though He *comes to rest* after motion but as the immoveable determination of His same Will, by which He limits all things so that they remain in the immutable stability of their reasons" (453a). "For properly speaking," the Philosopher concludes, "there is in Him neither rest nor motion. For these two are seen to be opposites one of the other. But right reason forbids us to suppose or understand that there are opposites in Him—especially as rest is, properly speaking, the end of motion, whereas God does not begin to move in order that He may attain to some end" (453a).

A Dialectically Coherent Treatment of the Cardinal Contradiction

Thus Eriugena gives the followers of his innovative logic to clearly see that *a dialectical unity of the opposites*, which alone is fully appropriate to the universal nature of the absolute whole (and, hence, to the *spiritual* truth of the Scripture), proves in fact to be the way the infinite being of God may be coherently thought of. It is consequently the opposites taken in their unity (as *recta ratio* would require with a view to overcoming the division of the Divine) that actually become a means of advancing the fundamental knowledge of the true being as such, in accordance with which human being truly enters the substantial reality of creation, where nothing alien to God himself does ever subsist. But since, furthermore, the opposites attain their unity through the *contradiction* dialectically resolved, it cannot also be denied that at the heart of the fundamental knowledge in question (and subsequently of the way God's being is conceived of) there must lie that *cardinal contradiction* which Eriugena is really after from the very outset of developing the *Periphyseon*'s doctrine of the fourfold division of Nature. It is this contradiction which, as we understand, truly allows him to overcome any opposites that impede the mind to proceed any further ahead in its attempt to know one and indivisible God. Unlike the oppositions formed, as discussed above, by the four species of Nature divided into pairs, the cardinal contradiction may not improperly be identified as the one made up by the *contraries* (opposite definitions) that are predicated of *one and the same* subject. And within the account of the fourfold division it is undoubtedly the case with God alone: as being *uncreated*, he is found to be not unfairly associated both with the *first* and the *fourth* forms of Nature. This is actually what Eriugena unambiguously means therefore when says about the cardinal and most intriguing pair of opposites, upgrading them to the status of the *contraries*: ". . . the first creates and is not created; it therefore has as its contrary that . . . which neither creates nor is created" (442a).[26]

Taking into account what has already been said about the only possible way in which the opposites may be properly treated, it is scarcely needful to explain here that the *contrary* definitions of the Nature *uncreated* should not be considered in conflict with the spiritual understanding of the Divine truth. In other words, these contraries should not be considered as referring to God in their temporal succession, according to which he would *first* appear to create and *then* to refrain from creating, as if taking "rest" after hard labor of bringing all things into being, as a naïve attitude to the scriptural message could suggest. On the contrary, in like manner to "motion" and "rest" which cannot be, as shown above, separated from one another without putting at risk the integrity of God's being, the *first* and the *fourth* forms of Nature ought to be coherently understood as being mutually inseparable in time and, therefore, simultaneously related to the one and indivisible

26. The words omitted in this quotation are given in the text in square brackets, which indicates, according to *Sigla* to Books 1–3 of the *Periphyseon* (see Eriugena, *Periphyseon, Book 1*, 33–34), that they refer to *later additions* to the text of M. S. Rheims, 875. Not unreasonably therefore, though held to be of *supposedly* Eriugena's autograph, they may be treated as those of *problematic origin*, especially when prove basically irrelevant to the implicit meaning of the context at 441a–442a, where from the very outset *the fundamental division* of the entire being is brought into focus. Indeed, to the extent the matter of division is being discussed, it is actually nothing other but the *fundamental division* of Nature (or, more specifically, the *oppositio* as it appears within its four forms) that is supposed to be more fully elucidated and, for this reason, to remain throughout the whole fragment (and onwards up to examining the modes of understanding of *being* and *non-being*) a real pivot of the author's discourse.

God. Otherwise, if only it were possible that each of these forms of Nature might be considered on its own (i.e., regardless of its counterpart), then *neither of the two would actually be true*. Indeed, only the opposites *taken together* (or, more precisely, in their unity) do overcome the finitude as such and along with it (for the reason of its incompatibility with the living reality of *the whole*) the very ground of any falsehood (i.e., discrepancy between knowledge and the reality proper).

As follows, solely in the result of a dialectical approach to the matter (namely, after the contraries are taken for being true when simultaneously applied to one and the same subject), the Nature *uncreated* proves to be adequately understood as being the universal Principle of all which is said *to create* and *not to create* at the same time. Causing everything come into being, it does remain the same unchanging Principle caused by nothing, because beyond its infinite nature there is absolutely nothing that might oppose and, therefore, exist apart from it. In this sense, it is fair to assert that properly speaking, there is no such God who *only* creates or *only* refrains from creating. Actually, he does both, and does it at the same time; otherwise his being would be found relevant to the realm of temporality only.

Thus, as we may deduce from what Eriugena means, the *cardinal contradiction* comes to the fore. So that, if divided into *thesis* and *antithesis* that make up the antinomy (where neither counterpart is conceivable without the other), it may take the following shape:

Thesis: God creates

Antithesis: God does not create

Having found the cardinal contradiction like this for being intrinsic to the fundamental knowledge of God (or the way he is really conceived of), the mind does not however stop at this as a final result of its efforts. Obviously, not for its own sake is any contradiction in general (and above all the one specified as *cardinal*) sought by the mind, but for the purpose of turning it into an effective instrument of overcoming the finitude of knowledge as being utterly incompatible with the infinity of the absolute whole. The proper significance of the contradiction identified must therefore consist in its genuine *resolution*. This is certainly the resolution that comes about not in the way of choosing one of the contraries for being true and rejecting the other, but in a dialectically coherent way of establishing the truth of both by getting them perfectly reconciled in the absolute whole. Indeed, no antinomy, as well seen before, can be really resolved in *either-or* manner, when each of its constitutive contraries may be alternately taken for being true or false. All the more, such a mode of treatment proves to be altogether irrelevant when the antinomy highlighted above is concerned, since neither of the contrary predicates in it, as the Scripture and the scrutiny of Eriugena's thought undertaken here convince, can be false. Consequently, as far as both *thesis* and *antithesis* are recognised for being simultaneously true when predicated of God, this antinomy may only be resolved if its counterparts are found to be reconciled in a dialectically proper way, as follows:

Thesis:	God creates
Antithesis:	God does not create.
Synthesis (or resolution of the antinomy)	God creates and does not create at the same time.

The Infinite Reality from the Metaphysical and Dialectical Perspectives

Therefore, in so far as the reality of God's creation is consistently thought of in its absolute totality, it is not hard to further deduce from this that *no single creature* (which is supposed to come into being not otherwise than from the only Principle of all) may ever be understood to *abandon* the universal integrity of its Principle, not improperly defined as the Divine Nature. For as it follows from 860b, within the Divine Nature the whole "of the created universe of things visible and invisible" (including those of the "primordial causes") is really meant to be contained.

This logically sound conclusion follows of necessity from the synthetic resolution of the antinomy above, but it inevitably comes into collision with common belief which traditionally tends to *alienate* the creature from the Creator.[27] The fact nevertheless is, and the logic carefully followed through-

27. Thus, for instance, speaking on behalf of Orthodox theology, G. V. Florovsky finds it possible to relegate the idea of the Divine *all-unity* as it is developed and widely employed throughout the tradition of speculative thought from Neo-Platonism to German idealism (notably, Schelling and Hegel) to nothing more than a mere remnant of the philosophical "naturalism" and "determinism." In contrast to these false doctrines (of any links with which, to tell the truth, the doctrine of *all-unity* is falsely accused), Florovsky offers the one to be associated with a faithful view of God's creation and to agree with what he calls "a metaphysical split of being": "In the religious experience the world is given as a creation of God's free will, as a surplus which might have not been at all" (Florovsky, "Метафизические предпосылки," 258). The cornerstone of this belief, according to S. N. Bulgakov, is undoubtedly the principle of God's absolute *transcendence*: "Between the world and God there is an absolute and insuperable [for the world] distance. As the transcendent, God is infinitely and absolutely remote from the world and alien to it. . ." (Bulgakov, *Свет невечерний,вып. 1, кн. 1*, 94).

out the present inquiry does convince of this, that such a belief may only fit the finite knowledge of sensible things that divides the whole of reality into the immanent and transcendent parts (as those lying within and beyond the mind's grasp respectively). It is also clear from the same logic that no belief such as this may have anything to do with the living reality of creation as it truly is according to the substantial order of things that do not subsist beyond the universal Principle of all they proceed from. For nothing universal by nature, as the logic itself requires, can ever be transcended. It is consequently nothing other but the *corrupt* (sense-dependent) mind that—breaking the Law of the Divine order by opposing the singular to the universal—actually envisions the created things as being *alien* to God. In this way, the created things (along with the human nature defiled by its *irrational motion*) are made to leave God or, speaking closer to what the biblical story tells, to fall out of the paradise of the true being of God's creation.

Indeed, this type of the mind entirely dominated by the *irrational motion* is actually forced, as previously seen, by the dictates of senses (whose power does not extend any further than the perception of externals) to treat God and his creation as *mutually countered*, and subsequently *mediated* in their relations by a similarly confined agent, not infrequently termed the "primordial causes." All the three thereby taken together—namely, God, creation, and the primordial causes—make up, as already mentioned, a *threefold model* of creation, which among Eriugena's four forms of the division of Nature obviously corresponds to the first three. As far as anything whatsoever is therefore grasped within the reality of creation modelled in this way, it inevitably proves to be merely *external* and, for this reason, lying only *alongside the other*: the creature alongside of God, the primordial causes alongside of both God and the creature. In the result of this, it might seem that not the integrity but the *division* alone dominates throughout the entire universe of creation, placing all things *outside* of God and making them in fact *separated* from him. Should it be the case, God himself would turn into nothing more than just a *confined being*, utterly distinct from the rest of reality and opposed to it, which might be appropriate to transient things only that are understood to come into being and pass away.

As known from the inquiry above, however, the situation defined by this threefold model of creation (which is found to be deeply rooted in a non-dialectical mode of thinking and basically akin to the Augustinian type of discourse) radically changes as soon as the fourth form of Nature emerges in the account of its division offered by Eriugena. Along with the introduction of this decisively "iconoclastic" form, a new, integral, perspective of the entire universe of creation opens up before the mind so as to leave no room there for God as a *confined being*. For it is undeniably true, as in the words of Hegel, *dialectic* teaches those who are concerned about the knowledge of God's being, that the truly infinite God should not be considered "merely as what is beyond the finite."[28] Indeed, as Hegel further explains, "God is not merely *an* essence" (among other essences) "and not even merely the *highest* essence either. He is *the* essence."[29] God is *the only* essence because *outside* and *alongside* Him as "the genuine Infinite" there can be no other essence: "Whatever else is 'given' outside of God has no essentiality in its separateness from God; on the contrary, any such things lacks internal stability and essence in its isolation, and must be considered as a mere semblance."[30] And the *fourth* form of Nature, as it appears in the *Periphyseon*'s doctrine to be all about bringing the created things back to the infinite Principle of their being, proves in fact to be—when properly viewed, as *recta ratio* requires, in its contradiction with the *first* one—a means of revealing this profoundly *dialectical* truth. According to this truth, nothing singular (the finite) can ever subsist apart from the universal (the infinite), nor a single whole is divided into parts that may be found outside it.

In the light of this truth, therefore, one can clearly see that such a flagrant misconception of God as that of positing his absolute distinction from the creation produced by him, does solely result from the *mind's corruption* (or its subjection to the power of the exterior senses) that is explicitly manifest in full measure in a common sense approach to the infinite as being sharply distinguished from the finite (or the particular). In accordance with this common sense delusion entailed by the *irrational motion* of the mind corrupted, both the infinite and the finite are thought to counter each other in like manner to the opposite entities, as if either could exist not otherwise than depending on its contrary as something substantial. Meanwhile, the fundamental truth concerning both requires that neither can the infinite depend in its existence on anything whatsoever, nor can the finite as such be substantial, when taken in contrast to the infinite. For as follows from the aforesaid (and is confirmed by Hegel's argument again), such a dualism of the entities set apart,

> which makes the opposition of finite and infinite insuperable, fails to make the simple observation that in this way the infinite itself is also just *one of the two*, [and] that it is therefore reduced to one *particular*, in addition to which the finite is the other one. Such an infinite, which is just one particular, *beside* the finite, so that it has precisely its restriction, its limit, in the latter, is *not*

28. Hegel, *Encyclopaedia Logic*, 166, §104 ad. 2.

29. Ibid., 177, § 112 ad.

30. Ibid., 166, §104 ad.2.

what it ought to be. It is not the Infinite, but is only *finite*. In this relationship, where one is situated *here*, and the other over *there*, the finite *in this world* and the infinite *in the other world*, an *equal dignity* of *substance* and independence is attributed to the finite and to the infinite; the being of the finite is made into an absolute being; in this Dualism it stands solidly on its own feet. If it were touched by the infinite, so to speak, it would be annihilated, but it is supposed to be not capable of being touched by the infinite; there is supposed to be an abyss, an impassable gulf, between the two; the infinite has to *remain* absolutely on the other side and the finite on this side. This assertion of the solid persistence of the finite vis-à-vis the infinite supposes itself to be beyond all metaphysics" (as common to faith positing itself in contrast to reason), "but it stands simply and solely on the ground of the most vulgar metaphysics of the understanding.[31]

Therefore, although erroneously following this division as intrinsic to a non-dialectical (or metaphysical, in terms of the Hegelian logic) type of mentality that common belief normally rests upon, "thinking means in this way to elevate itself to the Infinite, what happens to it is just the opposite—it arrives at an infinite which is only a finite, and the finite which it had left behind is, on the contrary, just what it always maintains and makes into an absolute."[32] And this result is obviously incompatible with the true knowledge of God *unconfined*.

So that, as long as the upholders of metaphysics who remain captive to a non-dialectical paradigm of thinking "regard God only as the 'highest essence' in the Beyond, then they have the world in view as something firm and positive in its immediacy. They are forgetting, then, that essence is precisely the sublation of everything immediate. As the abstract essence in the Beyond, outside of which all the distinction and determinacy must fall, God is in fact a mere name, a mere *caput mortuum* of the abstractive understanding. The true cognition of God begins with our knowing that things in their immediate being have no truth."[33]

Therefore, in order that God as he truly (infinitely) is might be adequately known, so as to be really worshipped in accordance with "what we know" (John 4:22), all things that only seem to exist on their own need to be brought back—as Eriugena insists on it (see 860b–c)—to the bosom of all-embracing universality of the Principle of their being, outside which nothing can actually be. And for this, they all ought to be released from

31. Ibid., 151, § 95 ad.
32. Ibid.
33. Ibid., 177, § 112 ad.

the grips of the mind corrupted by its perverse (*irrational*) motion—that is, the mind that, under the dictates of the exterior senses always focused on the singular, divides all things according to their appearance, and thus mistakes a mere construct of them for a substantial reality. Indeed, only the things that are sensually perceived from without and mentally held in their separateness may be assumed, as though fully distinct from the infinite, to stand in a diametrical opposition to God. Once they are contemplated however by *recta ratio* according to their proper nature that never abandons the universal Principle of their being, all things appear then as it were transformed in the light of a new insight. By this insight they are revealed as they genuinely are, while enjoying their intimate unity with him whose *essence* and *existence* are meant to be *one*, so as to identify him by the name '*I am Who I am*' that permits neither chasm nor discrepancy between the One himself and his manifestations.

From this, it would be sound to infer therefore that since it is nothing but the *corrupt* mind who makes all things leave God to form a sensible world opposing him, it is consequently the mind itself that must be restored to the proper ways of its operation. This restoration would allow the mind to overcome the alleged opposition between God and the creature, and thus to bring all things back to the place they are supposed to occupy in creation—that is, in the reality coming into being from the only Principle of all, whose universal nature, though giving rise to everything particular, remains never transcended.

As follows, it would be right to suggest with respect to this that it is not in space and time that the return of things should be understood to come about, but *in the mind itself,* when the latter is thoroughly disciplined in accordance with its proper nature,[34] as previously discussed. For this return, no doubt, is all about the restoration of the *right perspective of being as a whole,* in line with which all things are perspicuously seen as they truly are in the reality properly ordered. And all this is brought about through

34. As it follows from what Willemien Otten for example suggests while discussing the fundamental principles of Eriugena's anthropology, the return as such can hardly be understood in a coherent way unless it is considered from the perspective of man's nature real state: "Since there is no chronological distinction between man's pre–and post–lapsarean states, there is also no fixed point in time at which his procession ends. Neither is there a definite take-off point for the movement of nature's return. Instead, there is adopted a rational criterion by which one can discriminate between man's inner state of integrity and his outer life of the senses, regardless of any time-factors whatsoever. In accordance with this understanding, it can only be through a rational rehabilitation of man that *natura* can start on its movement of return"(Otten, *Anthropology*, 165). Not improperly therefore should the return of the immense universe of creation be understood, she points out, to come about through "the subtle clarity of human reasoning" (ibid., 189).

the mind's comprehension of the reality where nothing subsists outside the Universal Principle of all. Otherwise, unless the mind is restored to the true state of conformity with its deeply inherent *rational* motion (where senses do not dominate any more nor break the proper order of creation by positing the singular prior to the universal), the Divine reality cannot reveal itself according to its true (infinite) nature, which does subsist in the way of retaining its self-identity—that is to say, in the way of Return of the only Principle of all from itself through itself towards itself.

All this certainly gives us to realise that the restoration of the mind *concurs* with the way the reality of the Divine truly is (while proceeding from the universal to the particular), by virtue of which all things come to be no longer known as existing on their own but as being brought back to the place they originally belong to. Indeed, by allowing all things to come back from their captivity in the bonds of the sensible world to the bosom of the universal Principle of their being, the mind itself comes to be perfectly adequate in its operation to the way the reality of creation truly is. Giving rise to all particular things, the only Principle proves to actually subsist solely by *unfolding itself* as a single whole that is never transcended by the particular. In this sense, therefore, it would be not improper to conclude that in so far as the "reasonable senses" properly guided by *recta ratio* turn to contemplate all things according to their true nature (that never subsists apart from the Source of being),[35] any division within the entire universe of creation, including its alienation from the Creator, gets overcome. For as the truth standing for the correspondence of knowledge to the reality requires (and the logic of the present inquiry into the meaning of Eriugena's doctrine of the division of Nature does convince us of this), there is no other reality of creation save the one where, as mentioned above, there "is the one beginning of all things, and there one end, in no way at discord with itself" (459a).

That is why being chiefly devoted to the profound investigation of the mind and sense relationship as it is explicitly unfolding through the collision of the *rational* and *irrational* motions of human nature, the central task of the entire Book 4 of the *Periphyseon* proves in fact to be all about finding the way to true knowledge as such, which, strictly speaking, is that of God himself. It is for this reason—as claimed at 743c and confirmed again at 860b—that Eriugena seeks "to consider the Return of all things into that Nature which neither creates nor is created." In agreement with this task,

35. In this sense, perhaps, it would be right to suggest that the matter of Return might be considered by analogy with that of *conversion* described by Plato in the *cave simile*, as it particularly appears at 514b–517d of his *Republic* (see Plato, Сочинения, 321–25).

the mind's construct of the sensible world, made up of the things perceived from without and erroneously associated with the being itself, is meant to be decisively dismissed as the most pernicious blunder ever made by the mind, that is, the blunder leading human being astray to an illusory world of sensible phantasies which give rise to nothing other but finite things only.[36] This dismissal would definitely allow the mind to see anew the whole of "the created universe of things," namely as staying *within* the universal Principle of being (the Beginning and the End of all). From this perspective, the Return of all things, including their "primordial causes" as those "contained within the Divine Nature," may be fairly acknowledged to be brought about, and the things themselves to be perspicuously seen as they truly are according to their original nature.

Thus the author of the *Periphyseon* comes to convince all careful readers of Book 4 that the Return, without which the knowledge of the truly One God is unattainable at all, should not be understood as brought about in spatio-temporal terms as a sort of *reversio* succeeding the initial *processio*. In other words, it should not be understood in like manner to contraction as a sort of movement of the entire creation backward to its original centre from the utmost periphery of its expansion. In accordance with the *rational motion* of human being (where the mind and the sense are rightly ordered, as due to *recta ratio*), the Return is rather to be properly known as a *spiritual* process going on in the human mind[37] hand in hand with its recovery, which is apparently all about bringing its perspective to conformity with the substantial order of the universe of creation. For in coherence with Eriugena's train of thought, it appears undeniably true that any procession of natures in creation cannot be really understood otherwise than in the way of being *at the same time* the return[38] of the same natures "into their

36. According to Hegel, it is basic to *dialectic* in general that the "immediate knowing of the *being* of external things is deception and error, and that there is no truth in the sensible as such, but that the *being* of these external things is rather something contingent, something that passes away, or a semblance. . ." (Hegel, *Encyclopaedia Logic*, 123, §76). As a paradigm of thinking originating from Plato, *dialectic* " is concerned precisely with considering things [as they are] in and for themselves, so that the finitude of the one-sided determination of the understanding becomes evident" (ibid., 129, §81 ad.).

37. While being focused on "the detailed analysis" of the ontological dimension of *reditus-reversio*, Stephen Gersh admits that it would be quite unfair to refer to it in Eriugena's context as merely "a cosmological principle" regardless of its relation to the mind's perception of the creature (see Gersh, "Structure of the Return," 110–11). If *reditus* were considered as a purely natural process similar to cyclic motions found in abundance both in the physical and intelligible world, it would remain obscure then, he argues, why the return "is included in the order of things by the Creator" (ibid., 111).

38. As Willemien Otten rightly says (referring to 526a in particular), "Eriugena stresses the fact that *processio* and *reditus* are complimentary movements, to the extent

primordial causes and into that Nature which neither creates nor is created, that Nature which is God Himself" (860b). Not improperly therefore, when he expounds the meaning of the expression "that Nature which neither creates nor is created," does the Philosopher say in conclusion to Book 4 that the Divine Nature is fairly

> believed not to be created because It is the Primal Cause of all, and there is no principle beyond It from which It can be created. On the other hand, because after the Return of the created universe of things visible and invisible into its primordial causes which are contained within the Divine Nature, there is no further creation of nature from the Divine Nature nor any propagation of sensible or intelligible species; for in It all will be One, just as even now in their causes they are One and always are so. Therefore we can rightly believe and understand that this Nature creates nothing. For what should It create when It alone is all in all things?" (860b–c)

The Unity of the Infinite Self-Identical Being

After all this, therefore, it would be not unreasonable to say that the One God *does not create* indeed. This statement is true in the sense that in the course of creating God creates nothing different from himself, and because of this encounters in creation nothing other in fact but himself, that is to say, him who is rightly understood to be *uncreated*. On the other hand, however, it cannot be denied either as almost a commonplace that in order that God might encounter himself in creation, the creation itself needs to be produced; and God then, evidently enough, is to be plainly thought of as him who *creates*. As long as it is the case, an obvious paradox develops here to cause a great deal of perplexity to common sense. Indeed, while creating nothing alien to himself, the One God does not actually manifest himself in creation otherwise than in the way of being at the same time, as it were, *created*, and thus not inadequately known as him who, as Eriugena puts it, simultaneously "makes and is made, and creates and is created" (452a). For in coherence with a dialectical approach to the truth of the absolute being (where the universal and the singular are properly ordered), it would be not unfair "to treat of the Divine Nature that not only does It create all things that are, but Itself also is created" (452a) in the sense that "in all things the

---

that one cannot act without the other" (Otten, "Universe of Nature," 204). The only thing to be additionally emphasized here is however that both *processio* and *reditus* are to be thought of as *simultaneously* complementing one another.

Divine Nature is being made" (or revealed[39]), "which is nothing else than the Divine Will. For in that Nature being is not different from willing, but willing and being are one and the same in the establishment of all things that are to be made" (453d).

Thus, actually in confirmation of the unconditional truth that the Divine being as a whole is inconceivable at all beyond a contradiction, another crucial paradox (basically complementary to the *cardinal* one, though latently present throughout the *Periphyseon*) apparently comes to the fore here: whereas on the one hand God is fairly known to be *uncreated*, on the other hand his infinite self-identical Nature cannot be thought of otherwise in fact than in the way of being *created* at the same time. And like the *cardinal* paradox considered above, this too gets resolved when both *thesis* and *antithesis* are reconciled in the way of presenting the ultimate Principle of all according to its *universal* nature. Being uncreated (i.e., determined by nothing), this Principle solely subsists by *unfolding itself*, that is, by *the return to itself*, since *nothing alien* to it may ever be brought into being. Indeed, in so far as God is truly known as the absolute being beyond which there is utterly nothing because he "fills out all things" and therefore "is always immutably at rest in Himself" (453b), to this extent it would be not improper to suggest that the Divine Nature "which is invisible in itself becomes manifest in all things that are" (454b). In this sense, the Divine Nature may rightly be understood as "created because nothing except itself exists as an essence since itself is the essence of all things" (454a). So that, when the Divine Nature is paradoxically said to be created, it is fairly meant to be created "not by another nature but by itself" (455a). "For when it is said that it creates itself," the Philosopher concludes, "the true meaning is nothing else but that it is establishing the natures of things. For the creation of itself, that is, the manifestation of itself in something, is surely that by which all things subsist" (455b).

And this is rightly so; for no true being (that never ceases to be) may ever be coherently thought of apart from the true infinity, which "consists in the going together with oneself in one's other."[40] Indeed, as Hegel, the great master of dialectic, would elucidate it in unison with Eriugena, the infinite as it truly is "consists rather in remaining at home with itself in its other, or (when it is expressed as a process) in coming to itself in its other."[41]

39. Eriugena is certainly well aware that the Divine Nature is quite "inappropriately said to be made" (454b). For this reason, it would be sound to offer some other terms (such as, for example, "revealed") that might prove to be closer to the meaning implied in the context.

40. Hegel, *Encyclopaedia Logic*, 173, §111 ad.

41. Ibid., 149, §94 ad.

From this, therefore, it is not hard to deduce that it is nothing other in fact but a thorough understanding of the *identity* as such[42] that really allows us to approach the fundamental knowledge of God as the absolute or self-identical whole, which "contains *the One* and *its Other*, both *itself* and *its opposite* within itself."[43]

"In its truth, as the ideality of what immediately is," the German philosopher holds in his *Logic*,

> identity is a lofty determination both for our religious consciousness and for the rest of our thinking and consciousness in general. It can be said that the true knowledge of God begins at the point where he is known as Identity, i.e., as absolute identity; and this implies, at the same time, that all the power and the glory of the world sinks into nothing before God and can subsist only as the shining [forth] of *his* power and *his* glory.[44]

"There is in fact," Hegel further argues,

> nothing, either in heaven or on earth, either in the spiritual or the natural world, that exhibits the abstract "either-or" as

42. "It is of great importance to reach an adequate understanding of the true significance of identity," maintains Hegel when discussing the basic principles of *dialectic*, "and this means above all that it must not be interpreted merely as abstract identity, i.e., as identity that excludes distinction. This is the point that distinguishes all bad philosophy from what alone deserves the name of philosophy" (ibid., 181, §115 ad.). As for an abstract *law of identity*, it reads, according to the German philosopher: "'Everything is identical with itself, A=A,' and negatively: 'A cannot be both A and non-A at the same time.'—Instead of being a true law of thinking, this principle is nothing but the law of the *abstract understanding*. The *propositional form* itself already contradicts it, since a proposition promises a distinction between subject and predicate as well as identity; and the identity-proposition does not furnish what its form demands"(ibid., 180, §115). "If someone says," Hegel goes on, "that this proposition cannot be proven, but *every* consciousness proceeds in accordance with it and, as experience shows agrees with it at once, as soon as it takes it in, then against this alleged experience of the Schools we have to set the universal experience that no consciousness thinks, has notions, or speaks, according to this law, and no existence of any kind at all exists in accordance with it. Speaking in accordance with this supposed law of truth (a planet is—a planet, magnetism is—magnetism, the spirit is—a spirit) is rightly regarded as silly; that is indeed a universal experience. The Schoolroom, which is the only place where these laws are valid, along with it logic which propounds them in earnest, has long since lost all credit with sound common sense as well as with reason"(ibid.). Before Hegel, the irrelevance of such laws to the cognitive tasks of philosophy entirely focused on approaching the absolute truth (which is that of God's Oneness) was perfectly obvious to those few who successfully applied the principles of dialectic to the knowledge of the true (infinite) being, and to whom among the first Eriugena, beyond any doubts, does belong.

43. Ibid., 188, §120.

44. Ibid., 181, §115 ad.

it is maintained by the understanding. Everything that is at all is concrete, and hence it is inwardly distinguished and self-opposed. The finitude of things consists in the fact that their immediate way of being does not correspond with what they are in-themselves.[45]

That is why as the true (infinite) being, which is "the *unity* of essence and existence"[46]or, more specifically, "free equality with itself in its determinacy"[47] (because outside it there is definitely nothing), God may be properly defined in accordance with John 4:24 as *Spirit*. This means therefore that in his truth he can only be known as "absolute Spirit,"[48] who in fact is the infinite being distinguishing "itself from itself . . . , so that it is at once mediation,"[49] for "God can only be called spirit inasmuch as he is known as inwardly *mediating himself with himself.*"[50]

It is consequently this train of thought (pivotal to which is a coherent understanding of the true nature of *identity*) that allows in effect any dialectically disciplined mind, Eriugena's one included, to see in *paradoxes*, concerning God's infinite and self-identical being, the way of approaching the absolute truth of Revelation. Approached in this way and understood as God's *self-disclosure* that is brought about in and through creation, Revelation allows the mind to grasp that fundamental truth that nothing particular does ever subsist on its own, that is to say, apart from the universal essence which brings it into being. Indeed, anything whatsoever (with no exception of human being) does subsist not otherwise than in unity with its ultimate essence to make it *manifest* or, speaking more precisely, to let it

45. Ibid., 187, §119 ad.2. From this, it is quite easy to see that any charges against pantheism which Eriugena's system has been so often suspected of are merely irrelevant for that simple reason, once suggested by Hegel in defense of Spinoza's philosophy, that *pantheism* is usually understood as "the doctrine that considers finite things as such, and the complex of them, to be God," which is altogether absurd "because no truth at all is ascribed to finite things or to the world as a whole. . ." (ibid., 227, §151 ad.). To this, I think, Eriugena himself might also add the following explanation: "For that which is of all belongs properly to none, but is in all in such a way as to subsist in itself" (467c). Furthermore, as the Dionysian theology suggests (and the author of the *Periphyseon* does agree with it), no finitude is compatible with God's being: "For it says that God is not one of things that are but that He is more than the things that are. . ."(462d). It remains unclear, therefore, how those accusing Eriugena of pantheism manage to keep ignoring such crucial things as the basic tenets of his speculation.

46. Ibid., 240, §163.

47. Ibid., 239, §163.

48. Ibid., 133, §83.

49. Ibid., 121, §74 ad.

50. Ibid., 120, §74.

really be, so that being truly *unconfined* this universal essence could actually be not *in itself* only but *for itself* as well. This is the way in which "the created universe of things" has been established. This is also the way to be followed in the mind in order that the only possible access to the substantial reality of creation might be provided. When a proper solution to any paradoxes concerning the true (unconfined) being is found indeed, human beings—prior to this, blinded by ignorance which the finite knowledge is inevitably fraught with—are let clearly see all things according to their true nature and enter thereby the reality as it substantially is.

To this extent, Eriugena believes, by analogy with the way the mind comes to manifest itself (while surpassing everything finite in any of its explicit forms), it can be not inadequately shown how the Divine Nature gets disclosed. In fact, the Divine Nature,

> although it creates all things and cannot be created by anything, is in an admirable manner created in all things which take their being from it; so that, as the intelligence of the mind or its purpose or its intention or however this first and innermost motion of ours may be called, having . . . entered upon thought and received the forms of certain fantasies, and having then proceeded into the symbols of sounds or the signs of sensible motions, is not inappropriately said to become—for being in itself without any sensible form, it becomes formed in fantasies—so the Divine Essence which when it subsists by itself surpasses every intellect is correctly said to be created in those things which are made by itself and through itself and in itself and for itself, so that in them either by the intellect, if they are only intelligible, or by the sense, if they are sensible, it comes to be known by those who investigate it in the right spirit. (454c–d)

Hence, if examined in full (up to the depth of a dialectically understood unity of the exterior and the interior as such), this analogy allows us not only to demonstrate the basic affinity between the proper order of the mind's operation and the way the absolute whole truly is "by itself and through itself and in itself and for itself"; it also indicates the clue following which anyone can actually cleave to reality as it truly is.

As a result, by offering this articulate analogy the author of the *Periphyseon* helps his readers to realise that the investigation in "the right spirit" mentioned above is to be all about an unambiguous disclosure of the absolute *unity*, which unceasingly pertains to the reality of the living whole that does subsist "by itself and through itself and in itself and for itself." This is the reality of creation where the creature and Creator are perfectly and inseparably one in the living and indivisible Spirit that the Holy Scripture is explicit about. For it is undoubtedly of Spirit's essence to have nothing to do with finite (or discrete) things, of whom it is fairly believed that he is living and ubiquitous, ever remaining the *invisible one* (John 3:8). The investigative task, therefore, is apparently the one to be solved, as follows from Eriugena's thoroughgoing approach to the matter, by means of *dialectic* (or the dialectical way of thinking, to be precise). In fact, being intolerant of finitude as such and, above all, of any attempts of illegitimate application of the principles of non-paradoxical reasoning to the knowledge of the Divine, dialectic alone enables the mind to get rid of all illusions of the sense-dependent knowledge and thus to clearly see the reality as it truly is *beyond any division*—the division that tears up the whole of being into separate pieces liable to decay only. This means that, irrelevant to the true being which never ceases to be, the total division proves in the light of dialectic actually to be nothing more than just an abstract construct imposed upon the living reality by the corrupt mind, who falsely accepts the sensible (i.e., the realm of finite things) for true.

From this perspective then, as long as the dialectically-disciplined mind embraces reality as it actually is beyond any finite being and division, the forms of Nature explicitly presented in the account of its division at 441b may not improperly be seen in the light of their new meaning. In particular, despite their appearance, they come to be seen not as a succession of separate species of Nature emerging as far as the division progresses, but rather as the distinct aspects of one and the same indivisible (though self-differentiating) Nature which unfolds through all the created things, so as really to be *all in all*. This is the vision which alone is perfectly appropriate to him who is called "the only true God" (John 17:3) and who indeed is *the One* or the infinite self-identical being.

As a matter of fact, since the Divine Nature as a whole may not inadequately be conceived (in accordance with the paradox dialectically treated above) as being *uncreated* and *created* at the same time, it should subsequently mean that the first, the second and the third divisions of Nature may be fairly considered not as taken at their face value, as though they respectively were just the Beginning, the Middle and the End of *creation* following one another in time. Instead, in accordance with the living integrity of the Divine Nature, they should be not literally but spiritually understood as an intimate *threefold unity* as it is expressly presented in the account of division by the *fourth* synthetic form of Nature. This is the form within which the Beginning, the Middle and the End of creation, as those *appropriate to the true (infinite) being that perfectly is in itself through itself and for itself,* are reasonably understood to be *inseparably and simultaneously one.* Likewise the absolute truth of God's Trinity requires of "the Cause of all things" to be "of a threefold substance" (455c) so as to be congruous to the totality of being, but not merely to the apex of a hierarchy-like model of it.

No wonder then, as Willemien Otten points out concerning the pivotal theme of the *Periphyseon*'s dialogue, that the "Master does not answer the suggestion of his pupil that the difference between the second and the third form is found in reality as well as in our contemplation thereof. His abrupt transition to the audacious rhetorical unification of all four forms in the one indivisible divine essence may prove that he is not interested in such factual differences, as he has set his mind on the attempting to restore all forms to the divine harmony."[51] "It is obvious," she concludes therefore with regard to the "real intentions" of the author of the *Periphyseon*, "that Eriugena endeavors to restore *natura* to its original undivided unity in God . . ."[52]

---

51. Otten, *Anthropology*, 35.
52. Ibid., 32.

Conclusion

ON COMPLETION OF THE present inquiry, we arrive at a clear vision that the prime concern of Eriugena (as well as the main objective of his intellectual endeavor) is to find the way of bringing human life to conformity with the reality of God's creation, which proves in fact to be hidden behind the layers of sensible images that turn the world, where human beings think they live, into a conglomerate of finite things—that is, the transient world of things that come into being and pass away. This profoundly philosophical vision of the liberation of human being from its captivity in the world of dichotomy, where fleeting human life is squeezed between the extremes of being and non-being, allows Eriugena to pose a soteriological question (ever central to Christian theology) as an essentially *anthropological* one, at the heart of which there lies both the epistemological and ontological agenda. And all this, in turn, raises a question of Eriugena's Christology. For the way the liberation of human race is brought about and the role Christ plays in the drama of salvation[1] appear quite a problematic issue in Eriugena's vision of Christian faith. Perhaps, a good deal of the influence of Eastern philosophy on his religious beliefs might give us a clue and shed some light upon the peculiarities of Eriugena's thought, as well as let us learn a lot from the genius of his philosophical-theological discourse as it develops, above all, within the framework of his *anti-division* project, commonly known under the title of the *Periphyseon*. In this sense, Eriugena's system still remains to us a good example of thinking consistently about bringing the whole of real-

---

1. Careful and thoughtful reading of Eriugena's texts brings us to impression that their author (though he is certainly inexplicit about this) is inclined to see the Savior as a teacher *par excellence*—that is *the teacher* whose unique teaching of the kingdom of God leads those believing in his divinity and resurrection to complete transformation of their mind and life, resulting in their perfect conformity to the substantial reality of creation, as appropriate to being at one with the One God.

ity to the bosom of God's creation and, as a result, of building a coherent theology of God's Unity.

In particular, students of Eriugena's thought should learn from it the way the transcendence and immanence could get reconciled to allow us today to cure the most regrettable misconception of God severed from his creation (i.e., the one guilty of many miscarriages of practical faith) by steering a safe course between the extremes of Radical Theology and Radical Orthodoxy[2], and thus to address a wide range of calamities that institution-

---

2. In their reaction to the crisis that the Church is undergoing, Radical Theology and Radical Orthodoxy stand for a thoroughgoing rethinking of the basics of Christian theology, though see it in different ways. Speaking in general, both movements of thought find it possible to achieve cardinal changes by introducing *a new language* into theology. The distinction between the two consists, however, in their different, and even opposite, approaches to this language (or "the way of speaking of God"). The radical theologians, such as John Robinson or John Spong, believe that the language of the traditional theism (including unintelligible notions of the Church dogmas) should be resolutely rejected as obsolete. In order that the remote God of theism might be brought closer to those to whom the old religious practices do not appeal any more, the language of faith should be translated, as the radicals suggest, into the terms of everyday life, meaningful and clear to the contemporary society as a whole (e.g., the "sinful" or "fallen" state of being into the "untrue existence"). Robinson calls his followers for the quest of a "middle way" between the religious supernaturalism and the humanist naturalism, and for a profound justification of this quest he refers to such key figures of the twentieth-century theology as Bultmann, Bonhöffer, and Tillich. In alliance with their teachings, and above all with the ideas of "demythologization," "irreligious Christianity," and God as the basis and the purpose of being, the radical theologians hope to succeed in the enterprise of bringing Christian faith in touch with the secular society. Unlike these attempts of the radical reconsideration of the traditional tenets of religion, Radical Orthodoxy (and John Milbank in particular) seeks to provide a contemporary apology of faith by presenting anew its old truths, expressed in Christian theology as early as the teachings of Aquinas and Duns Scotus, and thus to render active the fundamental ideas (as well as the notions they coin) latently present to Christian thought. Among these truths and ideas, according to Milbank, one of the central is that of the radical transcendence of the Divine, actuality of which is to be affirmed in contrast to the virtual immanence. Along with this restoration of the traditional tenets, however, the old metaphysics likewise, as the way of putting them in order, is brought back to life. As a result, the infinite comes to be treated, erroneously again, as belonging to "the transcendent height" that lies beyond the transcendental categories of mind and is understood in terms of reality alternative to the finite being. All this consequently means that no renewal of theology is attainable unless the very logic of the theological reflection is cardinally changed. The language of theology does not consist of the notions only; it should also include *the way of bringing these notions together*, which is obviously nothing other than the *inner logic* of the theological discourse. So it is in fact a reconstruction of the logic appropriate to the infinite nature of the truths revealed which alone would allow us in our attempts to restore the dignity of Christian faith to steer a safe course between the extremes of the old and new. And this appeal to a proper logic of the theological thinking is one of the main things indeed that we learn from Eriugena's system.

alized religion is currently undergoing in its deep crisis. For this, as Eriugena teaches us, the very paradigm of thinking applied to faith and theology has to be cardinally changed: Metaphysics that tends to divide the living reality in two (providing thereby the ground for dualistic dichotomies of any sort) need to be resolutely rejected as basically inappropriate to the truth of faith in the One God and, subsequently, be effectively replaced by Dialectic. As a way of thinking, which alone is perfectly fit for the task of conceiving the reality of the whole (where no room for the dichotomy between being and non-being can ever be found), Dialectic proves to be appropriate indeed for guiding human beings in their life in unity with him who is the One.

Furthermore, as a way of thinking the absolute whole that is brought about by means of contradiction (due to which, as seen from the *Periphyseon*'s discourse, the opposition of the eternal and temporal is overcome), this Dialectic is actually where Eriugena and Hegel meet to confirm the validity of Noack's words of the medieval genius as the "Hegel of the ninth century." Both Eriugena and Hegel are convinced that things in their truth are not as they *appear* to be. Moreover, just as Hegel does not stop at this principal postulate of the Kantian epistemology that seeks to legitimize the dichotomy between the phenomenal and noumenal, likewise Eriugena is not keen at all on setting apart the infinite and finite. They are both concerned about the way things can properly be thought of (and therefore known) as they actually are in the true reality of the infinite, living and indivisible, whole in order that—through the knowledge of the true things—human beings could actually *be* in the reality as it truly (unceasingly) is.

For this, according to both Eriugena and Hegel, true things should not be thought of in like manner to *finite* ones, which appear to oppose one another as if existing in the world divided into opposites mutually separated. All the more this is true about the infinite (unconfined) Being itself to be known as the absolute, self-sufficient and self-knowing, whole or God himself. God cannot be thought of as something *external* in like manner to external (*finite*) things—that is, as an *external object*, when he is assumed to be known by virtue of predicating attributes of his essence, which has always been, according to Hegel, a favorite preoccupation of *metaphysics*. Nor can the infinite God be known as a *subject* that is simply opposed to the object and therefore ever remaining to be the hidden (negative) inwardness only. The true God may only be known as *Spirit*, the living and indivisible whole, who ever makes himself adequately manifest. As Spirit, God is him indeed in whom there is no discrepancy between the inner essence and actual existence, and who therefore truly says of himself, "I am Who I am." To be consequently at one with the true God known as Spirit, human beings must likewise, as due to *imago dei*, make sure that the innermost essence of their nature (that really makes them distinctive among the whole creature) may find itself to be adequately manifest. This furthermore means that in order to live in the one indivisible reality of the infinite whole, and thus really worship and please the true God, human beings must actually be *spirits*—that is, the ones who make their *reason adequately manifest* as *Logos*. This is actually what both Eriugena and Hegel, though each in his own way, prove to teach the faithful to get them focused on the truth revealed by Christ—the truth of God's Oneness, according to which *all* men and women are to be nothing other but the children of the only Father in heaven.

This truth, central to Christian faith, is however incompatible with a dualistic vision of reality provided by metaphysics as a type of mentality. It is metaphysics indeed to which it is essential to divide the reality as such *in two* (being-non-being, infinite-finite, transcendent-immanent, sensual-supersensual, natural-supernatural, essential-superessential, etc.) and to understand the whole as resulting from the complementary counterparts added up. Despite its obsession with dichotomies, metaphysics has been traditionally chosen by theology as a reliable method of understanding and theoretical underpinning of its truths. By doing so, however, theology inevitably dooms itself to *dogmatism*, which is, as Hegel insists, the very nature of metaphysics. Indeed, of the two opposite definitions (as appropriate to the pairs of contraries indicated above) it has always to choose only one for true and reject the other as false or irrelevant to God's being. In the narrow sense of the word, as mentioned before, dogmatism therefore "consists in adhering to one-sided determinations of the understanding whilst excluding their opposites."[3] According to Hegel, in metaphysics "one is of the opinion that one can speak only of the truth *of a proposition*, and that the only question that can be raised with regard to a *concept* is whether (as people say) it can be truthfully "*attached*" to a subject or not. Untruth would depend on the contradiction to be found between the subject of the representation and the concept to be predicated of it."[4]

As for the theology that traditionally, as Hegel says, rested upon this metaphysics, "it was a science[5] of God that rested not upon *reason* but on the *understanding*, and its thinking moves only in abstract thought-determinations. Whilst what was treated was the *concept* of God, it was the

---

3. Hegel, *Encyclopaedia Logic*, 70, §32 ad.

4. Ibid., 71, §33.

5. By no means should Hegel's *Wissenschaft* be confused with *science* in the everyday use of the word. To Hegel, *Wissenschaft* is not a body of empirically ascertained and verified truths; it is rather a coherent system of speculative knowledge targeted at attaining the idea latently present to the reality as a whole.

representation of God that formed the criterion for cognition."[6] "In this account of God from the point of view of the understanding," Hegel further explains, "what counts above all is which predicates agree or not with what *we represent* to ourselves as 'God.'"[7] As a result, under the direct influence of metaphysics, and in attempt to avoid the dogmatism that this metaphysics imposes upon the church doctrine, theology turns at best into a body of external and accidental knowledge of an empirical sort. In fact, however, only under the direct impact of the critical philosophy,[8] the major task of which is fairly understood since Kant to consist in having the rights of reason identified and defended,[9] can the mind be awakened from the dogmatic slumber.[10] The same is true of Christian theology as well. It desperately needs an intimate union with a profoundly philosophical thinking to secure a proper access to the Truth of Revelation.[11] For, as previously considered, even the

6. Hegel, *Encyclopaedia Logic*, 74–75, §36 ad.

7. Ibid., 73, §36.

8. The *critical philosophy* (originally associated with Kant's three *Critiques*, beginning with the *Critique of Pure Reason*) is where the German idealism agenda comes from. The focal point of the German idealism on the whole may not unfairly be understood as an attempt to overcome *the naive way of thinking*, as Hegel calls it. This is a kind of thinking that squarely rests upon the belief that the reality is that of finite things, and thus mistakes the data delivered by the senses from without for its own content, perfectly appropriate, as assumed, to the world as it "objectively" is. Kant resolutely shattered this naïve belief by appealing to *a priori* forms of reason and suggesting that the world given in perception is that of "experience," and therefore is nothing more in fact than a *construct* of mind.

9. See Кант, *Критика чистого разума*, 443.

10. See ibid., 446.

11. As it is well known, Christian theology has always been suspicious of philosophy, and sometimes even hostile to it, as Tertullian, for example, apparently was. Paul Tillich is perhaps one of the recent notable exceptions to this predominantly negative attitude to philosophy. In comparison to Karl Barth, "the Tertullian of our days," Reinhold Niebuhr (in his *Biblical Thought and Ontological Speculation in Tillich's Theology*) calls Tillich "the Origen of our days," who seeks to bring the Gospel message close to the entire history of culture. Similarly to Tertullian, Barth vehemently resisted to a possibility of union between theology and philosophy: "Actually, there has never been a *philosophia Christiana*; for if it was *philosophia*, it was not *Christiana*; and if it was *Christiana*, it was not *philosophia*" (*Church Dogmatics* 1, 1:5). By contrast, to Tillich it is exactly philosophy, with its strong appeal to the problems and anxieties human beings have in their existence, that really allows theology to bridge the gap between church and society. Theology and philosophy therefore need, according to him, a constructive dialogue, so that their relationship may not unfairly be qualified as *correlation*. As a method, *correlation* substantially differs from other approaches that previously dominated in Christianity, such as *supranaturalism*, *humanism*, and *dualism*. The advantage of the new approach (i.e., *correlation* between philosophy and theology) Tillich finds to consist in its appeal to nothing other but God as *Being itself*, the infinite one, that is beyond the dichotomy between being and non-being. Thus philosophy and theology,

highest truth given through faith still remains a category of knowledge, and may therefore be available to proper knowledge only.[12] "If theology provides a merely external enumeration and compilation of religious teachings," says Hegel, "then it is not yet science. Even the merely historical treatment of its subject matter that is in favour nowadays (for instance, the reporting of what this or that Church Father said) does not give theology a scientific character. Science comes only when we advance to the business of philosophy, i.e. the mode of thinking that involves comprehension. Thus, genuine theology is essentially, at the same time, Philosophy of Religion, and that is what it was in the Middle Ages too."[13]

As clearly seen from the very beginning of the present inquiry, Eriugena likewise understands that, in order to conform to the truth they are both focused on, true philosophy and true religion are to be known not as two different things but one and the same.[14] And it is exactly a deep under-

---

when properly correlated, translate the basic ontological question of distinction of being from non-being into the question of overcoming *non-being* and *finitude* as such. This is, Tillich believes, the central issue of all human beings' anxiety; this is where their existence acquires its new meaning, and the way to the New Being in union with the infinite Being itself opens up. Therefore, only working together, philosophy and theology get human beings focused on the vision of the Being itself, that is the one living God, and thus give them a real opportunity of overcoming the finitude of their existence, threatened by non-being, and be re-united with God again. It is, hence, a proper correlation between philosophy and theology that, in Tillich's view, brings all human beings to the very center of the Gospel message, making their life meaningful (See Bintsarovsky, "Современное богословие," лекция 10, 3–7).

12. The famous *credo ut intelligam* of Anselm's theology does remind us about the validity of this approach to the Christian truth. The objective of faith, as articulated by Anselm, may also explain why it is him who first after Eriugena managed to take the next considerable step in the evolution of Christian thought.

13. Hegel, *Encyclopaedia Logic*, 74, §36 ad.

14. It is well known that Eriugena's theology was many times condemned by church authorities, and although the reasons for accusations were never explicitly articulated, it is likely the originality of Eriugena's approach to Christian faith that caused among the conservatives a great deal of discontent with his views. Even the first big treatise *On Divine Predestination*, written by Eriugena at the request of the church superiors, was followed by a series of condemnations in the 850s—first at the council of Valence in 855 and then at the council of Langres in 859 (see Moran, *Philosophy*, 33). Since then Eriugena remained unpopular with the senior churchmen, and in 1210 his works were condemned again. This time, it remained likewise obscure why the thinker's ideas were found inappropriate to the church dogmas. Only later, in 1225, Pope Honorius III more or less explicitly (though rather emotionally then rationally) expressed his attitude to Eriugena's legacy and "in a letter to the bishops of France condemned the *liber periphysis titulatur* and ordered that all copies be sent to Rome for burning, since the work was "teeming with the worms of heretical perversity"" (ibid., 89). What kind of the "heretical perversity" was meant there is still a mystery. Perhaps, the story of the 1210 condemnation could shed some light upon this riddle. "The events surrounding

standing of this unity (where finite forms of truth get overcome) that gave
Hegel reason, as already mentioned, to see Eriugena as the beginning of
philosophy proper. "Philosophy properly speaking," he maintains, "begins
in the ninth century with John Scottus Eriugena."[15] According to this view,
philosophy cannot develop on its own—that is, apart from its genuine interest in the infinite religious truth, in the sense that God himself, as Hegel
says, is the Truth. Likewise, theology cannot really approach its own truth,
unless philosophically disciplined thinking of the infinite whole is deeply

------

his condemnation," says Moran, "are unclear. He was associated with two Aristotelian
scholars who were teaching at Paris—David of Dinant and Amaury of Bene" (ibid.).
Both Amaury and David of Dinant "were denounced by Thomas Aquinas as panthe-
ists," who respectively considered God as being either "the form of all things" or "the
matter of all things," as Aquinas presents it (see ibid., 86). Unlike Amaury, however,
Eriugena "does not use the term "formal principle," but he does use the formula *forma
omnium* to describe God on several occasions (e.g., 1. 500a). He also says that God is
the *essentia* and *subsistentia omnium*" (ibid., 87). It does not follow from this, nevertheless, that Eriugena could share a pantheistic view of the Divine being, and those
who ever studied his writings would readily agree that he actually did not. Any charges
against Eriugena's pantheism, therefore, would only result from a substantial misunderstanding of his views, which was certainly the case with his accusers who did not
bother to read what Eriugena himself wrote about the principle irrelevance of pantheism (or what later acquired this name) to a coherent theology. In fact, a possibility of
a pantheistic interpretation of his views, as Moran admits, horrifies Eriugena, and he
firmly rejects any attempts of identifying the created world with God: "For God is not a
genus of the creature nor the creature a species of God any more than the creature is the
genus of God or God a species of the creature. The same can be said of the whole and its
part, for God is not the whole of the creature, nor the creature a part of God any more
than the creature is the whole of God or God a part of the creature. . ." (1. 523d). So
that those who simply believed that Amaury had "found his teachings in the writings of
Eriugena" (Moran, *Philosophy,* 87), in fact falsely accused the latter of the doctrine utterly alien to his theology. And although there is no direct evidence that the *Periphyseon*
was ever officially condemned in the thirteenth century, "the 1225 condemnation, however, refers to the *Periphyseon* as having already been banned by the "Synod of Sens,"
presumably referring to the judgement of 1210" (ibid., 89), made by the archbishop of
Sens, Peter Corbelius, and by the council of bishops at Paris with regard to the works
on natural philosophy by David of Dinant and Aristotle (see ibid.). Since then "it has
become a common place that Eriugena was a pantheist" (ibid., 88), by which the Medieval Church actually meant to recognize Eriugena's system to be unsuitable both for
the ecclesiastical doctrine and practice. Needless to say, nonetheless, how unfair (and
simply wrong) this judgement was about Eriugena's contribution to Christian theology.
As Moran argues, the phrase *forma omnium* used by Eriugena should be interpreted as
linked to "scriptural pronouncements, such as I Corinthians 15.28 that God will be all
in all (*Deus erit omnia in omnibus*), or John 1.3-4, that all things are in God as life (*quod
factum est in eo ipso vita erat*), a phrase that appears frequently in Eriugena." This means
that the "phrase can, of course, be interpreted purely devotionally to mean that God is
omnipresent and that all things depend totally for their being on God; otherwise they
would be nothing at all" (ibid.).

15. Hegel, *Lectures on the History of Philosophy,* 42.

implanted in its body. Similarly to Hegel, it is clear to Eriugena that until theology stops relying on metaphysics, it will continue to deal with nothing other than a mere *misconception* of God. In metaphysical theology, the infinite and living God proves to be reduced to nothing more in fact than just a fictitious construct correspondent to a twofold representation, according to which he is believed to be 1) *external* (no matter whether remote or closely present) and 2) *transcendent.*[16] By contrast, in the theology appropriate to the unity of philosophy and religion, as Eriugena understands it,[17] the emphasis is to be made not on the conception of God as such but on *the way*

---

16. Representations of this sort, the metaphysical nature of which is undoubtedly obvious, are so deeply inherent in theological reflection that they may hardly ever be completely eradicated from it. Little wonder therefore that, despite a good deal of innovative developments in the Postliberal age, a twofold construct of Divinity goes on to survive in theology. In particular, in the Barthian theology that appears to have heralded a new dawn in understanding of Revelation and has really opened up a broad way to postliberal endeavors, the doctrine of "complete otherness" still insists that the Voice communicating the truth of God does come from "out there."

17. As seen in Chapter 1 with regard to Eriugena's argument developed within the context of the predestination controversy, a certain affinity between his thinking and the Mu'tazilah doctrines suggests that a philosophically coherent approach to faith should be understood to lie at the heart of the theology of the Divine Unity. This is the theology entirely based on *a new vision of creation*, according to which there is nothing alien in it to God who, as Mu'tazilites believe, is the absolute Good and who, therefore, cannot be held responsible for the existence of evil in the world. Moreover, as a philosophically rigorous thinking of the absolute Oneness further suggests according to them, God can neither create evil nor have power over it. Nothing at all subsists in the reality of creation otherwise than in the way of being determined from within; God himself cannot be known from without (by predicating attributes of his essence), for outside him who may only be known as the "Necessary Existent" (or the self-determined being) nothing at all can ever exist. Everything therefore can only subsist, as Mu'tazilites insist, by being at one with him who is the One and never acts contrary to his promise, because there is no discrepancy in him between his will and being. So it is by deviation from the inner essence of their genuine nature (or, in terms of the First Obligation doctrine, from the *speculative reason*, al-nazar) that all humans go astray, causing all wrongdoings and bringing evil into the world. Little wonder, therefore, that his Carolingian contemporaries were much confused when, arguing against the doctrine of double predestination, Eriugena put forward the arguments far removed from their traditional beliefs but close (which Carolingians might have been unaware of) to the doctrines developed within the *Falsafah* tradition. Surprisingly or not, in agreement with his Eastern contemporaries Eriugena strongly believes that life of human beings in defiance of their essential nature is the root of evil; God does not create hell: it is human sinfulness that is responsible for creating its own hell. Hence, salvation is available to all humans in so far as they take care of their genuine nature and live righteously in harmony with its *right order*, which is to be understood as its proper *rational* motion. All this consequently means that the *optimistic vision of salvation* (thoroughly essential to Christian faith) is impossible without a profoundly philosophical attitude to religion, which unlike his Western contemporaries Eriugena is obviously enthusiastic about.

God is conceived and, as a consequence, on *transformation* of human beings as a means of getting them prepared for the reception of the Truth revealed. The scriptural truths of *the renewal of the mind* (Rom 12:2) and *making straight the way of the Lord* (John 1:23) are therefore to be chosen for the pillars of a new theology to be built—that is, the theology of God's Unity, to which it is the most essential that *all* humans are known as *the children of the One God* that are *to be at one* with him (John 1:12).

The role of philosophy in this construction work, as Eriugena sees it, is perfectly obvious. It consists in offering the way of cleansing the mind of its alien (sense-dependent) content, loosely or tightly packed in the form of finite definitions, but unpacked by virtue of *dialectical contradiction*, tolerant of nothing finite.[18] This is the way in which to those who are spiritually transformed and liberated (i.e., renewed and purified in their minds) the knowledge of God as Spirit, that the Truth of Revelation is all about (John 4:23–24),[19] becomes available indeed. In other words, those who are spiritually free (i.e., not determined from without), and in whom therefore there is no discrepancy between the innermost essence of their nature and its adequate manifestation (actual existence), are summoned to be perfect as

18. As A. I. Brilliantov points out, an attention to Eriugena's philosophy was drawn only after the emergence of the German idealist systems, when there was found a certain affinity between those systems and Eriugena's views (see Brilliantov, *Влияние восточного богословия*, 420–21). A deep understanding of the role of the *dialectical contradiction* in philosophical thinking is undoubtedly one of the central themes common to Eriugena and Hegel. Since Kant's *antinomism* raised the question of irrelevance of finite concepts of human understanding (the categories of *Verstand*) to the knowledge of the infinite as such (and the divine being, in particular), Hegel insisted that the solution to antinomies was to be sought on the way of their *dialectical* treatment, which would also require that our attitude to epistemology and ontology should be cardinally reconsidered. Neither of them, according to Hegel, should be taken separately, in like manner to the "instrumentalist" approach of metaphysics. In other words, the dialectical treatment of antinomies required a complete *paradigmatic shift* in the mind towards a new type of mentality, based on the intimate interconnectedness of ontology and epistemology, and thus appropriate to the absolute reality of Spirit, ubiquitous and indivisible, transcendent and immanent at the same time. This paradigmatic shift in the mind also meant therefore a transformation of human being or, speaking more specifically, making it fit for living in the reality of the absolute whole.

19. Taking into account a great deal of Eriugena's interest in St. John's Gospel (obvious, for instance, in his *Homily on the Prologue to the Gospel of St. John*), we may not unreasonably refer to the *fourth* Gospel as one of the main sources of Eriugena's thought. Be it the case that Eriugena so highly valued this part of sacred writings, it would be hard to imagine that some of its most precious words could simply escape him. In this sense, it would be fair to let the Gospel speak for itself to hear the words of Jesus: "But the hour is coming, and is now here, when the true worshipers will worship the Father in spirit and truth, for the Father seeks such as these to worship him. God is spirit, and those who worship him must worship in spirit and truth" (John 4:23–24).

their Father in heaven is (Matt 5:48), and for this reason may fairly be called the sons of God. The new theology, hence, brings not a new shape to the old religious practices and beliefs, but *a new meaning to human life*, revealing the secrets of immortality and transfiguration. The ever-lasting being that never ceases to be, and the way all humans come to participate in it, is actually what appears to Eriugena central in theology, in so far as it is coherent with the heart of the message of Christ's *unique teaching of the kingdom of God.*[20] As our inquiry into the meaning of Eriugena's thought convinces us, this teaching should rightly be understood as that of the reality of God's *self-disclosure*, where the unity of the inner essence and its actual existence is utterly unshakable (Exod 3:14), and where therefore those capable of their *adequate self-disclosure* truly belong.

* * *

Such is a brief outline of Eriugena's understanding of a coherently Christian theology, as it may be reconstructed by an analysis of the voluminous and dense text of the *Periphyseon*, a monumental landmark in the history of Christian thought. It is the understanding which A. I. Brilliantov character- izes as Eriugena's *monism*, finding it firmly based on the Christian concept of God as "the self-knowing Spirit, analogous to the spirit of man," when he is restored to the integrity of his nature.[21]

Does this understanding matter to us today? It certainly does, to the extent that Christians are aware nowadays of the necessity of having their church-centered faith cardinally reconsidered to let it recover from the deep crisis it has at least been in since Christendom became the arena of the horrors and atrocities of the world wars. Eriugena's honesty and profundity encourage us to look at our faith anew in the hope of understanding where a fatal mistake was made—the mistake that led us astray so as to bring us to the nowhere of bestial and meaningless life. Was it collusion with state at Nicaea that resulted, as Leo Tolstoy believes, in the substitution of the

---

20. "It may be said," A. I. Brilliantov writes about Eriugena's work, "that the whole system of the Philosopher aims to banish non-being from the Universe, and thus to retain in it being alone" (Brilliantov, *Влияние восточного богословия*, 289). Moreover, Brilliantov believes that Eriugena's *opus magnum* is largely focused on what may be understood as the prime concern of Christ's teaching—that is, "restoration of the whole of human nature to its ideal state or, in a sense, liberation of all with no exception from evil, sin, and death . . ." (ibid., 381). "This is to happen," the Russian theologian further comments on Eriugena's doctrine, "with the Second Coming of Christ, . . . understood in the sense of the universal and full revelation of Christ as truth to all men and women" (ibid.).

21. See ibid., 260, 263.

Sermon on the Mount by the Creed?[22] Or was it the church itself, as Dostoevsky thinks, an institution of human enslavement built on the principles of miracle, mystery, and authority?[23] Or are the genuine reasons of the perversion of Christian faith even deeper than these and should be searched for, say, in ourselves, as Eriugena teaches us—that is, in our mind, in the way we think and impose our thoughts on the world we live in? No matter how many other questions of the kind can be raised, the only thing we ought to understand is what is wrong with us that for so long we fail to adhere to the truth revealed to us two millennia ago. To me, Eriugena seems to have come very close to the answer we are looking for, and this is why his legacy is immensely important to us today.

22. In his *The Kingdom of God Is Inside You: Christianity As Not a Mystical Doctrine But a New Vision of Life*, Leo Tolstoy particularly says: ". . . what we are taught by clergy is not Christianity" (Tolstoy, *Закон насилия и закон любви*, 369). "Churches," he further holds, "face a dilemma: Sermon on the Mount or the Nicene Creed, one excludes the other. If one sincerely believes in the Sermon on the Mount, then the Nicene Creed will lose its meaning and sense, likewise the church and its representatives. If one believes in the Nicene Creed, . . . the Sermon on the Mount will become needless" (ibid., 371). Understanding of Christ's teaching "puts churches and their meaning to an end" (ibid.). Churches "have always been, and cannot be otherwise, institutions not only alien but even hostile to the teaching of Christ" (ibid., 361). There is nothing in common between churches and Christianity, "except for the name; these are two completely opposite and mutually hostile principles. One is pride, violence, selfishness, stagnation, and death. The other is humility, penitence, submissiveness, movement, and life. It is impossible to serve these two masters at once; one or the other has to be chosen" (ibid.).

23. In his *Legend of Grand Inquisitor*, Dostoevsky features three powers able to conquer and hold captive forever the conscience of those disobedient to the rule of the Church, and these powers are *miracle, mystery,* and *authority* (see Dostoevsky, "Современное богословие: *Богословие и секуляризм*.", par. 12).

Bibliography

Adorno, Theodor (Адорно, Теодор). *Проблемы моральной философии*. Перевод М. Л. Хорькова. Москва: Республика, 2000.

Al-Kindi. *On First Philosophy*. With Introduction and Commentary by Alfred L. Ivry. Albany, NY: State University of New York Press, 1974.

Altizer, Thomas (Альтицер, Томас). *Смерть Бога: Евангелие христианского атеизма*. Перевод Ю. Р. Селиванова. Москва: Канон, 2010.

Amangaliev, V. (Амангалиев, В.). "Несторианство, Православие или Ислам?" Официальный сайт Митрополичьего округа Казахстана. http://rusk.ru/st.php?idar=1001036.

Aristotle (Аристотель). *Сочинения в 4-х ТТ. Т. 1: Метафизика*. Москва: Мысль, 1976.

Armstrong, Karen. *A History of God. From Abraham to the Present: The 4000-year Quest for God*. London: Vintage, 1999.

Augustine of Hippo (Августин Блаженный). *О граде Божием*. Москва: Издательство Спасо-Преображенского Валаамского монастыря, 1994.

Basil the Great (Василий Великий). *Василія Великаго Архіепископа Кесаріи Каппадокійскія Творенія. Часть I*. Москва: Типографія Августа Семена при Императорской Медико-Хирургической Академіи, 1845.

Beierwaltes, Werner. "The Revaluation of John Scottus Eriugena in German Idealism." In *The Mind of Eriugena*, edited by John J. O'Meara and Ludwig Beiler, 190–98. Dublin: Irish University Press, 1973.

Bely, Andrei (Белый, Андрей). *Символизм как миропонимание*. Составитель, вступительная статья и примечания Л. А. Сугай. Москва: Республика, 1994.

Berdyaev, Nikolai A. (Бердяев, Николай А.). *Русская Идея*. Санкт-Петербург: Азбука-классика, 2008.

———. "Философия свободного духа: Проблематика и апология христианства." In Бердяев, Н. А., *Философия свободного Духа*, 230–316. Москва: Республика, 1994.

———. "Я и мир объектов: Опыт философии одиночества и общения." In Бердяев, Н. А., *Философия свободного Духа*, 1–98. Москва: Республика, 1994.

Bergson, Henry (Бергсон, Анри). *Творческая эволюция*. Москва: Академический проект, 2015.

Bintsarovsky, Dmitryi (Бинцаровский, Дмитрий). "Современное богословие: Богословие и секуляризм." http://www.ersu.org/ru/video.

Brilliantov, Alexander I. (Бриллиантов, Александр И.). *Влияние восточного богословия на западное в произведениях Иоанна Скота Эригены.* Москва: Мартис, 1998.

Buber, Martin (Бубер, Мартин). *Два образа веры.* Москва: Республика, 1995.

Bulgakov, Sergei N. (Булгаков, Сергей Н.). *Свет невечерний: Созерцания и умозрения.* Москва: АСТ, 2001. Reprint, в 3-х выпусках. Санкт-Петербург: Чтение, 2001.

Diogenes Laertius (Диоген Лаэртский). *О жизни, учениях и изречениях знаменитых философов.* Москва: Мысль, 1979.

Dionysius the Areopagite (Дионисий Ареопагит). *О божественных именах. О мистическом богословии.* Санкт-Петербург: Глагол, 1994.

———. *О небесной иерархи.* Электронная библиотека Одинцовского благочиния. http://www.odinblago.ru/sv_otci/dionisiy_areopagit/dionisyareoagit/.

Dostoevsky, F. M. (Достоевский, Ф. М.). *Братья Карамазовы. Часть вторая. Книга пятая. Великий инквизитор.* Интернет-библиотека Алексея Комарова, 2005. http://www.ilibrary.ru/text/1199/p.37/index.html.

Eriugena, John Scottus (Эриугена, Иоанн Скотт). *Гомилия на Пролог Евангелия от Иоанна.* На латинском и русском языках. Вступительная статья, перевод, примечания В. В. Петрова. Москва: Греко-латинский кабинет Ю. А. Шичалина, 1995.

———. *Treatise on Divine Predestination.* Translated by M. Brennan. Notre Dame: University of Notre Dame Press, 1998.

———. *The Voice of the Eagle: Homily on the Prologue to the Gospel of St. John.* Translated with introductions and reflections by Christopher Bamford. Foreword by Thomas Moore. Great Barrington, MA: Lindisfarne, 2000.

———. *Iohannis Scotti Eriugenae Carmina.* Edited by Michael W Herren. Dublin: Institute for Advanced Studies, School of Celtic Studies, 1993.

———. *Iohannis Scotti Eriugenae Periphyseon (De Divisione Naturae).* Books 1–3 edited by I. P. Sheldon-Williams. Book 4 edited by E. Jeauneau, translated by J. O'Meara and I. P. Sheldon-Williams. Dublin: The Dublin University for Advanced Studies, 1968–1995.

Florensky, Pavel A. (Флоренский, Павел А.). "Обратная перспектива." In Флоренский, П. А., *Сочинения в 4-х ТТ. Т. 3 (Часть 1),* 46–103. Москва: Мысль, 1999.

Florovsky, Georgyi V. (Флоровский, Георгий В.). *Восточные отцы IV века.* Медиатека Предание.ру. http://predanie.ru/florovskiy-georgiy-vasilevich-protoierey/book/69629-vostochnye-otcy-iv-veka/.

———. *Восточные отцы V–VIII веков.* Православная интернет-библиотека Азбука веры. http://azbyka.ru/tserkov/svyatye/s_o_bogoslovie/florovskiy_vizantiyskie_otsy_v-viii.shtml.

———. "Метафизические предпосылки утопизма." In Флоровский, Г. В., *Из прошлого русской мысли,* 265–92. Москва: Аграф, 1998.

———. *Пути русского богословия.* Интернет-версия под общей редакцией Его Преосвященства Александра (Милеанта), Епископа Буэнос-Айресского и Южно-Американского. Православная интернет-библиотека Азбука веры, 2003. http://azbyka.ru/otechnik/Georgij_Florovskij/puti-russkogo-bogoslovija/.

———. "Спор о немецком идеализме." In Флоровский, Г. В., *Из прошлого русской мысли,* 412–31. Москва: Аграф, 1998.

Frank, Semyon L. (Франк, Семён Л.). *Реальность и человек: Метафизика человеческого бытия*. HPSY. RU. http://hpsy.ru/public/x1911.htm.

Gaginsky, Alexey M. (Гагинский, Алексей М.). "Онтологический статус Бога у Свт. Григория Богослова." *Историко-философский ежегодник: История западноевропейской философии* (2010) 33–53.

Gersh, Stephen. "The Structure of the Return in Eriugena's *Periphyseon*." In *Begriff und Metapher. Sprachform des Denkens bei Eriugena,* edited by Werner Baierwaltes, 108–25. Heidelberg: Karl Winter Universitätsverlag, 1990.

Grenz, Stanley J., and Roger E. Olson. *The 20bth- Century Theology: God and the World in a Transitional Age*. Chicago: InterVarsity, 1992.

Gregory of Nyssa (Григорий Нисский). *Об устроении человека*. Перевод, послесловие и примечания В. М. Лурье. Под редакцией А. Л. Верлинского. Санкт-Петербург: Axioma, 1995.

Gregory the Theologian (Григорий Богослов). *Собрание творений в 2-х ТТ*. Минск: Харвест, 2000.

Gribbin, John. *Almost Everyone's Guide to Science*. London: Weidenfeld & Nicolson, 1998.

Gromadka, Joseph (Громадка, Йозеф). *Перелом в протестантской теологии*. Москва: Прогресс, 1993.

Guzel, P. K. (Жузе, П. К.). *Мутазилиты: Догматико-историческое исследование в области ислама*. Казань: Типография В. М. Ключникова, 1899.

Hegel, Georg Wilhelm Friedrich. *The Encyclopaedia Logic*. Translated by T. F. Geracts, W. A. Suchting, and H. S. Harris. Indianapolis, Cambridge: Hackett Inc., 1991.

———. *Lectures on the History of Philosophy 1825–1826. Volume 3: Medieval and Modern Philosophy*. Revised edition translated and edited by G. F. Brown. New York: Oxford University Press, 2008.

———. (Гегель, Г. В. Ф.). *Лекции по истории философии. В 3-х Книгах*. Санкт-Петербург: Наука, 1993–1994.

———. *Лекции по философии истории*. Санкт-Петербург: Наука, 2000.

———. *Работы разных лет. Сочинения в 2-х ТТ. Т. 1*. Москва: Мысль, 1970.

———. *Философия религии. Сочинения в 2-х ТТ*. Москва: Мысль, 1976–1977.

———. *Энциклопедия философских наук. Сочинения в 3-х ТТ. Т. 1: Наука логики*. Москва: Мысль, 1974.

Heidegger, Martin. *Basic Writings from Being and Time (1927) to The Task of Thinking (1964)*. San Francisco: Harper, 1977.

———. *What Is Called Thinking*. Translated by J. G. Gray. New York: HarperCollins, 1976.

———. (Хайдеггер, Мартин). *Бытие и время*. Перевод В. В. Бибихина. Москва: Ad Marginem, 1997.

———. *Время и бытие*. Перевод В. В. Бибихина. Москва: Республика, 1993.

The Holy Bible, New Revised Standard Version. Anglicized edition. The Bible with Apocrypha. Oxford: Oxford University Press, 1995.

Innokentiy, Hieromonk (Иеромонах Иннокентий Павлов). "Санкт-Петербургская духовная академия как церковно-историческая школа." In *Богословские труды: Юбилейный сборник, посвящённый 175-летию ЛДА*, 211–68. Москва: Московская Патриархия, 1986.

Jasper, David. *Sacred Desert*. Oxford: Blackwell, 2004.

Jaspers, Karl (Ясперс, Карл). "Радикальное зло у Канта." In *Феномен человека*, 168–88. Под редакцией П. С. Гуревича. Москва: Высшая школа, 1993.

Kant, Immanuel. *Critique of Pure Reason*. Translated by Norman Kemp Smith. New York: St Martin's, 1965.

Kant, Immanuel (Кант, Иммануил). *Критика чистого разума*. Москва: Мысль, 1994.

Karsavin, Lev P. (Карсавин, Лев П.). *Сочинения. Т. 6: О Началах (Опыт христианской метафизики)*.Медиатека Предание. ру. http://mreadz.com/new/index.php?id=36386&pages=1.

Kartashev, Anton V. (Карташёв, Антон В.). *Вселенские соборы*. Москва: Республика, 1994.

Kenny, Anthony. *A Brief History of Western Philosophy*. Oxford: Blackwell, 1998

Klizovsky, Alexander I. (Клизовский, Александр И.). *Основы миропонимания Новой Эпохи. В 3-х ТТ. Т. 1*. Рига: Виеда, 1992.

Kuvakin, Valeryi A. (Кувакин, Валерий А.). *Религиозная философия в России: Начало XX века*. Москва: Мысль, 1979.

Lebedev, A. V., ed. *Фрагменты ранних греческих философов. Часть 1*. Под редакцией А. В. Лебедева. Москва: Наука, 1989.

Le Goff, Jacques (Ле Гофф, Жак). *Цивилизация средневекового Запада*. Послесловие А. Я. Гуревича. Москва: Прогресс, 1992.

Levandovsky, Anatolyi P. (Левандовский, Анатолий П.). *Карл Великий*. Москва: Молодая гвардия, 1995.

Lobachevsky, Nikolai I. (Лобачевский, Николай И.). *Полное собрание сочинений в пяти томах. Т. 2: Геометрия. Новые начала геометрии с полной теорией параллельных*. Москва: ГИТТЛ, 1949.

Löhr, Winrich. "Christianity as Philosophy: Problems and Perspectives of an Ancient Intellectual Project." *Vigiliae Christianae* 64 (2010) 160–88.

Losev, A. F., and A. A. Takho-Gody (Лосев, А. Ф.; А. А. Тахо-Годи). *Платон. Аристотель*. Москва: Молодая гвардия, 1993.

Lossky, Nikolai O. (Лосский, Николай О.). *История русской философии*. Москва: Советский писатель, 1991.

Lossky, Vladimir N. (Лосский, Владимир Н.). "Очерк мистического богословия Восточной церкви." *Богословские труды* 8 (1972) 1–388.

Marler, James C. "Scriptural Truth in the *Periphyseon*." In *Iohannes Scottus Eriugena: The Bible and Hermeneutics. Proceedings of the Ninth International Colloquium of the Society for the Promotion of Eriugenian Studies*, edited by G. Van Riel, C. Steel, and J. McEvoy, 155–72. Leuven: Leuven University Press, 1996.

Martin, Richard C., et al. *Defenders of Reason in Islam: Mu'tazilism from Medieval School to Modern Symbol*. Oxford: Oneworld, 1997.

Maximus the Confessor (Максим Исповедник). *Вопросоответы к Фалассию*. Электронная библиотека Одинцовского благочиния. http://www.odinblago.ru/sv_otci/tvorenia/5/.

McGinn, Bernard. "The Originality of Eriugena's Spiritual Exegesis." In *Iohannes Scottus Eriugena: The Bible and Hermeneutics. Proceedings of the Ninth International Colloquium of the Society for the Promotion of Eriugenian Studies*, edited by G. Van Riel, C. Steel, and J. McEvoy, 55–80. Leuven: Leuven University Press, 1996.

Men, Alexander V. (Мень, Александр В.). *Сын Человеческий*. Москва: Фонд им. Александра Меня, 2006.

Moran, Dermot. *Introduction to Phenomenology*. New York: Routledge, 2000.

————. *The Philosophy of John Scottus Eriugena: A Study of Idealism in the Middle Ages.* Cambridge: Cambridge University Press, 1989.

Mutahhari, Ayatullah M. "An Introduction to Ilm-al-Kalam: Mu'tazilah." Translated by Ali Q. Qara'i. http://www.al-islam.org/al-tawhid/vo13-no2/introduction-ilm-al-kalam/mutazilah. https://www.al-islam.org/al-tawhid/vol3-no2/introduction-ilm-al-kalam/mutazilah

Nicholas of Cusa (Николай Кузанский). *Сочинения в 2-х ТТ. Т. 1: Об учёном незнании.* Москва: Мысль, 1979.

O'Hear, Anthony, ed. *German Philosophy since Kant.* Cambridge: Cambridge University Press, 1999.

O'Meara, Dominic J. "The Metaphysical Use of Mathematical Concepts in Eriugena." In *Begriff und Metapher. Sprachform des Denkens bei Eriugena,* edited by Werner Beierwaltes, 142–48. Heidelberg: Karl Winter Universitätsverlag, 1990.

O'Meara, John J. *Eriugena.* Oxford: Clarendon, 1988.

————. "Introduction." In *The Mind of Eriugena,* edited by John J. O'Meara and Ludwig Beiler, I–XIV. Dublin: Irish University Press, 1973.

Otten, Willemien. *The Anthropology of Johannes Scottus Eriugena.* Brill's Studies in Intellectual History 20. Leiden: E. J. Brill, 1991.

————. "The Universe of Nature and the Universe of Man: Difference and Identity." In *Begriff und Metapher. Sprachform des Denkens bei Eriugena,* edited by Werner Beierwaltes, 202–12. Heidelberg: Karl Winter Universitätsverlag, 1990.

Parmenides (Парменид). "О природе." In *Фрагменты ранних греческих философов.* Часть 1, под редакцией А. В. Лебедева, 274–98. Москва: Наука, 1989.

————. "О природе." In *Эллинские поэты VIII–IIIвв. до н. э.,* под редакцией М. Л. Гаспарова, 178–82. Москва: Ладомир, 1999.

Pattison, George. *Philosophy Guidebook to the Later Heidegger.* London: Routledge, 2000.

Peacocke, Arthur R. *Theology for a Scientific Age.* Oxford: Blackwell, 1991

Peters, Francis E. *Aristotle and Arabs: The Aristotelian Tradition in Islam.* New York: New York University Press, 1968.

Plato (Платон). *Сочинения в 3-х ТТ. Т. 3. Часть 1: Государство.* Москва: Мысль, 1971.

————. "Парменид." In Платон, *Сочинения в 3-х ТТ. Т. 2,* 401–77. Москва: Мысль, 1970.

————. *Timaeus.* Translated by Benjamin Jowett. Elpenor: The Internet Classics Archive. *http://www.ellopos.net/elpenor/physis/plato-timaeus/world-soul.asp.*

Plotinus. *The Six Enneads.* Translated by Stephen Mackenna and B. S. Page. MBS Library: Micro Book Studio. http://www.microbookstudio.com/.

Plotinus (Плотин). *Эннеады.* Перевод С. И. Еремеева, Б. Ерогина, А. Ф. Лосева. Киев: УЦИММ-ПРЕСС, 1996.

Rauschenbach, B. V. (Раушенбах, Б. В.). "Икона как средство передачи философских представлений." In *Проблемы изучения культурного наследия,* 316–25. Под редакцией Г. В. Степанова. Москва: Наука, 1985.

Reale, G., and D. Antiseri (Реале, Дж.; Антисери, Д.). *Западная философия от истоков до наших дней. В 4-х ТТ. Т. 2: Средневековье.* Санкт-Петербург: Петрополис, 1995.

Roberts, Elizabeth, and Ann Shukman, eds. *Christianity for the Twenty-First Century: The Prophetic Writings of Alexander Men.* New York: Continuum, 1996.

Sagadeev, Artur V. (Сагадеев, Артур В.). "Статус философии в теологизированном обществе средневекового мусульманского Востока." In *Средневековая арабо-мусульманская философия. Т. 1.* В переводах и под редакцией А. В. Сагадеева, 8–28. Москва: Марджани, 2009.

Sartre, Jean-Paul (Сартр, Жан-Поль). *Бытие и ничто: Опыт феноменологической онтологии.* Москва: Республика, 2000.

Schweitzer, Albert (Швейцер, Альберт). *Мистика апостола Павла.* Библиотека Гумера. http://www.gumer.info/bogoslov_Buks/Philos/Schw_Mist/.

Seliverstov, Juryi I., ed. *О Великом инквизиторе: Достоевский и последующие.* Составитель и предисловие Ю. И. Селиверстов. Москва: Молодая гвардия, 1991.

Sextus Empiricus (Секст Эмпирик). *Сочинения в 2-х ТТ. Т. 1: Против учёных.* Москва: Мысль, 1976.

Sheldon-Williams, I. P. "Eriugena's Greek Sources." In *The Mind of Eriugena*, edited by John J. O'Meara and Ludwig Bieler, 1–14. Dublin: Irish University Press, 1973.

Soloviev, Vladimir S. (Соловьёв, Владимир С.). "Кризис западной философии: Против позитивизма." In Соловьёв, В. С., *Сочинения в 2-х ТТ. Т. 2.*, 3–138. Москва: Мысль, 1999.

———. "Об упадке средневекового миросозерцания." http://www.vehi.net/soloviev/upadok.html.

———. "Чтения о Богочеловечестве." In Соловьёв, В. С., *Собрание сочинений. Т. 3*, 3–185. Санкт-Петербург: Просвещение, 1966.

Spengler, Oswald (Шпенглер, Освальд). *Закат Европы: Очерки морфологии мировой истории. Т. 2: Всемирно-исторические перспективы.* Москва: Мысль, 1990.

Spinoza, Baruch (Спиноза, Барух). *Избранные произведения в 2-х ТТ. Т. 1: Этика.* Москва: Политиздат, 1957.

———. *Богословско-политический трактат.* Харьков: Фолио, 2001.

Suzuki, Daisazu, and Sakida Kazuki (Дайсацу Судзуки и Сэкида Кацуки). *Основы Дзэн-Буддизма. Практика Дзэн.* Библиотека восточной религиозно-мистической философии. Бишкек: Одиссей, 1993.

Teilhard de Chardin, Pierre (Тейяр де Шарден, Пьер). *Феномен человека.* Москва: Наука, 1987.

Thyssen, Heinrich (Тиссен, Г. К.). *Лекции по систематическому богословию.* Под редакцией Вернона Д. Дерксена. Санкт-Петербург: Логос, 1993.

Tolstoy, Lev Nikolaevich (Толстой, Лев Николаевич). *Закон насилия и закон любви: О пути, об истине, о жизни.* Составитель и предисловие О. А. Дорофеев. Москва: Рипол Классик, 2004.

———. "Религия и нравственность." In Толстой, Л. Н., *Полное собрание сочинений в 90 ТТ. Т. 39*, 3–26. Москва: Художественная литература, 1956.

Trubetskoy, Evgenyi N. (Трубецкой, Евгений Н.). *Миросозерцание Блаженного Августина.* Библиотека Вехи, 2000. http://www.vehi.net/etrubeckoi/avgustin1.html.

Valiuddin, Mir. "Mu'tazilism." In *A History of Muslim Philosophy*, edited and introduced by M. M. Sharif. Islamic Philosophy Online. http://www.muslimphilosophy.com/hmp/title.htm.

Wensinek, A. J. *The Muslim Creed.* Cambridge: Cambridge University Press, 1932.

Wolf, Marina N. (Вольф, Марина Н.). "К вопросу интерпретации доксы у Парменида: В поисках космологии." *Историко-философский ежегодник: История западноевропейской философии* (2010) 5–32.

Made in the USA
Monee, IL
14 January 2022

88966211R00128